The Hebrew Prophets
after the Shoah

The Hebrew Prophets after the Shoah

A Mandate for Change

HEMCHAND GOSSAI

Foreword by Walter Brueggemann

PICKWICK *Publications* · Eugene, Oregon

Pickwick Publications
An Imprint of Wipf and Stock Publishers
199 W. 8th Ave., Suite 3
Eugene, OR 97401

www.wipfandstock.com

ISBN 13: 978-1-62564-004-8

Cataloging-in-Publication data:

Gossai, Hemchand.

The Hebrew prophets after the Shoah : a mandate for change / Hemchand Gossai ; Foreword by Walter Brueggemann.

xviii + 194 pp. ; 23 cm—Includes bibliographical references and indexes.

ISBN 13: 978-1-62564-004-8

1. Bible. Prophets—Criticism, interpretation, etc. 2. Political theology—Biblical teaching. I. Brueggemann, Walter. II. Title.

BS1505.52 G67 2014

Manufactured in the USA

For Viera

Contents

Foreword

Hemchand Gossai has written an exposition of the ancient prophets that voices an immediate contemporaneity from their message. The term "mandate" in the subtitle is exactly correct; the book reflects the urgency of the prophetic message that pertains to our contemporary social crisis. With responsible imagination, Gossai has transposed the dynamics of the ancient prophets from *uncredentialed poets vis-à-vis the numbed urban elites in ancient Jerusalem* into a *textual tradition of ethical imagination vis-à-vis the self-destructive conduct of the US empire*. That transposition is in my view compelling, and the "vis-à-vis" of opposition of the textual tradition to the empire is on target. Gossai exhibits a telling interpretive gift in his witness to the Promethean struggle for truth that is under way in our society.

One version of truth is that offered by the empire in the midst of which we live. Gossai notes many marks of that empire, but here I will single out three for notice. First the empire is rooted in a deep and unexamined conviction about exceptionalism. That powerful notion holds that the United States is chosen to be the carrier of economic freedom that gives it a pass on moral questions. Second, the enactment of that exceptionalism, in an imperial mode turns out, as it does with all empires, to be an extraction of wealth from the occupied territories to the "Homeland," as in "Homeland Security." This extraction depends upon an immense military investment to enforce control and domination. Third, Gossai notes that the various articulations of empire culminate in violence that is perpetrated against any vulnerable outsider to the orbit of privilege that the imperial effort is designed to serve.

In the face of this force of exceptionalism-cum-military-violence, Gossai places the prophetic tradition and offers a textual interpretation that is well-grounded but that surges with contemporeneity. He notices that in that ancient world such voices were readily slotted as "madmen," that is, those who did not subscribe to the force of domination, regularly articulated in protective religious phrasing, were simply crazy people not to be taken seriously. But of course his exegesis will show not only that the "madmen" of ancient Israel were impressively sane, but perceptive and courageous in articulating an alternative truth that exposed the pretend-truth of the empire. The force of the book is to review that prophetic tradition, in its textual expression and in its contemporary embodiment, as truth-telling that is indispensible for the health and well-being of our body politic.

This Promethean struggle for truth is now, as always, an uneven contest. But Gossai shows how and why the articulation of an alternative truth continues and must continue to be voiced. I am currently reading the biography of Sumner Welles written by his son Benjamin. Welles is a now forgotten diplomat of the US State Department in mid-twentieth century who served as Undersecretary of State under Franklin Roosevelt. Though his brilliant career ended early and tragically, he developed unparalleled expertise concerning US policy in Central America. I mention his life and work because at the height of his influence he published an extended study of US policy in Central America. With knowing irony, he titled his study *Naboth's Vineyard*, thus a deliberate allusion to the Elijah narrative of 1 Kings 21 that Gossai cites to such good advantage. That ancient narrative concerns the action of the powerful queen and king in Israel (Jezebel and Ahab) who usurped the land of a vulnerable peasant farmer. Welles intends to expose the usurpatious policies of the United States that were allied with the aggressive policies of the "fruit companies" who preyed upon the poor in Central America in exploitative ways. The linkage between ancient text and Welles's policy statement is a telling case in which the prophetic text functions as a truth-teller in a venue of power. It is this old truth in the face of contemporary false truth that Gossai champions.

Gossai's analysis is "post-Shoah" in the sense that the Shoah has caused the ungluing of all old assumptions and all old certitudes—social, political, and religious. That new context creates new responsibilities and new possibilities, and waits for new acts of imagination. The book is a welcome harbinger of new acts of imagination that will permit the old tradition to have its say. It will surely turn out in our context, as in the ancient context, that the purveyors of empire are indeed the madmen who host destruction. This Promethean contest here continues with boldness!

Walter Brueggemann
Columbia Theological Seminary
August 26, 2013

Preface

I typically begin my classes with one of several questions/statements in order to set a stage for what my expectations are from my students. Thus, I may ask: "Why do we read?" While I am aware of the distinct possibility that reading might not be a priority for some, I do not teach to what is currently popular and in vogue but what I consider essential and important. Beyond the commonly expected, I am invariably surprised and heartened by some of the responses. I tell my students, paraphrasing a comment that is attributed to C. S. Lewis, that we read so that we know we are not alone. We find ourselves in the narratives of others, and perhaps mysteriously, and even miraculously, their stories become our stories. We laugh, we weep, we wonder. We identify with characters whose worlds are so immediately different from ours, so distant from ours, literally and figuratively, that on the surface one might wonder what could possibly be the connection, and yet we find ourselves connected, and indeed in defining moments we are transformed. We cannot only read books that simply reflect, confirm or underline our particular perspectives, ideologies or truth claims. This sadly is somewhat pervasive when it comes to the Bible and biblical material. "Reading the Bible is not an unmediated meeting of reader with biblical author(s), but is rather like pulling up a chair at a feast that has been underway for some time. However, this image carries another, sobering implication, for not all diners bring nourishing food to the feast."[1] There is a well-established tendency to read sections of the Bible that simply reflect one's ideology. So for example one is not surprised that for some obedience is the principal guiding principle in which one approaches the Bible; for others taking every word or circumstance literally, is essential and then it becomes very difficult, if not impossible to follow fully every iota of the Bible. So what are the alternatives? Is it to make an arbitrary determination that some parts of the Bible do not apply, and therefore should not

---

1. Callaway, "Exegesis as Banquet," 221.

be obeyed? Is it to employ a variety of means to justify and uphold one's ideology? At the very least these are myopic, and have the mark of being simultaneously destructive.

The Hebrew Bible has much that will resonate and inflame at the same time, but the issue is not what should be redacted and discarded, but rather to learn even from those parts for which we have a visceral reaction. So, I advocate a hermeneutic of engagement; a relational approach. Among the many virtues in this approach is the fact that it will expand the angle of our thinking, while allowing us to engage with the rich layers of the text. Reflecting on books and ideas of several writers and activists, each coming from different circumstances, Robert Coles notes that there are three essential questions that form the foundation of their works. How does one live a life? What kind of life? And for what purpose?[2] Our lives chronicle moments of violence, pain, oppression and injustice but also freedom, peace, redemption and grace. These questions and the choices are often made in the face of devastating moments, universal and profound in their relevance. What is essential for us in exploring the Hebrew Prophets critically is the idea embedded in these questions, namely that finally we do not live unto ourselves and in a vacuum. Our lives are inextricably tied to each other, and so how we live our lives, the kind of life we live, and the purpose, are all immediately relevant, and interconnected with each other. These questions are not to be forgotten. We must not forget who we are, for in so doing we will not forget the moral calling that we have, and the universe that beckons us. "Maybe we forget because maybe not to forget is more than we can bear; we ourselves . . . take stock morally, spiritually, humanly—we confront the great existential questions that Camus and Sartre and Simone Weil and others have put on us."[3]

The world faces something of a challenge with a critical component of the prophets' message, namely the particular emphasis on individualism in many societies, and the challenge of embracing community that the biblical text invariably emphasizes. When a well-known axiom such as "it takes a village" is used in American political discourse, it is frequently pilloried in some quarters, and at other times cast aside as socialist or some such remark meant to be disparaging and dismissive. Yet, many who hold the very distinct view that individualism is the core of the American worldview also

2. Coles, *Handing One Another*, 181.

3. Ibid., 197.

seek to emphasize their rootedness in the biblical tradition. It is, I believe, a challenging chasm to bridge.

> According to Israelite understandings, it is not as isolated individuals, but as members of a community that we realize our being ... The moral soundness of the community, moreover, is mostly clearly manifest in its treatment of its most vulnerable members ... Individual responsibility is not ruled out by this sense of solidarity; yet it gains an essentially social meaning. I act not simply for myself, but for the wellbeing of the whole people. I am answerable not simply to myself and my own principles, but to the whole people and its foundational principles.[4]

Ogletree's idea regarding the essential tension between the individual and the community is one that strikes at the biblical core. Not only within the political realm does one hear the language of individualism extolled as a principal virtue, but within religious communities, where faith, narrowly construed as individualistic, is viewed as the ideal.

> The essence of being human is that one does not seek perfection, that one is sometimes willing to commit sins for the sake of loyalty ... and that one is prepared in the end to be defeated and broken up by life, which is the inevitable price of fastening's one's love upon other human individuals ... Many people genuinely do not wish to be saints, and it is probable that some who achieve or aspire to sainthood have never felt much temptation to be human beings ... One must choose between God and Man, and all "radicals" and "progressives," from the mildest Liberal to the most extreme Anarchist, have in effect chosen Man.[5]

Some such as Socrates or Jeremiah or Joan of Arc or Gandhi or Mother Theresa or King or Wiesel may be thought of in such regard, but none of whom sought to be a saint; whatever such titles are bestowed on them by others, it is not what they set out to be or do. Neither the saint nor the prophet sets out to be the saint or the prophet.

The incontestable reality is that a person's faith does not develop in a vacuum without the influence and nurturing of others within the community. Some Christian communities have embraced this idea, and e.g., within the Roman Catholic and Anglican traditions, before one can enter into the ordination process, one must first journey through a discernment process

---

4. Ogletree, *Use of the Bible in Christian Ethics*, 80.

5. Orwell, "Reflections on Gandhi."

where members of the community engage with the candidate precisely to discern the person's calling. It is this idea that must be extolled, namely that one functions within the community and in the context of what is in the best welfare of the community.

> In the case of communities growing out of biblical tradition, the courage to speak with impartiality at times when popular opinion is being swayed by materialistic individualism, myopic expediency, racism, sexism, economic elitism, or nationalistic self-interest will be fostered by the prophetic tradition . . . and especially by the central reality of the God of compassionate justice.[6]

On the issue of individualism and community, Ezekiel is frequently cited as the prophet whose words regarding the role of the individual is the fulcrum upon which the shift occurs from communal responsibility to that of the individual.[7] This however is an oversimplification of Ezekiel's message. Even as one reads and interprets this text in the context of the exile, it seems much more evident that in fact Ezekiel not only is not radically shifting the focus from community to individual, but rather he is reorienting the moral responsibility of the community in light of the exilic experience.

> Ezekiel 18 suggests that the prophet is not elevating the individual so much as he is seeking to reconstitute moral community in the face of exilic sentiment that they are simply the victims of the sins of a previous generation . . . Ezekiel criticizes the notion of inherited guilt in order to call the present generation of exile to repent, turn, and live (vs. 20–29). It is not to individuals that Ezekiel speaks, but to a generation in exile.[8]

One might say that in entering the life of another in a meaningful way is one pathway through which we might further discover who we are. It is the reality of an unavoidable interconnectedness. Referring to E. M. Forster's "only connect" and Martin Buber's "I–Thou," Coles underlines the significance of this interconnectedness. "All of this reminds us to trust, finally someone else, and thereby finally some self-respect that is more than one's own egotism. What good is it to accumulate knowledge, know the theories, know the means of earning a living; know the intricacies of how to work the system, but not be human, how to be kind and loving to ourselves and

---

6. P. D. Hanson, *Isaiah 40–66*, 216.

7. See Ezekiel 18.

8. Birch, *Let Justice Roll Down*, 297.

others?"[9] Or as Mandolfo observes, "According to Bakhtin, we are all co-authors of one another's identities. In other words, the whole story about us cannot be told by us alone . . . Part of the job of authoring others involves listening to them as responsibly as we can, listening and responding fairly."[10] In recent years, our lexicon has included the language and the horrific circumstances surrounding what has been coined "blood diamonds." Such diamonds with their beauty, and patrons with the natural impulse to buy these beautiful pieces of nature now have to face the reality that the only way these diamonds are possible and available are on the backs and lives of those who have been crushed to produce them. The diamonds are mined for the sake of the insatiable appetite of others for the opulent life, and for those who are willing to sacrifice the lives of others to accumulate such wealth and beauty. Such is the devastating cycle. Less we imagine that this is a moment that does not affect all of us, we are mistaken. In fact, this idea has everything to do with us who look to God as the architect of our existence and God's ongoing presence that guides us. Ultimately, the issue here is neither about the diamonds nor the wealth accrued. There are rather two things to note. It is about the *source* of the wealth, and then what one *does* with the wealth; that is finally at issue. Fretheim has observed, "while wealth as such is apparently not condemned, the wealthy often are, because wealth is so easily, indeed it is almost always gained on the back of the underprivileged and misused once it has been procured."[11]

This is a distinction not to be overlooked. There is nothing evil or condemnatory about wealth in and of itself. But the manner in which it is accrued is of deep concern, and a subject of prophetic indignation. The prophets are unequivocal that there is no such thing as accruing wealth singularly by oneself. There are always others who are used to generate wealth for others. One cannot misconstrue the profound straightforwardness of the prophet Micah who says, "Your wealth is full of violence."[12] We know that among others Isaiah was connected with the "powers that be" and perhaps even had access to wealth. So it is not a matter of wealth and access. Indeed it is egregious enough to gain wealth crushing the poor which we know existed in ancient times and throughout history, and has been documented, but, wealth invariably becomes a platform for further

9. Coles, *Handing One Another Along*, 196.

10. Mandolfo, "Perseverance," 53.

11. Fretheim, "Interpreting the Prophets," 104.

12. Mic 6:12.

accumulation. What transpires is that one lives lavishly at the expense of the other through the other's "sweat and tears" and perhaps unavoidable and inherited circumstances. It is about the abuse and infidelity of an indelible relationship. For the prophet to be able to make such pronouncements to the people many of whom are his own people, there must be a dramatic transformation. Speaking from a psychological perspective, Kast argues that mood swings might have an important and perhaps positive function. We are accustomed to concluding that mood swings are a bad sign; an even temperament is sought and hoped for. It strikes me that as a metaphor Kast's idea is precisely what one might seek for the people as they hear the words of the prophet. Even temperament at that point is neither noble nor hoped for. It has to be a radical change of mood as one sees oneself, and one sees the world. It is a mood swing that is not involuntary but voluntary, one that is intentional. As Kast has suggested, a mood swing might very well be an indication that something has gone out of tune and must be changed to put us back in tune again.[13]

> The nature of moral community in its covenantal commitment to justice, righteousness, and shalom has not changed, but its way of being in the world has changed. Its suffering in the midst of the empire is for the sake of the empire and not Israel alone. This is to have profound implications for future generations of the faithful community of God's people, because the way of national political power for that community was not to be possible.[14]

Invariably when discussing the issue of what YHWH seeks or what might be YHWH's perspective in a matter of gravity or substance, there is a call to the prophet. In this regard, for example one hearkens to the 1 Kings 22 narrative.[15] When Jehoshaphat inquires of Ahab as to whether God's imprimatur has been sought in the matter of war, Ahab refers to his four hundred prophets; Jehoshaphat wonders aloud to Ahab as to whether the perspective of any other prophet was sought. This is all by way of saying that when God's perspective is sought, the prophet is invariably the one who enters the scenario, and is not left to those under the employment or presence of the king. Ahab is not thrilled at the prospect of having Micaiah prophesy, but nonetheless expects nothing but the truth from him. He feels obliged to hear the prophet's pronouncements despite his disinclination

13. Kast, *Joy, Inspiration and Hope*, 25–26.

14. Birch, *Let Justice Roll Down*, 300.

15. 1 Kings 22 will be explored in detail in chapter 7.

to do so. He knows the truth. Perhaps in contrast to Ahab is Sophocles's, Creon, King of Thebes, who in his obstinacy is not only responsible for the death of his son and wife, but the public humiliation of Polyneices, in death, and the vengeful and barbaric punishment of Antigone. Yet, when he is faced with Teiresias, the blind prophet, he is forced to see what the prophet tells him. The prophet's word will be heard, and unlike Ahab, there is a change of heart on the part of Creon, but even here such dramatic transformation is not enough, as the people who mattered most to him die at their own hands; finally they die because of him. As is the case here and in the biblical text, the prophets must have distance from the ruler.

Immediately after the terrorist attack on September 11, 2001, Archbishop Rowan Williams wondered about the tragedy and the response that was sure to come. He insightfully notes, with a generalization that has merit: "the hardest thing in the world is to know how to act so as to make the difference that can be made; to know how and why that differs from the act that only relates or expresses the basic impotence of resentment."[16] Williams' words following September 11 are apropos here. Because the US has not experienced anything quite like the tragedy and horror that befell us on that day, not only did we not have the language and vocabulary, we did not know how to gather our emotions and how to channel them. We have witnessed war and terror from afar, but now it was at our doorstep. Williams suggests that "there is a particularly difficult challenge here, to do with making terms with our vulnerability and learning hope to live with it in a way that isn't simply denial, panic, the reinforcement of defences."[17]

When spoken or written, my words and ideas are never generated in a vacuum. I am shaped singularly by those who have read, listened, dialogued, reflected, critiqued, debated with me, and who unreservedly have committed themselves such conversations. My sincere thanks to Walter Brueggemann who graciously agreed to write the Foreword to this book. His works have been enormously influential on my scholarship, particularly the manner in which I interpret the biblical text in the context of contemporary society. My heartfelt thanks to my Graduate Assistant Aaron Roberts who not only read the manuscript and made copious notes, but formatted the work and created the indices. Many thanks to K. C. Hanson for his ongoing support and acceptance of this work, and the staff at Wipf

---

16. Williams, *Writing in the Dust*, 47.

17. Ibid., 57.

& Stock for their attentiveness and professionalism. It is a privilege to work with them.

Most of all thanks to my family for countless moments of grace, bidden and unbidden. So my heartfelt thanks to Annika, Chandra, Clara, David, Joshua, Krista, Maren, Nathan, and Rachel. Known or unknown, they have all left their mark on this work. And my deepest thanks to Viera for her love and unwavering encouragement and support; she has journeyed with me at every turn, and it is to her that I dedicate this book.

1

The Post-Shoah World

O n the anniversary of the killing of Osama bin Laden, and in the midst of the politics and often politicizing of that moment, it was not unusual to hear the statement, "Of course if I were in power I would have made the same decision." Perhaps for a little while, that statement will score political points with those who are supporters, and ideologically aligned with the speaker. But finally to have such a momentous event as the capture and death of a terrorist, where the decision was so extraordinary, to look in retrospect and use the language of "of course" is at best self-indulgent and self-aggrandizing. Indeed, I would argue that in seeking to show compassion, to listen intently, to console, etc. the vocabulary of "of course" should be stricken from our lexicon or used sparingly and with circumspection. Finally, one does not absolutely know. So then where does that leave us? Is this an implied suggestion that one cannot do anything; that one must have a particular experience in order to speak, console, show compassion? In a rather extraordinary document, Lawrence Langer in a prelude to interviewing Shoah survivors notes, "A statement like, 'to understand, you have to go through with it,' however authentic its inspiration, underestimates the sympathetic power of the imagination."[1]

> The Shoah evokes a redefining that permits and requires us to reread all else as fragment. It does not distort the Shoah nor does it trivialize to take the Shoah as the lens for reading the world of horror, abuse and violence everywhere all around, in forms of

---

1. Langer, *Shoah Testimonies*, xv.

terrorism or in more institutionalized forms of capital punishment, and welfare reform and so on.[2]

The issues of understanding and memory are arguably no place more poignantly present and urgent, as in remembering and speaking about the
Shoah. The ubiquitous statement "You have to go through it to understand"
and the many variations, do have truth, but along the lines of Langer's observation that in fact while absolute identification is not ever fully possible, the
story nonetheless has to be told. One might say with some certitude that no
two Shoah experiences are in fact identical; the experiences are also shaped
by worldviews, internal capacity for faith, fortitude, religion, etc. Yet, the
story must be told and personal identification cannot become a moment
of silencing the voice or truncating the story. One must step away from the
comfort and boundaries of lived experiences, and modes of thinking, and
find a way of entering into the stories so that we might give voices to the
memory. We must give voices, for we, unless we are survivors ourselves,
cannot remember, and so we give voices to the memory of those who lost
their voices, and those who have remembered and left us their memories.
Listening to the voices of witnesses, we in turn become witnesses.

One of the most challenging ideas is that of the role of war as a means
of punishment, or for injustices which often necessitates the resources for
military power and might, over and against the need for bread. YHWH's
use of war and cosmic artillery in a variety of forms as punishment for a
people who are involved in systemic and systematic injustices suggests two
things. First, this level of violence and the magnitude of declaring war or
cosmic cataclysm raises ethical questions, and the challenging prospects of
reconciling the idea of God as one who is merciful and slow to anger with
that of a God who launches a war and unleashes cosmic havoc on a people.
Platitudes and clichès will not suffice here, nor will simple points of justification. Indeed, in large part this kind of challenge leads some to conclude
that the "violent" and "warring" God is the God of the Old Testament and
the God of Love is the God of the New Testament and with this comes
salvation, redemption, etc. This kind of thinking creates an untenable and
troubling dichotomy, and it is a variation of the flawed "promise and fulfillment" distinction that has for the most part been dismissed as indefen-
sible. Second, one might argue that the issue of oppression and injustice is
such that it transcends petty acts, but points to that which is systemic and
systematic, and therefore must be met with a kind of punishment that is

2. Brueggemann, "Fissure Always Uncontained," 73.

commensurate; hence war and acts of cosmic violence. Thus, with considerable reflection and circumspection one is compelled to ask: is genocide a proportionate response to injustice and idolatry? Janet Tollington has raised several pertinent and urgent questions in this regard. "'Is war a divinely approved method of establishing justice, of settling territorial claims, of resolving power claims?' 'Is war divinely instigated and part of the overarching order between the nations?' 'Is war an inescapable fact of life and therefore understood as inevitable within Hebrew Bible traditions?'"[3] The very questions in the context of injustices point to that which is significant in the lives and dynamics of the peoples' lives.

One of the undeniable and unprecedented struggles that the victims of the Shoah face analogous to the experience of Jewish exiles in Babylon, is the loss of identity where not only are they stripped of their clothes and homes and land and temple, but are faced with the real possibility of death, family separation, and ongoing violence. There is also, in both instances, the real possibility of losing faith, whatever faith they might have had in God, and for that matter in humanity. In the Babylonian exile the Israelites are told that they will return home one day, and indeed God has plans for them. Yet, how could one realistically function in such a foreign and hostile society, and still maintain the level of faith, and believe that in fact God the architect of their exile, is the one who will deliver them, again. In both the Babylonian Exile and the Shoah is the fact that one could not quite fathom the new reality with the inherent questions. Certainly in the case of the Shoah it very quickly became apparent that staying alive was no longer a self evident reality but one had to reach into the recesses of one's physical and mental strength, where it took all of the resources to simply stay alive. Langer suggests, "Once the impulse to stay alive begins to operate, the luxury of moral constraint temporarily disappears. Tainted memory then replaces judgment as it deposes guilt."[4]

Rarely pursued is the issue regarding the prophets' voice on behalf of the people to God. In this regard, Jeremiah and Amos are notable exceptions among the prophets, though Abraham, Moses, and Job also stand in the tradition of advocates though the divine responses vary. In the first instance the issue focuses on engaging God, but unlike Jeremiah and Amos, Isaiah is silent! God responded positively to Amos on both occasions, and

---

3. Tollington, "Ethics of Warfare," 72.

4. Langer, *Shoah Testimonies*, 150.

Abraham stopped asking on behalf of Sodom and Gomorrah, not God. So, one is left to wonder about Isaiah's silence.

> Then I heard the voice of the Lord saying, "Whom shall I send, and who will go for us?" And I said, "Here am I; send me!"
> And he said, "Go and say to this people:
> 'Keep listening, but do not comprehend;
> keep looking, but do not understand.'
> Make the mind of this people dull,
>   and stop their ears,
>   and shut their eyes,
> so that they may not look with their eyes,
>   and listen with their ears,
> and comprehend with their minds,
>   and turn and be healed."
> Then I said, "How long, O Lord?" And he said:
> "Until cities lie waste
>   without inhabitant,
> and houses without people,
>   and the land is utterly desolate;
> until the Lord sends everyone far away,
>   and vast is the emptiness in the midst of the land.
> Even if a tenth part remains in it,
>   it will be burned again,
>   like a terebinth or an oak
>   whose stump remains standing when it is felled."
> The holy seed is its stump.[5]

While much has been written and spoken about the call of Isaiah, the details of the text beyond the well known and foundational "'Whom shall I send, and who will go for us?' And I said, 'Here am I; send me!'" lies a very problematic and challenging outline of what is at the forefront of the call. Indeed the call of Isaiah is not only a matter of sending the prophet to proclaim a message to the people that contains a quality of indictment because of injustices, and perchance a possibility of redemption. Rather, this message given to Isaiah to be pronounced to the people, and in so doing be effected, is one of utter devastation. The principal message is to destroy and sever the relationship. There is no point of restoration, but rather an utter annihilation of the present. If the message that is given to Isaiah is taken for what it is, and not even to imagine it to a logical conclusion, it would be of apocalyptic proportions. The prophet is to speak to the people

---

5. Isa 6:8–13.

and cause them to lose their relational quality: no intellect, no hearing, no sight, no capacity to comprehend, no healing. But beyond their personal incapacities, the people are scattered, and land, homes are destroyed. No longer is there a sense of home or belonging, even as communities and families will be separated and scattered. One is left to wonder what is God's end plan. The vocabulary in this text itself tells the devastating story: no comprehension; no perception, dull; deaf; blind; no healing; wasteland; forsaken; desolation; burnt to the ground; displacement; emptiness! With such destruction, the prophet's response is encapsulated in, "How long?" Just as well that the prophet is not given an inkling of the message before he accepts! One is reminded that the "How long, O Lord?" question has more to do with a lamentation than a quest for a timeline. Yet, surely this cannot be enough. Such devastation cannot only be met with a sigh that suggests a sense of resignation. If the prophet does not raise his voice under such circumstances, then what is the message to those who today face such devastation and genocide by those with power to destroy? Painful as it is to say and acknowledge, Isaiah at this point is complicit with God's and this complicity underlines the destructive role of silence under these circumstances. What might have been the difference or consequence had he said, no?

"In the end, Isaiah becomes complicit in the evil proposed by YHWH for the people by his failure to act."[6] While it almost certainly will not be overwhelmingly embraced or accepted, there is, I believe, truth to Sweeney's observation. When translated into the context of the Shoah, and indeed in contexts such as Darfur, Rwanda and Kosovo, and certainly in the context of domestic abuse, the truth is much more striking, and cannot be dismissed casually or uncritically. The voice of the victim cannot be silenced, and be blamed for his or her suffering, as is far too often the case. This is not to say that there are no consequences to certain actions, but the one with power cannot routinely be protected and the powerless who are victimized routinely be blamed and silenced.

Posing the Difficult Questions

In reading biblical texts interpreters must not only resist the temptation of navigating around the many challenging acts attributed to God, but resist the very tempting notion of seeking to justify divine acts of violence that

---

6. Sweeney, *Reading the Hebrew Bible after the Shoah*, 91.

by any measure under different circumstances might be extraordinarily difficult to justify.

> Our world no less than the world of our ancient forbears is a world of violence. Whether it is at home, in the schoolyard, on the city streets, or on the shores of another country, violence would appear to be sown into the fabric of our domestic, social, and political lives. We all, in one form or another, are caught up in violence's vicious play, either as victims or victimizers, or more likely, a bit of both . . . Divine violence cannot be treated in isolation from other language about God. If God is violent, God is also loving, benevolent and compassionate, all powerful and wise. And for Christians the violence of the cross itself represents preeminently, the revelation of the non-violent love of God, God's solidarity through Christ with us as victims of violence and the promise of God that violence and counter violence of this world will not win out in the end.[7]

In Dobbs-Allsopp's astute encapsulation, he observes that to overlook, or for that matter minimize the importance of divine violence is to marginalize the central act of the crucifixion in Christianity. The crucifixion in Christianity has been a dividing point for many denominations and Christians, namely its centrality in the faith. There seems to be two options for many Christians. Some seek to hasten the distance between crucifixion and resurrection. The darkness for some is so overwhelming that they cannot bear the thought of living through the darkness, and so it is brushed aside. "In an age after Auschwitz such a risk, even if unwitting, cannot be tolerated."[8] In *Lamentations*, the malevolence of God's silence and inattention is not so much represented or inveighed against, as it is felt, evoked in the reader, and thus implicitly criticized. "It is self-destructively sentimental for Christians to allow their understanding of the God who is Love to be separated from the hidden God. We must be willing, religiously and theologically, to face the dialectic of the revelation of God's radical hiddenness as we—and the Bible—experience that hiddenness in life."[9]

Many Jewish thinkers, including some who survived the Shoah have raised significant questions about God, about divine silence, about the role of humans after the Shoah. Where was God? Why was God silent and perhaps even absent during the Shoah? These questions, difficult as they are,

7. Dobbs-Allsopp, *Lamentations*, 45.

8. Ibid., 48.

9. Tracy, "Hidden God," 13.

must be posed and pursued. Buber has argued that ultimately it is humanity's idolatry that has been the basis for the historical moments of punishment in different forms. Buber does develop this idea with particular reference to the Shoah, but one is left to wonder somewhat given that this idea is articulated in a volume published in 1952. Could one make and sustain this argument about the Shoah and what led to the Shoah? Buber's idea is predicated on the notion of *hestēr pānîm*, that is, the hidden face of God as espoused in Jewish thought. Sweeney notes that this idea "posits that the all-powerful and righteous G-d sometimes chooses to remain hidden in times of crisis."[10] Certainly this idea raises substantial questions about God and the manner in which God is involved in the affairs of the world and the lives of the people. An immediately apparent issue would be, if God does not act, and is in fact absent during times of crises, then what might be God's role. Indeed as Sweeney notes, there are several essential questions that have been raised, and indeed must be raised. Thus for example Sweeney responds to Ignaz Maybaum's *The Face of God after Auschwitz*, in which Maybaum argues that Jews are destined to suffer and the Shoah was theologically justified in order to save the world. That is, there is a greater good and importance to the slaughter of six million Jews, for such is their lot in this life; thus their suffering and death will witness to and save the world. Not surprisingly, Maybaum's ideas have not generated widespread support, and indeed have met with astonishment by many. However, this notwithstanding, Sweeney notes that there are a number of critical questions that might be raised. "Can G-d's love and justice be understood in relation to the Shoah? Is it even possible for the Shoah to be understood as a form of punishment? What sins would justify the punishment the magnitude of the Shoah?"[11] This idea can certainly be expanded to include other genocides, exiles and such altering and dramatic moments that transform the landscape of human life. Indeed after such extraordinary events, one might very well be left to wonder how a human-divine relationship might continue, and if so in what re-designed form. Even if one wanted to, one cannot overlook the exile or the Shoah as a defining event, and in light of these it is impossible not to wonder about the role of God.

Elie Wiesel places the most dramatic reading of God's role in his novel, *The Accident*. The protagonist, not coincidentally named Eliezer, concludes that God is malevolent, and abuses his power by using humans for his own sport and entertainment, and there is nothing that humans can do about it.

---

10. Sweeney, *Reading the Hebrew Bible after the Shoah*, 8.

11. Ibid., 9.

David Blumenthal's examination of abuse, as a particular way of exploring God's action and inaction on behalf of Israelites in Exile and Jews in the Shoah raises further questions, and places the issue squarely within the category of human experience that affects the ordinary person, regardless of race, ethnicity, nationality, or religion to identity. Could God be an abuser? Referring to Blumenthal's study, Sweeney notes,

> Taking an analogy from contemporary concern with the abusive behavior of spouses, parents, clergy, and so forth, Blumenthal posits that G-d may be viewed as an abuser insofar as the Shoah constitutes abuse perpetrated or permitted by the ultimate figure tasked with the well-being and security of the Jewish people and humankind in general. In such a model, the abusive perpetrator is one who is known to and loved by the victim; the abuser breaches and takes advantage of a relationship based on trust; the abuser blames the victim; and the abusive relationship seeks the continued commitment of love while continuing to perpetrate the abuse.[12]

Like all analogies, this too ultimately breaks down, but like all good analogies, this too has truth to it, with the particular complexity of divine-human relationship. Thus, the questions and statements of abuse between human perpetrator and human victim might also be voiced here, namely, "why don't you leave," "sever the relationship," and "carve out a new direction for life." Indeed many who have suffered have done these very things, and many who have suffered in the Shoah have lost their faith in God and severed their relationship with God. One of the components of this analogue of abuse is the particularly egregious level of suffering of the children, given that children are often equated somewhat with innocence; and in this case divine abuse takes on a very difficult and painful quality. As if to underline the extraordinary drama of violence against children, only recently has the world witnessed the massacre of twenty-seven persons in Newton, Connecticut, twenty of whom were little children. The world mourns and the phrase "this is different" reflects the painful unparalleled act of the slaughter of children.

The Hebrew word for "question" is *she'elah*, which as Elie Wiesel notes, has *el*, God in it. God is thus in the questions, and someone might say that there is something divine about the great questions, including the questions that are posed to God. Perhaps one might equally say that answers should

12. Ibid., 13.

not be the logical conclusion to every question. As we explore the various themes that surround exile, punishment, redemption, ritual, injustice, among others, we are led inexorably by the prophets to the matter of divine righteousness, justice, power, and inevitably to the issue of theodicy. What is God's role and intention in the punishment and suffering of the covenant people? Sweeney notes that the book of Isaiah raises some very disturbing questions. One of the factors that seems to have characterized many interpreters of the Hebrew Prophets is the very particular reluctance to raise sustained questions about the issue of theodicy and the disturbing realities of prophetic complicity in the punishment of the people. More disturbing is the matter as to God's role in intentionally creating a circumstance that makes it impossible for the people to come to a realization of what they are doing, and what needs to be done in order to change their actions and rectify the relationship. "To what extent does YHWH consign the people of Israel, Judah and Jerusalem to suffer by rendering them blind and deaf and therefore unable to repent? To what extent is their suffering explained by their own wrongdoing, even when they are prevented from recognizing that wrongdoing and changing their ways? What might have become of the people had Isaiah done more than simply ask, 'How long, my L-rd?'"[13] In this last question, is there a sense that Isaiah has simply decided that the punishment that is meted out is justified, that YHWH will not listen, that the decision is a *fait accompli*? Yet, one must ask, "what if?" This is more than simply a rhetorical device. It is a way of saying that in the face of what is about to transpire, one cannot say that belief in God is central, and yet decline to ask what might be the final and defining question.

The conventional view among the majority of scholars is that the Hebrew prophets based their pronouncements on the verifiable and defensible fact that God was faithful and Israel repeatedly was unfaithful, and therefore the prophets over the course of centuries would also repeatedly prophesy with sharp and piercing invectives. While this perspective is substantially true, there are still notable moments where questions to, and about God and the role and actions of God are brought into question. The reason for the questions or occasional challenges is not to usurp the role of God or for that matter tarnish the character of God. Rather it is to walk in the footsteps of those biblical characters who have questioned or wondered aloud about God's actions, and indeed have not been cast aside by God for blasphemy or arrogance. Questions about the nature of punishment and the depth of

13. Ibid., 103.

the judgment, from bondage to exile, to the remarkably defining moment of the Shoah must be voiced.

> I believe that it is important, even ethically mandatory, to recognize and resist dangerous thinking wherever it occurs including and perhaps especially in the Bible. To be faithful, I believe demands recognizing the problems of biblical texts, how they participate in the web of power relations that are toxic . . . I believe that [the Bible] has to be read responsibly, with eyes wide open. To attempt to "fix" the problems of the Old Testament by reading it selectively or making excuses for it is, in my understanding, not only dishonest, but also dangerous.[14]

It is the capacity to raise substantial and existential questions to, and about God that reflects that depth of confidence and faith, and belief in God who is indeed God of the universe and is unafraid to face major questions. Not to question strikes me as a weak sign of faith. Sometimes a question must be posed even if it remains unanswered. Ignoring or diminishing the 'Why?' questions is often a remarkably easy way to escape from our own complicity in such matters. Sweeney poses a number of questions that are generated from Job that have universal claims, and thus must be asked beyond the parameters of the story of Job. "Why do the righteous suffer? Does G-d indeed protect the righteous? Is a human being capable of questioning G-d? Is it sinful for a human to question G-d? Is it futile for a human to question G-d? Is suffering the lot of human beings because humans must ultimately die? Can humans correct G-d? Can humans challenge G-d's power? . . . Rather than condemn Job and the readers of the book for asking such questions, the book of Job is designed to elicit and affirm such questions, even if the answers are not easily forthcoming"[15]

INCOHERENT FRAGMENTS

A recognizable note from the biblical text reminds us of the reality that we live in a world that is ever changing, and while God is understood as both inscrutable and unchangeable, nonetheless, the manner in which we are to embrace and interpret the biblical text also must reflect the world in which we live. Thus, while for some interpreters it might seem noble

---

14. O'Brien, *Challenging Prophetic Metaphor*, xxi.

15. Sweeney, *Reading the Hebrew Bible after the Shoah*, 198–99.

or wise to conclude that they have a sense of certitude about God and the text, it seems to be a dangerous proposition, as one perhaps imperceptibly usurps the place of God, and ignores the world around. In this regard it is impossible to think of the role of God in the world as being the same as before and after the Shoah. It seems that the questions are more pronounced, more pointed, more wide-ranging and strikingly resistant to the impulse to remain locked in a time gone by. The Shoah in modern times, recalls the exile and the dramatic landscape of biblical times. Everything has changed! Simply to leave things as they are; to refuse to broach questions under the well established veil of only being human and therefore unable to know the mind of God, is unconscionable and a dereliction of faithfulness.

> The truth is in fragments . . . In the face of fragments, the empire and its theologians fling out coherence—all coherent, all reasonable, all accounted for, all understood, . . . For most adherents of such coherence, however, the claim becomes a recipe for denial, censure and pretense, all of which issue in violence.[16]

Coherency certainly has its place, but in the midst of a fragmented society, the idea of coherency born out of an artificial construct or coercion is not only unacceptable, but destructive. Coherency of this sort simply awaits a time for further and worsened disintegration. Fragmentation cannot be made whole by a patch work or being "band aided" together. The etymology of *sincere* is instructive here. The common background of the word combines *sin* (without)+ *cere* (wax). The word is generally associated with marble sculptures in Roman times, some of which had imperfections that were filled with wax, which to the average eye, unskilled to discern imperfections would assume that the piece is not flawed or fragmented. A society cannot be waxed together in the face of fragmentation. In 1936, the Nazi regime "waxed" its deeply oppressive and violently fragmented society into a showpiece for the 1936 Berlin Olympic Games. Regarding the question of a boycott of these Olympics, Avery Brundage, president of the American Olympic Committee, stated: "The very foundation of the modern Olympic revival will be undermined if individual countries are allowed to restrict participation by reason of class, creed, or race."[17] Creating another "waxed laden" moment, Brundage was invited for an inspection tour which, following the "waxed" script of Hitler, he saw what he was meant to see, and indeed what he wanted to see. Brundage stated publicly

---

16. Brueggemann, "Fissure Always Uncontained," 73.

17. Bard, "Nazi Olympics," n.p.

that Jewish athletes were being treated fairly and that the Games should go on, as planned. He even alleged the existence of a "Jewish-Communist conspiracy" to keep the United States out of the Games. This is the problem when coherence trumps all else, and when coherence further generates fragmentation, and when personal ideology forges ahead for the world to see. Many who thought and might have felt otherwise, over the fragmentation, settled for the faux coherency. Even though many nations including the United States knew of this "waxing," they nevertheless participated and closed their eyes to Hitler's prohibitive "waxing" that was put into place. "Hitler's Nazi dictatorship camouflaged its racist, militaristic character while hosting the Summer Olympics. Soft-pedaling its antisemitic agenda and plans for territorial expansion, the regime exploited the Games to bedazzle many foreign spectators and journalists with an image of a peaceful, tolerant Germany."[18]

The word *survival* means living through or living over. Those who have survived a particular horror such as the Shoah or particular wilderness experiences such as the Babylonian exile must face the daunting reality of how does one live through such an event, precisely because one must live through such moments if one is to survive. The idea of survival intimates a mandate to live again, but this kind of living through can never be as it once was, for the landscape has been transformed. Fretheim correctly observes, "We need to be confronted more directly and more often with our known and our unknown participation in the causes of suffering, and reflections on such questions can be helpful to that end."[19] Fretheim points to a two-fold imperative here. It might be a deep seated reluctance to face oneself and thereby one is unable to ever face the reality of one's complicity. As suggested elsewhere in this study, I would argue that facing oneself in whatever way, and for whatever reason, has to be one of the most difficult and challenging things that one does, and yet it is only in so doing that the possibility exists for a beginning to clarity as to why certain things transpire. So the "why" must be asked not to diminish faith, but to face the possibility that the answer lies within our human purview. Moreover, the "why" question must not be silenced by others either by casting misplaced fear, or the suggestion that asking such questions reflect a lack of faith. We might very well learn from Job an essential lesson in terms of how humans might relate to God, and not only on the occasion of one's personal pain

18. Ibid.

19. Fretheim, *Untamed Creation*, 101.

and suffering, but particularly in times when one is not personally involved. What is of significance here is the fact that one who takes the relationship with God seriously, must in fact have the level of confidence to ask personal and existential questions. In matters of gravity, one should have to face the devastating statement, "you should have asked," or "you should have said something." Job asked, and after the "God Speeches" in which Job seems to have been taken to task by God, God then extols the sustained righteousness of Job. One of the qualities that we might determine from the "God Speeches" is not that Job should not have asked questions, persistently so, as is sometimes concluded by some interpreters, but that the questions of Job might not have been encompassing and universal enough. It is not that Job should not be concerned about himself, but God invites Job to think of all of creation, and even the inherent realm of divine responsibility. In this regard, Job invites all interpreters to pose significant and large questions to God not only about oneself or for that matter one's community or nation, but for all people wherever there might be evidence of injustice, and particularly circumstances where God might be held accountable. It is precisely God's encounter with Job at the end of the book that suggests something of a divine mandate to question in a wide-ranging way. Among the many pertinent questions that we are compelled to ask, perhaps the most challenging is that of God bringing suffering on the innocent for reasons that only God knows; reasons that are never told to the suffering, and to those who wonder and lament. Thus, it is that the prophetic voice today must not focus narrowly but be attentive and accountable to the entire world where there is injustice and oppression in whatever way.

With life comes suffering in a variety of ways, not simply the possibility, but the certainty of suffering. And regardless if this is the result of human finitude, limitations or fault still human acknowledgment leaves us wondering, perhaps about what we perceive as the unfairness of it all. Or as Hall sees suffering, "Life depends in some mysterious way on the struggle to be . . . If nothing were inaccessible, nothing out of reach, and there were no unfulfilled dreams or wishes, there would also be no wonder, no surprise, and no gratitude."[20] Hall's point regarding the struggle to be is well taken, and it certainly underlines humankind's ongoing journey, one that is not unencumbered, but is filled with hills and blind corners. However, it still seems somewhat more of a justification of that which we cannot fully understand, and in a way are forced to embrace, comes from God. Are we

20. Hall, *God and Human Suffering*, 58–60.

then given pain so that we can understand the value and the wonder of joy and happiness? When one takes this to a logical conclusion, it seems that we encounter the Shoah along the way and we are then left speechless. What possible justification is there!

Cost of Saving Nineveh

As one reflects on the book of Jonah, and moves beyond what has become something of a simplistic tale of "Jonah and the Whale," and indeed beyond the ill-conceived idea of Jonah being xenophobic and the purveyor of ideas that historically have lead to an anti-semitic perspective, we once again encounter the issue of theodicy. We know now, and the prophet and the people knew then, that the Assyrian kingdom had a propensity for the abuse of power, and impulse for violence, as witnessed when the Assyrian Empire destroyed the Northern Kingdom of Israel in 721 BCE. Given this, the searching and difficult question must be asked: why would God set out to save a nation, particularly with the somewhat extreme measures witnessed in Jonah, knowing that Assyrian Empire would in fact come to destroy Israel? So then, the question arises as to whether God should be proactive in saving Israel knowing that destruction looms or simply allow Israel, the people, including the innocents, and land to be punished? Part of the complexity in *Jonah* is the fact that it not only points to the theme of divine mercy for all people, including the Assyrians whose track record for abuse of power and violence is known and documented, but also the question of divine justice. Thus, would a just God save the Assyrians, or for that matter invite the Assyrians to repentance knowing that with the possibility of repentance, these very Assyrians will indeed destroy Israel? In this regard, perhaps one might argue that Jonah, aware as he was of the Assyrian history and propensity for violence, and the execution of unbridled power, simply did not want to have God exercise what is very much a part of who God is, namely a God of justice and mercy. One might also argue with some justification that one should not be condemned on the basis of what one imagines might happen in the future. This is a philosophical principle that humans might employ in pondering human realities, but it poses greater complexities with regard to God. It is far too easy and perhaps even simplistic to speak of devastating punishment and violence such as exile and Shoah; slavery or war, as ordinary suffering. Those who have had these experiences and have survived to have a memory can never be the same; the landscape of their lives has been irreparably altered.

> God does not seem to take the evil with all of the necessary se-
> riousness. Jonah began by addressing himself to *ra'atam* of the
> Ninevites (1:2) and he brings them back *middarkam hara'ah*, from
> their evil way (3:10), thus averting their punishment. God repents
> of the *ra'ah* which he had intended to do to them (3:10). But this
> is precisely *ra'ah gedolah*, a great evil (4:1) in Jonah's eyes . . . Jonah
> clearly expected the literal fulfillment of his oracle of doom against
> Nineveh. He preached to the Ninevites, not in order to bring them
> to repentance, but in a spirit of vengeance that is without parallel
> in Israelite prophecy . . . For ancient Israel, being is inseparable
> from performing. Abraham *is* the one who leaves Ur and becomes
> the father of faith; Jacob *is* the one who fights with the angel and
> deserves to be called Israel; Amalek *is* the wicked one who tries to
> thwart the fulfillment of Israel's destiny. Similarly Nineveh *is* the
> destroyer of Jerusalem, the concentration camp for God's people.
> God's decision to spare it perpetuates a fatal threat to Israel. One
> must always bear in mind the historical character of the reality
> of which the Bible speaks. It is furthermore in the name of the
> historical integrity of the "actors" and their acts that Jonah is also
> as much message as messenger. He feels totally implicated in the
> Nineveh affair, vis-à-vis which he keeps no objectivity. When the
> oracle's outcome is the antipode of the prophet's expectation, it is
> clear that Jonah is left with an unbearable split of his personal-
> ity. He was wholly committed to his message "yet forty days and
> Nineveh shall be overthrown." A reprieve of the sentence or, worse,
> a verdict of cancellation is violation of his person.[21]

One of the arguments, legitimate and arguable, is whether one can make such judgments suggesting a kind of determinism that punishments are made on the basis of what one might expect or anticipate in the future. Indeed the entire fabric of repentance would unravel if indeed a person of tomorrow would always reflect the person of yesterday particularly in terms of evil intent or actions. And this is surely a message of redemption, that is, one is not left to wither and die in one's present reality. The reason why YHWH would have repented of the evil even after the announcement by Jonah that Nineveh would be destroyed in forty days underlines why one must attend to repentance seriously, and not make judgments on the basis that one's repentance cannot be believed to carry over into the future.

21. LaCocque and LaCocque, *Jonah*, 139.

Yet, this decision by YHWH and the decision to allow Babylon to become another prison of the Israelites led to the razing of the Temple and the destruction of Jerusalem. The LaCocques argue that in fact, while this kind of dramatic change is possible, it would in fact take a miracle, and since the history of change is not predicated on miracles, this kind of dramatic change by the Ninevites is not likely.

> The Nineveh of tomorrow is not necessarily the Nineveh of yesterday. This, in part, is the lesson of the book of Jonah. But for this metamorphosis to happen, no less than a miracle must occur. Only a miracle can alter the unswerving course of heavenly bodies, but Jonah's "logic of faith" militates against such a hypothesis, not only because history is not made up of miracles, but when they do occur it is in Bethlehem, in Judah, in Palestine. That they can actually happen in Nineveh is in Jonah's eyes a remote possibility that is not to be envisaged. For all practical purpose, Nineveh is what it represents; it represents evil. Jonah's anger does not, therefore, emerge from solipsism and parochialism. It is a righteous wrath for which Jonah feels no shame.[22]

In this narrative, fundamental conventions are overturned. We are fully expecting that the prophets will listen and obey whatever it is that YHWH has told them to pronounce, even though they might be reluctant or even refuse or be in a state of question. Finally the expectation is that they will listen and follow. In *Jonah*, both expectation and convention are overturned as Jonah refuses, and the Ninevites listen, and thereby have a reprieve and Nineveh lives; in time Nineveh will return to destroy Israel. Thus, one wonders whether this is a sign of God's mercy, weakness, or as the Wisdom of Solomon testifies that this is indeed an expression of God's omnipotence. The fact that God is creator, is both able and willing and perhaps compelled precisely to act in the manner because God is God.[23] Perhaps, it is the case that Jonah is not disappointed as he knew from the beginning that God would likely do this and so now he must decide if in fact this will undermine his credibility as a prophet. He made a pronouncement as mandated by God only to see his words lead to a divine reprieve not to the punishment that he believes the Ninevites deserved. The circumstances that emerged might very lead him to wonder if he misconstrued his calling and the message. That is to say, it is not simply that Jonah knew that the

22. Ibid.
23. Wis 11:23–24.

mercy of God was such that it will likely be given to the evil Ninevites but that he will begin to wonder about his role. Given, that he might have concluded that YHWH's decision will inevitably lead to the demise of Israel, along with other prophets such as Elijah and Jeremiah, he might wonder if it is not better to die than endure this sense of doubt and divine betrayal. But as is the case with all of the prophets who saw death as an option, God would have none of it.

> Jonah's theology is not one-sided; he cannot be accused of believing an authoritarian God who would lack the attributes of mercy and compassion . . . Jonah, therefore, simply *chooses* to call into question the exercise of divine mercy toward Nineveh. This, he thinks, is tantamount to warming a snake on one's breast . . . Clearly the prophet does not seek to protect himself; he, rather, puts himself in jeopardy, as he did on the boat, showing to all that he is not a coward . . . He rejects any idea of an absurd existence where justice is flouted by the very one who is its initiator, its founder and its guardian.[24]

Given this, one of the ongoing questions that continues to be in the forefront of our consciousness, and one which needs to be reckoned with is that of the quality of redemption. Is redemption possible in every instance even in evil hearts and those who have a perpetual evil inclination and impulse? To point to the defining instance of our time, the Shoah, is it possible to imagine redemption for Hitler and the Nazis? Is the mercy shown to Nineveh an indication that even for the Ninevites, knowing their historical propensity for evil and what in fact they did to Israel later, there is still hope for transformation and the justification of redemption? In a dialogue between Origen and Jerome regarding this very issue, the two early Church Fathers came to radically different conclusions. "Origen insisted upon the full pardon of the repentant sinner; at the end even the devil will be converted. Jerome reacted to this opinion with indignation, rhetorically asking whether ultimately there will be no difference between the Virgin Mary and a prostitute, between the angel Gabriel and the devil, between the martyrs and their torturers."[25]

---

24. LaCocque and LaCocque, *Jonah*, 143.

25. Ibid., 145.

MEMORY AND SHAME

There have been instances in which those who have been the victims of injustice or oppression have survived and have themselves gained power, proceed to perpetuate the cycle of violence. Victims having had the experience of what it means to be oppressed and who lived under tyranny cannot in turn become oppressors, particularly under the guidance of, and relationship with the God who delivers them from, and breaks the bonds of oppression and injustice. In this regard, one reflects on the major infrastructural undertaking by Solomon, including the building of the Temple and the manner in which the success of such a massive enterprise eventuated. Slave labor of the Hebrews by the Pharaoh was such a bane that the memory of it has lingered in the consciousness to this day and it is surely one of the defining moments in the life of ancient Israel. Yet, once again, either there is a lapse in memory at the highest level or a disregard of the lessons and experiences of history. In order to build extensively, Solomon conscripted his people and so engineered a new era of forced labor, and from all indication, those who were the principal workers were his people, those with little power to avoid such conscription. As we are aware today, those with power have the voice and position to avoid such conscription for reasons that may not be accessible to all. Certainly in ancient Israel, not everyone was viewed equally. The fact is, forgetfulness has devastating consequences, because we are destined to repeat our mistakes and have no context from which to understand the consequences of our actions. In forgetting what is central, two elements are to be noted. First, forgetfulness shifts the focus of our attention and core conviction to other now privileged idols in a sort of hedonism. The prophet Hosea pronounces:

> Israel has forgotten his Maker, and built palaces;
> and Judah has multiplied fortresses;
> but I will send a fire upon his cities,
> and it shall devour his strongholds.[26]

This pronouncement from Hosea encapsulated three particular aspects of grave concern: forgetfulness of the creator; extravagance by rulers; the multiplication of its military prowess. In this case, forgetfulness of God is directly connected to the confidence of the military protection and a lifestyle of opulence and extravagance. Yet, such confidence is self-indulgence and military fortresses will not withstand the divine inferno that will destroy

---

26. Hos 8:14.

the strongholds. That is the result of forgetfulness. It allows the people, in this case the leaders and the powerful, to find a new center. Here, tellingly the two foci are opulence and fortification of the military. But there is an even more devastating consequence of the people's forgetfulness, and that is, God will in turn forget them. This in effect places the relationship on very thin ice.[27] Moreover what the people of Israel were told, and the essential message for contemporary society and religious institutions, remains for the most part the same, namely, perish. Given the nature of *our* society and its unbridled preoccupation with commodity and more commodity, and the dramatic expanse of the divide between wealthy and poor, it would be easy perhaps to dismiss such a pronouncement as unfounded or explain it away as archaic and no longer applicable. But this kind of dismissal also reflects what society has come to believe, namely that might, particularly military and imperial might, might hint that such pronouncements do not apply or affect. The act of not forgetting or remembering is neither abstract nor theoretical; it must be active. One's life must be a testimony to remembering the one or those to whom one belongs and what that means. "Memory of the painful past corrects an amnesia of both divine and human identity . . . Memory and shame: taking responsibility for past actions and acknowledging our failures—Ezekiel affirms repeatedly that this kind of self knowledge is necessary if a future of hope is to open before us."[28] The importance of memory not only significantly ensures that the past injustices are not repeated, but even moreso not to remember is not to live. How can one really live without a memory, without being attentive to what has gone before, and how might one be shaped in light of this? There is an existential issue to be reckoned with here, namely our capacity for self-reflection and self-critique. This surely is one of the most difficult undertakings if for no other reason than it poses the real possibility that we might discover within us that which must be changed, altered, transformed. So today, as it was in ancient Israel, many simply choose not to reflect and in so doing make a decision that the path on which they travel is one that will never be changed. Perhaps there is fear in facing who we are, and yet we must wonder about the cost of no self-reflection.

Without self-reflection, how might we possibly have a sense of what our sins are, our errors, the pain which we might have wrought, and indeed the joy that we might have been the subject of? In other words, self-reflection

---

27. Hos 4:6.

28. Lapsley, "Genius of the Mad Prophet," 136.

and self-critique are not simply an afterthought, a luxury, but a necessity. But there is also the matter of being ashamed of what we have done in the past, call it sin or some other term, and the capacity to face the past and to acknowledge our actions and seek repentance, repair and restoration. Self-assessment and reflection are certainly very difficult and many have made the choice to avoid them, perhaps with the hope that the challenges might disappear. Of course whatever challenges there might be do not simply disappear. In the United States in general we are very reluctant to have any kind of collective national self-critique and as a consequence, whatever it is that confronts us it is very difficult to take particular responsibility for what occurred. Memory was also significant for the ancient Israelites. They must remember YHWH and the history of redemption and salvation, given that forgetting or neglecting inevitably leads to acts of injustice. Moreover, one must remember both in times of suffering and in times of prosperity. In the case of punishment and suffering, when painful and persistent questions about belonging and abandonment abound, divine absence, divine silence, and fear all are woven together, it was important to remember the times when they were given assurance and hope in the midst of despair; judgment and punishment are not the last word. Such memory cannot be confused with reminiscence as good as the latter might be under the right circumstances, but an active sense of remembering. Indeed extravagance generated by injustices and lavish lifestyles are no more the last word than is suffering. "Memory alone would not have been enough on which to base hope for exiles. As an end in itself it becomes a preoccupation with the past . . . Memory served to enable discernment of God's new thing for Israel's future. That future was to be no mere repeat of the past. Even when the prophets use a familiar image for them from the tradition it was often transformed in keeping with trust that God was doing a 'new thing.'"[29]

> See, the former things have now come to pass,
>   and new things I now declare;
> before they spring forth,
>   I tell you of them.
> Sing to the LORD a new song,
>   his praise from the end of the earth![30]

"The people's failure to know themselves is revealed especially whenever Ezekiel refers to the benefits of shame, yes, the benefits of feeling ashamed.

29. Birch, *Let Justice Roll Down*, 294.

30. Isa 42:9–10a.

For Ezekiel, shame is a profound gift, and an essential element of self-knowledge . . . Remembering our sins is a crucial part of self-knowledge . . . and remembering the past is always accompanied by an appropriate sense of shame, spurred by the recollection of our past actions."[31] There is certainly something of a difference between being "shamed" by someone and having a sense of shame. The point is not being forced into shame, but to come to that moment for the right reasons. Within the context of the Hebrew prophets, one notes Jeremiah's pronouncement.

> They acted shamefully, they committed abominations;
>> yet they were not ashamed,
>> they did not know how to blush.
> Therefore they fall among those who fall;
>> at the time I push them, they will be overthrown, says the LORD.[32]

That is to say, shame has to do most fundamentally with an acknowledgement of actions gone before. Indeed an essential component of shame is confessional in nature. It is an acknowledgment that what has happened by way of injustices, oppression or atrocities must not happen again. Not to be ashamed of these acts on behalf of those who have gone before us, and in whose footsteps we travel, is not only to show a wanton disregard for the pain and suffering, but to give the impression that a lack of shame is an indication that it is likely to occur again. To be sure, there is nothing simple or easy about being ashamed; indeed it is particularly difficult if the shame must be on behalf of our ancestors. Yet, the alternative is even more painful and destructive. Thus, not to feel shame for slavery, or indentured servant-hood or genocide is to live with a belief that whatever the form of injustice, we cannot be responsible for the actions or perhaps even the belief. This invariably may lead to the conclusion that whatever the actions were, they must have been justified, or of no import. To hold in tension the positive regard that we have for our ancestors and the counter intuitive reality that their actions might have been destructive is difficult. The challenge is not simply to know intellectually or logically that what transpired was unjust and oppressive, but to be able to engage the heart as well. While we may have deep affection for our ancestors, the test of our sense of justice is to have the will to be engaged with our moral agency even when we must face ourselves in the persons of our ancestors. "Prophetic calls to shame in the

---

31. Lapsley, "Genius of the Mad Prophet," 134.

32. Jer 6:15.

context of history are not calls to a paralyzing guilt or humiliation. It is a call to recognize the constant failures of living according to alternative ideals and values . . . Shame therefore is not a psychology, it is a politics."[33] To feel shame for our ancestors is at the same time to face ourselves. At every level and under every circumstance shame must be felt and not be simply an embarrassment that is concluded with a passing *mea culpa*. Michael Sells has pointed out the refusal of the Serbian Orthodox Church to not even acknowledge the genocidal policies of the Serbs. This is the first step to feeling shame and if there is intransigence on the part of the Church, and if the Church will not acknowledge such heinous atrocities then could the church bear witness to God's justice and the centrality of confession and forgiveness.[34]

The juxtaposition of Isaiah and Jeremiah is very instructive both for an understanding of the progression and relationship of the prophetic message and also for the interpreters, and their understanding of the importance of memory. Thus, we know that Jeremiah challenged Hananiah on the latter's proclamation that Jerusalem will be safe and there will be peace. Isaiah had prophesied that while Israel will face severe judgment through the conquest by Assyria, Jerusalem will be saved and delivered from such punishment. One of the fundamental lessons here is the fact that one must learn from one's past, and the history that surrounds and encompasses us. We see the evidence of this in two important ways. Hananiah was inattentive to the fact since the time of Isaiah, the behavior of Jerusalem had changed dramatically and thus a reprieve from the Assyrians did not commit Jerusalem to a *carte blanche* freedom from judgment. Jeremiah on the other hand was cognizant to the fact that the messages of those who came before and prophesied have to be remembered. The prophets and their message therefore did not function independently of each other; the one constant being God. What Jeremiah knew was that unless Jerusalem heeded the mistakes of Israel, judgment would be meted out to Jerusalem as well. If ever there was a universal lesson to be heeded here, it would certainly be that we must have a memory that is beyond the recent past, and perhaps most importantly, we must have a memory that does not assume that which has gone before us cannot be replicated. For that matter we ourselves who do not carry the blood stained hands of our ancestors, howsoever faints these stains might be, are not above reproach. Those who

33. Smith-Christopher, *Theology of Exile*, 76.
34. See Sells, "Kosovo Mythology," 180–207.

in the past have taken on this posture have done so at their own peril. What is particularly striking about Jeremiah's message, specifically in his *Letter to the Exiles*, is the recognition that there were prophets among the exiles who were preaching a message of empty and painless deliverance. It is not that there was no recognition that the people were in exile, but rather the unwarranted belief that life in exile will be brief and the judgment will pass quickly and life will return to the way things were. This, for Jeremiah would not be, for he was compelled to pronounce very specifically that they must in fact live their lives fully in Babylon. Jeremiah was not in any way relishing the pronouncement of judgment, but he recognized that as painful as it was, the truth must be told. We are further reminded that before all else in Jeremiah, words of restoration, to build; to plant (Jer 1:10) are made; it is also made clear that what was about to transpire in terms of judgment and punishment will not be the last word. However the moments of "darkness" so to speak cannot be circumvented or for that matter navigated away. If anything, Jeremiah's message is that all of life must be lived even in the midst of exile and among those who are deemed the enemy. Having said this we are still faced with difficult questions, such as divine judgment not predicated on any kind of sustained evil or sinful behavior.

Jeremiah tells the people not to listen to the more popular but false assurances that the exile is nothing more than a "passing glitch" and will soon be over. Indeed Jeremiah's younger contemporary Ezekiel points to the rebuilding of the Temple and Jerusalem, but does so on the heels of having made clear that the reason in the first place that this is even necessary is that all creation has been corrupted through idolatry. While one may not dispute this reality, we are to equally recognize that such an idea as this cannot be applied universally. Ezekiel has been particularly concerned about the problem of evil and what might have precipitated the evil of exile and the devastating punishment that was the exile. Ezekiel believed with justification that the destruction of the Temple and Jerusalem were the result of the people's intransigence and attitude of ritual self-indulgence that ultimately led to judgment. Certainly, there were many moments of resistance and reluctance to bring such devastating message to the people. No prophet took pleasure in bringing a message of doom and destruction, and on occasions the reluctance was so sharp that the prophets not only brought the message, but even cast derisive comments against God's decision and the divine insistence on severe punishment. The prophet's life is such that his identification with his people (and one thinks most notably about Jeremiah in this regard) that his loyalty and deep compassion only made his message so much more unbearable and difficult to proclaim. Indeed Jeremiah grieved and was pained for his people, the people whom he loved and with whom his life was deeply invested. But it is precisely a prophet such as Jeremiah that reminds us that as much as he cared deeply for his people, he could not casually approach the message, nor was he crazy about the idea of delivering it, yet his principal and first loyalty was to God. The people's pain would be his pain, and in this respect, his words first pierced his heart along with the people. While a prophet such as Amos made pronouncements and then left, and though his words would live on with him, and his words would be the framework for future prophets' ethical imperatives, it is entirely different when the prophet lives among the very people, and to whom his words will serve as a devastating indictment and judgment. The challenge with Ezekiel's message is not only that it has unequivocal truth with regard to Judah and Jerusalem of the sixth Century, but how might one translate this message for today, particularly in light of some systemic and devastating evil such as the Shoah.

The fact remains that in some very striking ways, memory, and the act of remembering might very well be a double edge sword. Some memories are so very deep that one cannot get out from under them. It is not to suggest that one must forget, but the deep memory is such for some that it becomes another remarkable burden that cannot be shared. Former President Jimmy Carter relates the story of the meeting of Egyptian President Anwar Sadat and Israeli Prime Minister Menachem Begin meeting at Camp David to work out a peace treaty, which would emerge as the Camp David Agreement. In the first face to face to meeting between Prime Minister Begin and President Sadat, Prime Minister Begin was so aggrieved about the ancient Hebrews being in bondage in Egypt, that he spoke about such Egyptian oppression and reached so far back in the history and memory of what transpired that such deep memory had the potential to unravel the fragile talks before they ever settled into forming something permanent and formidable. So the question is whether the possibility exists that imagination can be born out of such deeply set memory? The answer must be "yes." Though it comes with substantial challenges, it can be a road that leads to redemption. "In some way too, with the exception of surviving victims, all are witnesses to memory rather than remember themselves. They have an 'unstory' to tell."[35]

35. Langer, *Shoah Testimonies*, 39.

2

Prophecy and Prophetic Literature

A rguably it is the case that biblical scholarship over the last 400 years or so has been shaped principally by the Reformation/Counter-Reformation and the Enlightenment. In large part what this has done is to emphasize the centrality of rationalistic thinking and somewhat later, historical criticism. Indeed for a prolonged time these methods have been granted a privileged status in biblical scholarship, and in all of this time, while surrounded by the presence and influence of imperialism and colonialism, biblical scholars have been remarkably reluctant to employ other methods in shaping the trajectories of biblical hermeneutics.

> There are two greater dangers within the field. One is an uncritical acceptance of the principal tenets of the discipline, and the other, its failure to relate it to the society in which its work is done. Biblical Studies is still seduced by the modernistic notion of using the rational as a key to open the text and fails to accept intuition, sentiment and emotion as a way into the text. By and large the world of biblical interpretation is detached from the problems of the contemporary world and has become ineffectual because it has failed to challenge the status quo or work for any sort of social change.[1]

It is sometimes quite difficult for us to understand the encounters between the Hebrew prophets and the communities and peoples with whom they related, and the relationship between God and these prophets. For the most part these kinds of divine and prophetic encounters are absent, or at best sparese in today's world. Invariably when I speak to groups about the

---

1. Sugirtharajah, *Postcolonial Biblical Reader*, 18–19.

Hebrew Prophets, I ask the question, "who are the prophets in our generation or who have been the prophets in the last century or so?" Without providing too many details, I have suggested to the various audiences that they use the Hebrew Prophet as something of a model. In posing this question I typically have not had any preconceived names that I am seeking to elicit in particular, but the responses that I have received have been quite revealing. There was often a challenge to generate names and while Gandhi and Martin Luther King invariably made the list, it was typically not long before names of popular preachers or even celebrities were cited. It is not to suggest in any way that many of those named did not have merit in terms of who they were and what they did, but to speak of a prophet is distinctive. Occasionally one confuses a minister or priest with a prophet. And while it is true that a member of the clergy might be prophetic in his or her message from time to time, it should never be the case that the roles are seen to be interchangeable. Certainly within the Hebrew Bible there is no confusion between the prophet and the priest. Why might there be confusion between the roles of clergy and prophet today? And indeed why is it that many find it difficult to embrace the role of prophet today, along the lines of the manner of the Hebrew prophet?

First, we live in a world where the technological and scientific developments have generated a healthy element of cynicism for most people in terms of that which might be prophetic. In part because of the quest to have empirical proof for practically everything, there has developed a kind of division between what can be believed and what must be proven. We witness from the various topics on which the Hebrew prophets spoke that all of life was rooted in God and therefore one could not proceed with arguments that separated one section of life from the other. This was an intensely important issue as the people of ancient Israel sought to remove the practice of worship from the ethical elements of life. In effect they sought to separate the care of the neighbor (understood to be a secular matter) from the worship of YHWH (a sacred matter). This division was to trigger sharp invectives from Israelite prophets. Certainly this unity of the sacred and the secular was not unique to Israel, for it was also present in other Near Eastern societies and it continues to be an essential aspect of the spiritual and biblical inheritance of both Jews and Christians.

Second, in today's society, there are some who have laid claims to have had private revelations from God. While there are loyal groups of believers who are willing to subscribe to and follow such religious figures and the revelations they claim to have received, it is often through their monetary support that they sustain such persons. Many others view such "private revelations" available to the public for a price with a certain degree of justifiable suspicion. The "private line to God" is not a saleable feature of religious experience in contemporary society. Recent experiences of this sort have only served to intensify the suspicion about the nature and role of prophecy. This however was not the atmosphere under which the Hebrew prophets delivered their message. While there were questions regarding the motives of some prophets and indeed there were questions about the essence of their message, nevertheless the religious experiences of the Hebrew prophets have not only survived, but their message have maintained a remarkable and striking relevance and resonance. The prophets of ancient Israel had the deep rooted conviction that God was actively involved in the affairs of the people, and because of the covenant with Israel, God would communicate his will to the prophets to ensure that the relationship was kept intact not only in a vertical way with God but in a seamless horizontal way with each other.

Brueggemann is certainly on point when he says that there is an element of urgency to disconnect "the academic community away from self-preoccupied triviality that is such a waste, the ecclesial communities away from excessive certitude that is idolatry and the civic community away from brutality rooted in autonomy."[2] An unmistakable and deeply rooted feature of the Hebrew prophets that cannot be negotiated away is the fact that what they have to say will happen within the context of history. The prophets in this regard are not appealing to an apocalyptic vision for the practice of justice. While there are instances when there is a vision of the next life, when there will be no more tears and the old life will pass away, the prophets for the most part are preaching for transformation and justice in this world. What this means for the prophets is that punishment, destruction, exile, scattering will all happen in this world and in the concreteness of societal settings. It might seem to some that what the prophets proclaimed will be fulfilled in the afterlife, and others who are too entrenched in places of comfort and security might in fact dismiss the prophetic call as utopian. But one is reminded that utopia carries the meaning of *nowhere*, and indeed the call for justice will in fact take place, and it is somewhere, and it is in our time and will be in other times as well. But most assuredly it is not *nowhere*. The prophets experienced God in a variety of ways, some of which

---

2. Brueggemann, *Deep Memory*, 122.

are shocking to us. Despite those who today say that they take the Bible literally and follow it as in a textbook, hardly would they consider walking around naked as Isaiah did or others who exhibited ecstatic behaviors. But there is more to this sacred experience. Some today have intimated as much that God not only identifies with us as a people, as perhaps the "new chosen," but also with our system of government. But in fact as it is, God is not tethered to one political system; God's working is not tied to one worldview and indeed the message of the prophets is directed to every source of injustice regardless of the political system. "Like the God who appeared to Moses in the burning bush, such a God subverts rather than legitimates the social order."[3]

The prophets are so deeply entrenched in the system that they cannot begin to envision extricating themselves, assuming that there is even an impulse to do so. Martin Luther King Jr. in his "Letter from Birmingham Jail," where he speaks forcefully about what I would deem the "urgency of now," emphasized the significance of immediacy and urgency. In matters of injustice, justice delayed is justice denied and waiting is the equivalent of never, according to king. In the message of the prophets, there is no waiting. Tomorrow is now. While there are many similarities in the message of the prophets, nevertheless their different foci point to the spontaneous and contextual nature of their message. While we have inherited their message as part of scripture, it was first delivered within a particular time in history to a particular people. Further, a basic presupposition among scholars today is that not all the words that we find in the text can be ascribed to the prophets. This naturally only serves to compound the problem, because the system of redaction and refinement not only creates textual and redactional speculation, but adds an element of incoherency to the already complicated interpretive issue.

It is therefore impossible to place the prophets in well rounded categories. Depending on the emphasis which is placed, the prophets have been called "ethicists," "revolutionaries," "reformers," "traditionalists," "Yahwists," "poets," and "messengers" among others. This wide range of possibilities in itself underlines the difficulty which exists. Clearly to posit the prophets as exclusively or even primarily one of th   ese is to run the risk of overlooking significant textual evidence which might indicate differing notions. While the message of the prophets includes all of the elements listed above, I have suggested elsewhere that the prophets were fundamentally

3. Borg, *Reading the Bible*, 126.

"witnesses," as Abraham Heschel has convincingly argued.[4] There is also one other aspect of the role of the prophet that merits mentioning. The Hebrew prophets were not all from the same socio-economic situation, or from the same locations, or of the same status or station in life. In fact they are from North and South, urban and rural, politically connected and without political ties or intimate connection with social and political institutions. The prophets do however have one essential factor in common and that is their core message. Moreover, they do not have structural and institutional ties and are not beholden to anyone, including those on whose behalf they speak. And of course they are not beholden to "special interest groups" who wield their power to influence their message. As witnesses they spoke the words of God without diluting it. They were challenged, they were rebuked, they were ostracized, and they were excommunicated. Being a prophet was not a position with great job security, but there was no escaping the call.

The Hebrew prophets were more than predictors of the future. Rather than simply making pronouncements in which they were somehow not personally invested, the prophets embraced and invested themselves in issues that they spoke about. Heschel suggests that they were some place between human and divine.[5] One should not conclude as some are wont to do that the call and role of the prophet was an easy and sought after position. Indeed, there is no instance where a prophet sought such a calling. Moreover, there were many moments of resistance and reluctance to make such devastating announcements to the people. But there is also another factor. The words of the prophet is often so dramatic that at first glance one is sure to conclude that the prophet must be exaggerating, that surely his words cannot possibly be true. The prophetic words invite a vision that is so far reaching and dramatic, spoken to a people who are often deeply rooted in the present and the manner they imagine life will be, that such dramatic words might strike them as wholly untrue and impossible.

> It is embarrassing to be a prophet. There are so many pretenders, predicting peace and prosperity, offering cheerful words, adding strength to self-reliance, while the prophet predicts disaster, pestilence, agony, and destruction. People need exhortations to courage, endurance, confidence, fighting spirit, but Jeremiah

---

4. Gossai, *Social Critique by Israel's Eighth-Century Prophets*, 221–41.

5. Heschel, *Prophets*, 1–26.

proclaims: You are about to die if you do not have a change of heart and cease being callous to the world of God.[6]

For you shall go to all to whom I send you,
and you shall speak whatever I command you . . .
Now I have put my words in your mouth.
see, today I appoint you over nations and over kingdoms,
to pluck up and to pull down,
to destroy and to overthrow,
to build and to plant.[7]

Despite the somewhat common notion today of some who would willingly and casually take on the mantle of prophet and under this guise make pronouncements, often reflecting their personal ideologies, the Hebrew prophet was not one to flaunt being a prophet; not one to seek the role of prophet, not one who seemed enamored with the very idea of being a prophet. Rather, the Hebrew prophet is something of a solitary figure without the structural support that others might have, and we have no indication that the prophet returns to a family, to a place of belonging. Instead, solitude is his companion, as he seems to alienate all others. Heschel underlines the drama and pain of such calling in his rendering and commentary on Jeremiah's encapsulation of his call:

Oh, LORD, you have seduced me,
    and I am seduced;
you have raped me
    and I am overcome.[8]

Typically, this verse is translated in a way that seeks to capture more of a "PG" rating while the text itself is graphic and more of an "R" rating. In diluting the drama and radicalism of the prophet's confession, most modern translations have in fact done a terrible disservice under the guise of propriety.

The words used by Jeremiah to describe the impact of God upon his life are identical with the terms for seduction and rape in the legal terminology of the Bible. The call to be a prophet is more than an invitation. It is first of all a feeling of being enticed, or acquiescence or willing surrender. But this winsome feeling is only

6. Ibid., 17.
7. Jer 1:7b, 9b–10.
8. Jer 20:7.

one aspect of the experience. The other aspect is a sense of being ravished or carried away by violence, or yielding to overpowering force against one's own will. The prophet feels both the attraction and the coercion of God, the appeal and the pressure, the charm and the stress. He is conscious of both voluntary identification and forced capitulation.[9]

FACING THE TEXT

The prophets' message must not be relegated to a place of historical reminiscence, but instead must be deeply embedded into the fabric of what is pronounced and preached today. In many respects those who dare to proclaim the prophetic word today, and it is daring in the deepest sense, must know that what they are doing is in fact walking in the already challenging steps of the ancient prophets. If anything, the choice is as stark today as it was in ancient Israel. Even as wealth, power, and social and judicial inequities abound in our society and those who embody these realities as the dominant reality cast them as hegemonic, the prophetic world establishes a different hegemony. A creational hegemony reiterates and confirms that all persons are created equal, and it is the way that relationships are to be lived out. As with the Hebrew prophets, this kind of message comes with tangible risks. Yet it cannot be relegated to a mere option among many. It is *the* alternative. We are reminded that carrying the mantle of prophet does not mean that one escapes the vagaries and dangers of those with power to cause harm and use violence. No prophet is beyond such; Elijah being a prime example. The very interpretation of the biblical text suffers from a kind of division between those who have had for a long period of time unchallenged positions of privileged power of interpretation that seek to distance oneself or even disconnect from the text, and the circumstances and challenges, and those persons who have made a point of employing new methods of interpretations that bring a personal engagement where the text is not viewed merely as a historical artifact. With the emergence of a number of voices in the latter category, no longer is it possible to simply conclude that what lies behind the text is of principal value. Historical criticism thus has for a long time served to obscure, perhaps even conceal, the radicalism of the prophetic text.[10]

9. Heschel, *Prophets*, 114.

10. Cf. Brueggemann, *Word Militant*, 22.

Eric Hirsch has argued, "Valid interpretation is always governed by a valid inference about genre . . . Every disagreement about an interpretation is usually a disagreement about genre."[11] While there is truth to Hirsch's perspective, it is of a particular truth and may very well apply more to the area of scholarship, where it more likely reflects the differences between scholars and those who pursue the historical, cultural and *Sitz im Leben* of texts. However, by and large, the differences in interpretation lie more often in what readers bring to the texts and the ideologies that are either defended or promoted. One must be aware of three constant realities: the voice of the text, the methods used to interpret the text, and the voice of the one who reads the text. Each interpreter/reader is shaped by what he/she hears and the trajectories of the text. Moreover not all of the voices will form a kind of synchronicity—in fact there is likely to be dissonance and much of this has to do with who we are and what we bring to the text. What this tells us in part is that the message of the text is not monolithic and unilateral. Each of us brings a particular truth to the text that we read and we hear. When someone says, as some do, that they read the text "objectively" and they simply speak to what the text says, they are being either disingenuous, and aware of it, or unaware that they bring a point of view. The most basic truth in the interpretive endeavor is that we bring who we are to the text. This is neither an unwelcome nor a naïve thing; it is simply the way it is. The challenge is not to refrain and seek to refrain from bringing who we are to the text, but rather to be self aware and ensure that neither our voice nor the voice of the text is silenced. That is the challenge we face and it is one that is often dismissed ironically by those who do use their voices to shape the message of the text.

Stephen Fowl argues that one only has to observe the many and varied ways in which texts are read to elicit particular perspectives to conclude that texts in and of themselves do not have ideologies, but those who read them do.[12] Fowl's argument does have merit to the degree that often it is the case that one is able to dominate a text with one's ideological voice to the point that the text itself is forced to fit what the interpreter intends. This is neither new nor unique, for everyone who reads a text brings who he or she is to the text. Yet, this is not the entire truth for the text also has a voice, and within the text lies a worldview, and perspective that were brought into the text itself.

11. Hirsch, *Validity in Interpretation*, 98.
12. Fowl, "Texts Don't Have Ideologies," 15–34.

When we think of the various methodologies, including the well established archaeological and literary methods that are used in biblical studies, we are reminded that all, each in its own way, begin with certain presuppositions and assumptions. In the case of social scientific methods, the role is somewhat more challenging in arriving at conclusions, and one of the challenges is not to draw conclusions as if they are historically based. The social scientific criticism invites an examination of the socio-cultural aspects of the text or texts under exegesis, and in so doing provides insights into the world of the writers and the intended audience. Perhaps under ideal circumstances one would be able to discover such contexts and environments in some detail, but even if one is not able to do so fully, the method should serve to widen the angle, and add to the already well established methodologies that are used. Social scientific approach like other approaches is an important guide in the navigation of the sometimes murky and difficult waters of interpretation though in itself it does not establish indisputable evidence of a historical nature. It could be that cultural-evolutionary theory will also provide insight in the lingering and important question of identity. While we may not know the identity of the oppressors that the Hebrew prophets addressed, one should not necessarily conclude that the criticisms are generic, perhaps anonymous. In a way unanimity makes it applicable to everyone. Though not always an easy line to walk, it still remains the case that implications and meaning for today's society are not wholly shaped by historical contexts. Moreover, we do have some sense of the effects that oppression and injustices have had on the people and from these effects one is able to draw conclusions and implications. "A greater understanding of the contexts behind prophetic complaints against injustice might not only lead to a greater understanding of the world of those that wrote these texts, it could also reveal connections between ancient and modern cases of economic oppression."[13]

The insistence on prophetic justice carries with it a passion that is predicated on the partiality of God with regard to the care of the oppressed. It is not a dispassionate approach or as some would argue, sticking to objectivity and the established legal procedures. This kind of prophetic justice does force us to step away from the more secure space of doing what is narrowly construed as objective, knowing that objectivity in this regard is practically impossible, and not indeed a virtue for which to strive.

---

13. Coomber, "Caught in the Crossfire?," 399.

> Justice represented as a blindfolded virgin, while conveying the essential thought of the rightful caution of the mind against illusions and partiality of the heart, conceives of the process of justice as mechanical process, as if the life of man was devoid of individuality and uniqueness and could be adequately understood in terms of inexorable generalizations. There is a point at which strict justice is unjust.[14]

"Strict justice" as Heschel observes invariably upholds the status quo and a pronounced sense of order, and in a sense is an official conduit for injustice. What we have in the Hebrew prophet as spokesperson for YHWH is that injustice cannot be taken as a normal part of the human landscape, and cannot be accepted as simply the way things are. "Progressive justice activists frame their understanding inclusively, while conservatives frame it exclusively . . . Progressive prophetic activism is characterized by its concern for the *other*, for those who are marginalized. In the midst of the chaos and pain of the present, prophetic politics envisions an altered future in which human relationship to one another and their natural order are repaired."[15] One of the issues in the exploration of socio-political and economic injustices and exploitation in Hebrew prophets is the fact that it is not always clear as to who the perpetrators and the victims are. In particular a number of texts in the Eighth-Century prophets that have become standards for speaking to the injustices in ancient Israel are without identities of subjects and objects. While this may be true in general, it is the case in some instances that one is able to extrapolate from the text the identity of the perpetrators. Both Isaiah (5:22–23) and Amos (4:4–6) indict those whose heroics and bravery are in drinking wine and mixing drinks. This kind of courage and heroics stand in sharp contrast to the taking of bribes, acquitting the guilty, and depriving the innocent of their rights. In this instance the focus is on the Judges who have the responsibility and power to ensure that the innocent are not deprived of their rights. This is where the courage and the heroics should be, but the bribes taken by the judges crush the poor and innocent and provide the necessary lifestyle of the powerful. So who are the people responsible—the nobility, the haughty, those entrusted with the execution of justice, those who are deceitful, those who have replaced divine wisdom with their own, indeed all the people, the throngs. Not only will those in power, but everyone will be held responsible.[16]

14. Heschel, *Prophets*, 215.

15. Slessarev-Jamir, "Prophetic Activism," 676.

16. Isa 5:11–25.

The prophet knows that he must deliver the message, but he also wants to know the degree and the length of the devastation; and there is no taking joy in the suffering of the people and the devastation of the land, despite the ruinous behavior of the people, is not part of the prophet's constitution. To place an exclamation to the level of devastation, even a hint of life that might be left will be destroyed. It is noteworthy that the punishment is not only focused on the people and the lack of healing that will not be afforded to them, but the ravishing of the land, and every sign of hope. For the land itself, it will be a long time before healing will come; the devastation will be complete. The land, and the houses and the cities will be no waiting for the people to inhabit them again. Instead, everything will be crushed and there will not be joy and enjoyment of the wealth and power that had been gained at the expense of those members whose very lives have been crushed for their personal gain. It is tempting to take this text as something of an anomaly, and thus view it more as an exception, but in fact it is no exception. Indeed seven centuries after the prophet spoke these words that hearken to a punishment of unprecedented proportions, such words would again be voiced, in connection with Jesus. When society arrives at a point where the very elements of our ancient counterparts that invariably defined life then for many, and life today for others are cast aside or made irrelevant and understand self-determination in the narrowest way regardless of God, while simultaneously immersing in the liturgy of self indulgence, then the devastation meted out will be equally severe. It was difficult to comprehend then, in the time of Jesus, and equally today, but the truth of the prophetic words has, and will continue to stand the test of time.

Some who see the role of the prophet as a matter of moral superiority, and who believe that they are there to proclaim an ideological message to uphold certain personal agenda, or a particular project, do so at their own peril: they do so at the expense of the text and the core of the prophetic inheritance. The task of the prophet today is not to re-create contemporary society to fit the biblical world, and so erroneously conclude that if it does not fit, then the word is not relevant. The manner in which the message of the Hebrew prophets are appropriated and applied today does not neces-sarily depend on the manner in which the message was applied in the days of ancient Israel. Indeed the meaning of the message is not inextricably tethered to the circumstances of ancient Israel. Of course, having said this, it is incumbent upon modern interpreters to be acutely cognizant of the his-tory of the prophetic words and as much as possible the broad landscape of the issues of the prophets' time. Rather, the contemporary prophetic voice is called upon to do something even more challenging, namely re-imagine the world. The relevancy of the prophetic message does not depend on the world of the Hebrew Bible. Moreover, as were the prophets of ancient times, those who speak the prophetic word today cannot, and indeed must not be beholden to any group or person, ideology or institution. Does this perhaps make for a difficult life? Invariably so. Yet, such an enticing temptation must be resisted.

It is not possible to have a prophetic voice without causing a measure of offense. Even those who may benefit from the pronouncements of the prophet might be suspect and fearful about what change may come, and what pain they may experience as a consequence. It is more than likely that the prophet will bear a great burden precisely because she/he will be the only one upon whom scorn and ridicule might be cast. Ultimately, this might not be much of a comfort to the one who speaks with a prophetic voice.

Another notable feature of the prophets is the fact that they have a variety of issues that they address and thus they cannot summarily be all placed into a single group. Self evident in the reading of the Hebrew prophets are the wide-ranging issues and occurrences against which the prophets spoke. Indeed, the prophets cannot be taken off the pages of the Hebrew Bible and be applied to our time without some element of critical analysis. The invectives they pronounced have variations that are not only present today, but in many circumstances, either tolerated or for that matter embraced or woven into the fabric of our society. One of the many challenges in the Hebrew prophets as one seeks not only to understand their message in their historical context as much as this is possible, but also to ask questions as to their meaning and implications for contemporary society, is to understand the sometimes violent punishment pronounced by the prophets and meted out by God. The text simply does not spare us in the clarity with which the punishment is pronounced, and the image and the attributes associated with God. So in the oft overlooked opening verses of Nahum, God is described as vengeful and wrathful. "A jealous and avenging God is the Lord, the Lord is avenging and wrathful; the Lord takes vengeance on his adversaries and rages against his enemies. The Lord is slow to anger but great in power, and the Lord will by no means clear the guilty. His way is in whirlwind and storm, and the clouds are the dust of his feet."[17] I would just as soon not have these words associated with God, but

17. Nah 1:1–11.

the text does not seek to protect us from the complexities of God's character and nature. The God of love is also the God who is wrathful and angry; the God of mercy is also the God of judgment; to choose attributes that we would prefer to embrace at the expense of others is to compartmentalize God and in so doing undermine who God is. It is not to say that we can fully understand all of the complexities, but perhaps it is the case that it is a reminder that there will always be a mystery as to who God is; and that, we will have to live with, and seek to know God beyond what is being revealed. Weber has argued that the Hebrew prophets had a particular emphasis on the vocation as prophets. Their aim was not so much to institute social reform but rather to focus on foreign policy. He notes "[The prophets] concern was with foreign politics, chiefly because it constituted the theater of their god's activity. The Israelite prophets were concerned with social and other types of injustice and a violation of Mosaic code primarily to explain God's wrath, and not in order to institute a program of social reform"[18] I have suggested earlier, the role of the prophet is not to be social reformers, though there is a component of social reform in what they do. However, while foreign affairs were clearly of importance to the prophets, and the oracles against the nations among other pronouncements make this clear, it can hardly be called a preoccupation.

Rather the message of the prophet is such that by definition it will challenge the status quo and those within the power establishment. This kind of disruption and the possible unraveling of the settled fabric of society will in fact generate opposition that invariably leads to violence. It would certainly be too simplistic to suggest that a prophet will inevitably get killed, though in fact this has occurred more times than not. On a plaque outside the Civil Rights museum in Memphis Tennessee, at the site of the assassination of Dr. Martin Luther King, Jr. the following words are inscribed: "They said to one another, 'Behold here comes the dreamer. Let us slay him and we will see what becomes of his dreams."[19] So what might be the motive for slaying Joseph or Martin Luther King Jr.? Is it a matter as simple as jealousy as some have suggested? "The prophets were critics of their societies, condemning religious and social practices and institutions of their times. They cannot, therefore, be understood apart from their historical and cultural settings."[20] We are unmistakably reminded of this

18. Weber, *Sociology of Religion*, 50–51.

19. Gen 37:19–20.

20. McKenzie, *How to Read the Bible*, 69.

in Amos 7 where the priest who aligns himself with the king asks Amos to leave and take his message elsewhere for he and his message are not welcomed in the king's temple. The temple has been seized and the shift of language shows the usurping of God's role and ownership. It is not so much that the prophets are not welcome, however the message that they bring, a message that is very much a part of their very being and cannot therefore be separated, is such that it is disruptive and uncomfortable. "Instead of dealing with the timeless issues of being and becoming, of matter and form, of definitions and demonstrations, he is thrown into orations about widows and orphans, about the corruption of judges and affairs of the market place. Instead of showing us a way through the elegant mansions of the mind, the prophet take us to the slums."[21] And life in the slums is by any measure challenging and difficult. Indeed it is not only life in the slums, but is often the case with the prophet, it is life on the run, where invariably one's life is in danger and peril is imminent. So to whom does the prophet turn, but to God. Yet, even here, the encounter is not always what one expects and the prophets were keenly and even painfully aware of this. It would be easy to conclude that the prophets in their relentless attack against the injustices in society are focused on a particular group. And certainly while there are certain groups that are particularly excoriated in large part because of their systemic abuse and intransigence, there is certainly no privileged group that is beyond or above the prophets' invectives. Both Micah and Amos are told not to preach on matters of social injustice and oppression. In fact the religious establishment is equally under condemnation by the prophets. Perhaps the religious leaders are even moreso condemned because they purport to bring the "good news" to the people, but in fact they too sustain the status quo and align themselves with the institutions of power.

So, for example in Mic 2:6–11, the prophet is told not to preach in the manner he does.[22] It would be a variation of being told, "Here are the topics on you which you may preach and refrain from others." He is told that one should not preach about such things. However this is not an invitation for a leader who seeks to be prophetic to simply use his/her position merely for shock and ridicule or for his or her self-promotion and self-aggrandizement. This is as much an issue today as anytime; self promotion is rampant among religious leaders and what is promoted as prophetic word is in fact a promotion of a particular ideology. What has transpired is the fact that

21. Heschel, *Prophets*, 3.
22. Cf. Amos 2:12.

those who are placed in positions of power to ensure the care and welfare of the poor and disenfranchised have used their positions to further abuse the very people who have been placed under their care. There is something particularly egregious about abusing the very people who you purport to care for, and who assume that you will. For those who today might seek to prey on the disenfranchised, the voiceless, the marginalized, the deeply wounded are set apart for a particular level of indictment and punishment. Those who have been elected to power, or placed in positions of power precisely to care for others, the politicians, priests and prophets are taken to task precisely because they are being held to a particularly elevated standard. The prophets without exception have words of critique, for they look at the society and the machinations of the leaders, the wealthy and the powerful and call them to change. In Jeremiah's "Temple Sermon" (Jer 7:1–15), the prophet makes it clear that the mere repetition of the right words will not suffice. They cannot live unjustly and then hide behind the walls of the Temple and simply repeat the words: "the Temple of the Lord" as if somehow that in itself will have salvific value. Recently, a number of financial institutions both in the United States and globally have found themselves to be in a state of financial disaster that have been hidden over the years. Some have said that some of these institutions are too big to fail. Indeed some have been propped up, and the deep wounds tended to. Perhaps there is a place for this if only to remind us that wounds can be healed. However, they cannot be superficially bandaged without the requisite medication, even painful medication. Perhaps, then and only then, there will be a legitimate "turning back." But there is another aspect to this notion of being "too big to fail" that is apropos for our discussion of the prophets. The idea that one has too much power to tackle, or that an institution is too prominent or powerful to challenge, or that there are divisions too deeply within the fabric of the society and the expectations of the people that it is impossible to unravel them, are all eviscerated by Amos and other prophets. The point is, nothing, and no one is beyond the reach of God or beyond the capacity of God to change or punish. No nation, no people, no group, no Church, no Temple, no institution is too powerful to escape the divine mandate to change or to be nullified. There is no middle ground when it comes to matters of justice.

FREE AT LAST

It is simply not possible to extrapolate from the prophets any idea that freedom can be understood apart from the concrete. To say that one is now free, one must immediately, ask, "what now?" As I write this study, the United States is celebrating Memorial Day, and one News Network has a lead story about a returning soldier who survived the wars in Iraq and Afghanistan and from all accounts performed heroic service; he asked a simple, but profound question, "now what?" In the context of war, perhaps it is appropriate to ask whether a soldier can come home again, for surely the experiences are such that one's life is indelibly altered. So then, is one free in the sense that one is not involved in the theatre of war? Certainly freedom carries with it a variety of qualities and many of them have practical implications. One might say that freedom might most meaningfully be spoken of with the proposition "to" and "from." So, for example, it is therefore entirely disingenuous to say that a slave has been freed, but he or she has no resources at his or her disposal for basic sustenance. There is an inherent dishonesty in the somewhat empty statement "you are free" without the commensurate qualities that must accompany such a statement. So who must be attended to? What hunger must be satiated? Whose nakedness must be covered? Who must be given shelter? These are the questions that must be posed. This might not be fully embraced by everyone, but such is the nature of God that all of God's creation must be granted a quality of freedom.

> Is not this the fast that I choose:
>> to loose the bonds of injustice,
>> to undo the thongs of the yoke,
> to let the oppressed go free,
>> and to break every yoke?
> Is it not to share your bread with the hungry,
>> and bring the homeless poor into your house;
> when you see the naked to cover them,
>> and not to hide yourself from your own kin?[23]

On the basis of Isa 58:6–7, Gray argues:

> The struggle toward freedom properly entails the feeding of the hungry, sheltering the homeless, clothing the naked, and being available to those in need—that is addressing primal hungers for food and community . . . In a terrifying vision of a deranged world in which cannibalism is practiced and in which, significantly, in

23. Isa 58:6–7.

light of Isa 58.6–7, "no one will spare his brother," Isa 9. 19–20 pictures a situation in which people will devour and still be hungry . . . The idea of hunger in the midst of vast social dislocation is also sounded in 8.21–22 . . . So when the prophet urges those he addresses "not to conceal themselves from their own flesh and blood," the implication of the rhetorical development of 58.6 and 58.7 taken together is that anyone hungry or poor or naked or in need is to be considered as kin, even if they belong to a broader grouping that would normally be regarded as the enemy. The vision is of reconciliation emerging as the poor, and those prepared to stand in solidarity with the poor, reaching across traditional lines of enmity, exclusion and suspicion in a common search for justice.[24]

Micah describes the injustices by such persons as cannibalism. To do what they do is analogous to tearing the skin off the people. But there is more.

> Who tear the skin from my people
>   and the flesh from their bones;
> who eat my people's flesh,
>   strip off their skin,
> and break their bones into pieces;
>   who chop them like meat for the pan,
>   like flesh for the pot.[25]

The crime against the people is such that they not only tear the skin off, they rip the flesh off their bones, they eat the flesh and finally crush the bones and place it all in a cauldron! Among the many conclusions one might draw from this graphic, "R" rated type description is the relentless nature of the crime. The pursuit of the poor for their own gain demonstrates an insatiable appetite for crushing the needy and poor. Marginalization is insufficient. There will be utter and complete annihilation. Perhaps one might legitimately conclude here is that not only are the poor crushed, but those who do so seek to ensure that there is nothing of the people remains. In a way, by placing them in a cauldron, it is to ensure that not only is there no evidence, but their absence will lead to a kind of forgotten-ness; it is as if they never existed. To further exacerbate the injury, those who survive the onslaught of the relentless crushing at the hands of the politicians and priests and take their grievances to the judicial courts are met with Judges who have taken bribes and simply give the plaintiffs platitudes: don't worry,

24. Gray, "Justice and Reconciliation," 165–68.

25. Mic 3:2b–3.

all will be well; don't worry, you will find peace; don't worry, your reward will be in heaven. One of the many issues that Micah addresses that is unavoidable in its implications and relevance for contemporary society is the active pursuit of wealth and power at the expense of those who are on the margins of society, and whose very livelihood is at stake. The accused are people who lie awake on their beds and plot ways in which they might take advantage of those who can least afford it. Even a time of rest is desecrated for the sake of taking away from those who are already precariously perched on the edge of society. Neighborliness is no longer a quality that causes one to pause and wonder, for even the neighbor and all that he/she has is open for being coveted. The obscenity of wealth accumulation at the expense of the neighbor has reached new proportions.

A further quality that we have inherited from the prophets that must be proclaimed in every generation henceforth, is that all who feel and experience themselves as outcasts will resonate with the prophetic word. No one must be an outcast in the world in which we live where there are artificially created divisions that maintain the status quo and categories of people who are at the center, and those who are relegated to the margins. "We live in that place between trust and lament, just as the prophet did. Our broken world cries out for transformation today no less than in the days of Micah. Poverty, racism, war, disease, violence against women and girls, homophobia, political corruption; the challenges facing us are daunting."[26]

> For thus says the LORD:
> To the Eunuchs who keep my Sabbaths,
> > who choose the things that please me and hold fast my covenant,
> I will give, in my house and within my walls,
> > a monument and name better than sons and daughters;
> I will give them an everlasting name
> > that shall not be cut off.[27]

The prophet is unequivocal. All people will be included in the community of worshippers, and not simply as tokens but as full members of the community. For example, the artificial and disingenuous distinction that many have embraced, "love the sinner but not the sin" as a means of barricading gays from being active participants at all levels in the community of faith cannot subside. So, e.g., Eunuchs (Isa 56:4) are invited to join all others in worship. This of course stands in sharp distinction to the earlier

26. Sharp, *Old Testament Prophets*, 55.

27. Isa 56:4–5.

prohibition against such person from even entering the congregation let alone holding any kind of leadership. But now, according to the prophet, all are welcome.

Perhaps it is the case that when a people suffers as the Israelites did in the Babylonian exile, when all, regardless of status and station in life, experienced the pain of disenfranchisement, slavery and dislocation, then all, regardless of status or station in life are restored. There are no hierarchical levels of acceptance or any distinctions of class or whatever distinction society creates. Perhaps this is what it takes to have *tikkun*. Simone Weil, who after the indescribable horror of the Shoah was instrumental in advocating rights for women in France, rights that included notably reproductive freedom and specifically abortion choice. To some today to understand such advocacy by a Shoah survivor, might seem counter intuitive and incomprehensible, but once again perhaps it is the case that when freedom has been taken away and large groups of people have been made to be less than human through the wielding of human evil, that all persons must be treated with equality. All must be included and not marginalized by human structures and conventions. Difficult, yes, but necessary. Such would be the prophetic message inherited by us.

As we read and listen to the words of the prophets, it is evident that the message is not to be narrowly construed as only religious or spiritual in orientation. No one or a group can or should seek to take ownership of the prophet or the prophetic word. Discarding the prophetic message simply because the message challenges us beyond our ideological basis is at our own peril. When The Hebrew prophets create a vision of justice, and the freedom that comes with living in a just society, invariably there is the juxtaposition of the moral and the cultic, that is, the interconnectedness of what is done in the context of worship, Temple, and Church and how one lives one's life. This connection is indelible and inseparable. When there is the language of violence and bloodshed that is associated with the practice of cultic activities then the evidence is incontrovertible. The people's hands are full of blood, (Isa 1:10–17) and whether this is figurative or literal or both, what we know with certainty is that such a statement is a testimony to the devastation and the indictment that comes with the prophet's words. God wants no part of this and indeed unless and until the people change and begin doing that which is moral and just, YHWH will close off all communication, with ears and eyes that are shut.

The radicalism of the prophetic message is further accentuated even as Jeremiah and Ezekiel have crafted a new and radical way for Torah piety to be incorporated into the lives of the people. It will no longer be a clinical and external matter. Both have spoken of the heart as the center of newness. Jeremiah speaks of a new covenant inscribed on the heart, and Ezekiel speaks of crafting a new heart. This renewed focus on the heart invites a rethinking of the creed of the people. Now the creed of the people will be precisely shaped by the heart. The people can no longer speak of the love of God and the love of neighbor without such words and actions being rooted in, and generated from the heart.

MADNESS IN EAST OF EDEN

The prophets invite us to think of everything as pertaining to the relationship with God; if anything is a part of creation and affects the creaturely lives, then it must be addressed. There are some contemporary leaders following in the dubious footsteps of their counterparts who have made public claims that certain topics should not be spoken about by ministers and religious professionals. One quickly discovers a quality of disingenuity in this regard in that only a particular set of topics that might adversely challenge or undermine their theological or ideological positions are singled out. No one or group can or should seek to take ownership of the prophet or the prophetic word. By definition the prophet will take us places where we do not want to be and often we resist because such places are profoundly uncomfortable and perhaps even uproot us from our zone of settledness. Discomfort must not inevitably lead to resistance, and resistance must not lead to neglect.

> To us a single act of injustice—cheating in business, exploitation of the poor—is slight; to the prophets, a disaster. To us injustice is injurious to the welfare of the people; to the prophets it is a death-blow to existence: to us an episode; to them, catastrophe, a threat to the world . . . We ourselves witness continually acts of injustice, manifestations of hypocrisy, falsehood, outrage, misery, but we rarely grow indignant or overly excited. To the prophets even a minor injustice assumes cosmic proportions.[28]

In sitting at the "East of the City," the author of Jonah alludes unmistakably to the Cain episode where the latter is banished to the East of Eden and made to wander, as a punishment. In this instance, Jonah is "East of the City" by choice, but it is a choice that he has made because he does not

28. Heschel, *Prophets*, 4.

see an alternative. He simply chooses to create a sense of distance not only from the city but symbolically from God, for in a somewhat state of madness he seeks to be alone. As opposed to the man in Gen 2:16, where it is *not good* for the man to be alone, and thus the creation of community, here Jonah has no community, and he even seeks to separate himself from God. This aloneness is doubly challenging as it is intentionally from both divine and human community.

> God's answer to Jonah, stressing the supremacy of compassion, upsets the possibility of looking for a rational coherence of God's ways with the world. History would be more intelligible if God's word were the last word, final and unambiguous like a dogma or an unconditional decree . . . yet, beyond justice and anger, lies the mystery of compassion.[29]

Finally, it is the case that prophets do not fit within the parameters of society and often literally and figuratively they leave the human constructed confines. "All through history . . . prophets have left the city behind them to insist upon things greater than they are; but in the double nature of all phenomena, the abandoning of the city for the wilderness is also the pattern of madness: the psychotic leaves the social structure of sanity . . . Those left behind in the city define themselves as responsible and sane and see the wanderer as a madman. The wanderer defines himself as the only sane person in the city of the insane and walks out in search of other possibilities."[30]

Of course these "madmen" do not particularly see themselves as "mad" but for those who believe that all must function within the parameters that society has established, then of course it is madness and insanity of a disdainful order to cast oneself "east of the city." The Hebrew prophets like Moshe the Beadle[31] were more than messengers; they were witnesses. They witnessed and they were compelled to tell the truth even when the people would not listen, particularly when they felt that the truth was too painful to bear. Like Moshe the Beadle, Jeremiah could not understand why the people would not listen to him, and so he laments and grieves, but continues to be with the people, even those who vilified him. His life among the people, as one of the community was an essential part of his belonging and this further intensified his sense of loss. Moreover, self-awareness and one's human limitations and finitude must always be essential components

---

29. Ibid., 76.

30. Schneidau, *Sacred Discontent*, 119.

31. Wiesel, *Night*.

of who we are. To put in theological terms, the witness to God's justice must be aware that as vessels we are flawed. While it is the case that we might not be entirely aware, we must nonetheless be aware at all times that we too stand broken in the face of God's justice.

> The Jonah complex, as we see it, is a rejection of our Godlike potentialities . . . Indeed, to be concerned and feel responsible for others' welfare requires such an enormous amount of energy and compassion that seldom do we find anyone willing to make this existential leap. To do so, individuals must overcome the narcissistic preoccupations that bind them to solipsism . . . The Jonah complex means that, for all and always, there is a congenital fear of one's humanness and of one's vocation to universality.[32]

In 1 Kings 19, the conventional wisdom focuses on "the still small voice" of God over and against the more thunderous manifestations of God that reveal the power of God. But one is left to wonder if indeed this is the case. As blasphemous as it might be, the reality is that the principal issue surrounds Elijah's implied decision that enough is enough; he has had it being YHWH's prophet. This is a serious moment of power struggle between God and Elijah. Even though on the surface, it appears to be a mismatch, this is not to take away from the issue at state. There is certainly legitimacy to some of what scholarship has proposed over the years. Can one predetermine precisely how God will communicate with people? It perhaps makes for an interesting theological twist for God to communicate in a way that simply undermines the convention. The scholarly wisdom has been that God was not present in the loud demonstrations typically associated with God. In fact, a close reading of the text makes it clear that Elijah does not necessarily react any differently to the "soft voice over against the loud demonstrations." Indeed Elijah comes out of his cave, literally and figuratively, when he does not hear anything, and this is the moment that has been memoralized as the "the still small voice that speaks to Elijah." In fact it is entirely possible to conclude legitimately that YHWH had stopped speaking and not hearing anything he came out of the cave. One of the important themes that frames the narrative is that of Elijah's quest to be relieved of his calling. The narrative suggests that he has had enough and is seeking YHWH's release from his calling. The question is whether God will allow Elijah to walk away from his calling. What we know is that history is not on Elijah's side. God did not allow Moses to negotiate his way

32. LaCocque and LaCocque, *Jonah*, 202.

out of going to Egypt and Jonah fared no better in seeking to die rather than proclaiming on behalf of Nineveh. When Elijah awaits God's response, what he receives is a further assignment to continue. Perhaps then God will not take "no" for an answer. This text poignantly reminds us that being called to be a prophet brings with it such an element of angst and pain that cannot simply be explained away or overlooked. In a way Elijah wants to run away, to be by himself, to leave behind any kind of structure or even the divine support. He wants to be left alone. It is not so much that he did not believe in the importance of what he was doing, but rather he finds himself emotionally and perhaps physically unable to carry on. "Elijah is pictured as a broken, disappointed man. The picture of Elijah moping under an isolated, solitary tree . . . is a careful psychological touch . . . The narrative shows deep psychological insight in describing the generalized depression that sometimes results from stress, in this case the stress of fear. . . . The person suffering from depression sits alone, contemplating the idea of death."[33] The reality is that the prophets are very much human, even though as Heschel has astutely observed they are some place between human and divine, and as is to be expected, they suffer as humans. Fear is real; fear of failure is real; fear of being killed is real; fear of feeling ill equipped for what God has called one to do is real, and so Elijah has arrived at a point where all of the these senses have descended upon him and he is overwhelmed. In the case of Elijah, even the divine pyrotechnics will not be enough to entice him to leave his cave. Ultimately, psychologists have observed that it is not enough to leave one's cave; it is when he hears silence, when he believes that the conventional way of marking God's presence now has ceased that on his own terms he leaves his cave. In a real way, this is "Elijah's cave," the place of *his* hiding and *his* refuge. It is not the universal place of refuge, but it is the place where all who seek to be alone from the stresses of this world retreat. "This narrative explores the interplay between human despair and God's call in a way that speaks to the exiles of any age. God can be counted on to provide in the wilderness (vv. 5–7) . . . God's therapy for prophetic burnout includes both the assignment of new tasks and the certain promise of a future that transcends the prophet's own success or lack of it."[34]

None of us, howsoever committed we are or feel compelled to be, is above reproach, let alone perfect. Not surprisingly then, despite our best

---

33. Nelson, *I & II Kings*, 126.

34. Ibid., 129.

efforts, the conclusions that we draw from the Bible might in fact be flawed even if we have noble intentions. We often find ourselves employing axioms to reflect what is important to us. So it is commonplace to hear one pronounce that "honesty is the best policy" or "the Bible is my authority" or "I always speak the truth." In some manner each perhaps might be comforting to the person, but if one is truly honest most of all with oneself, then these statements must be examined and done so with the precision of a surgeon. Simon Wiesenthal, in the remarkably relevant book *The Sunflower*, explores the limitations of forgiveness. There is a moment at the end of the narrative, when Wiesenthal, the Jewish protagonist in the camp is made to listen to the confessions of a young dying Nazi who seeks forgiveness, and he is identifed as the one to grant him thus, but to whom he is unable to grant such forgiveness. After the soldier Karl dies and his belongings are given to Wiesenthal, he takes them to Karl's mother. Karl's mother, in her reflection remembers her son as a fine young committed Catholic boy, who though misguided in his loyalties was nevertheless a good boy. At this remarkable moment Wiesenthal could have thoroughly dismantled her memories and the recollections of her son, but instead he chose not to do so; he chose otherwise. He graciously allowed her to reminisce, and in his silence he did not tell her the truth; and in so doing, he granted her a measure of grace and a moment of such redemption that no maxim about honesty at all cost could displace.

Reflecting on the character Maggie in Henry James' novel *The Golden Bowl*, Martha Nussbaum suggests that Maggie sought to be like "a flawless crystal bowl, holding . . . pleasures without penalties." Nussbaum, taking the particularity of Maggie's character and applying it to humanity in general concludes insightfully that we humans are like "flawed crystals." But this realization for each of us as interpreters comes after that most difficult of undertakings, namely self-examination. I think of two examples in this regard, perhaps neither unique in itself, but they serve as a reminder to me of the importance of ongoing reflection, even when one arrives at what might be considered an informed and thoughtful conclusion or interpretation. First, after a number of readings and explorations on the book of Ruth, I have noted that the well known and equally well used text of Ruth 1:16–17 is the basis of the popular, *Song of Ruth* often sung in weddings. It is a beautiful song and a testimony to a sacrificial, compassionate love. But of course the biblical context for the text is that of a daughter-in-law expressing her loyalty to her mother-in-law, a moving and remarkable transformative moment. It is not a bride to a bridegroom or vice versa. I often felt that the song, moving as it is, did not seem to fit a marriage ceremony, as *I* saw it. But in the last several years as I have re-read the text, it has occurred to me that I have allowed myself to make determinations that seem absolute in their singular trajectory. One notable element in the text that I had overlooked is the situation in which Ruth and Naomi found themselves, and what might be argued as the pivotal factor in Ruth's decision. What makes this text relevant for a marriage ceremony are the promises made; in the context of powerlessness, weakness, loss, one will not leave the other. Second, I am unable to leave alone the Genesis 22 text, "The Binding/Sacrifice of Isaac." Perhaps the text refuses to leave me alone. I cannot imagine that this can be a text of such human obedience that Abraham has become nothing short of heroic in his faith. Yet, I wonder whether this kind of unimaginable act is what it takes to express faithfulness. I have long struggled with this text, and for the length of this struggle I have concluded that Abraham should have been more forceful and forthright in his interaction with God. After all if he is able to challenge God on behalf of Sodom and Gomorrah, why would he be silent on behalf of his son, the only son of Sarah and the son of the promise? But then I re-read Søren Kierkegaard's, *Fear and Trembling* and I was stopped in my "clear-cut" thinking about the role of Abraham. There is a sense that finally one cannot know what transpired in the heart of one who suffers to the degree that Abraham and Sarah suffered with such a divine request. The text repeatedly reminds us that Isaac and Abraham were so indelibly connected, that Isaac had become a part of Abraham. In this sense the divine mandate that Abraham sacrifice his son Isaac, could as well be understood as Abraham being asked to sacrifice himself. This changes the manner in which I was moved to see the text. I also came to the conclusion that in asking Abraham to make such a sacrifice, God also makes himself vulnerable. Such a test cannot but be vulnerable to the one who makes the demand.

No doubt there are many other instances in which one might point to moments where pausing is essential and changing interpretive directions could be cited. The point here is to invite us to do the challenging task and revisit texts even as we change and we hear and read the words with new ears and eyes. "It is, nonetheless, the entire conversation in the text that discloses an alternative world for us. Thus scripture revelation is not a flat, obvious offer of a conclusion, but it is an ongoing conversation that evokes, invites, and offers . . . my assumption is that there are no 'innocent' readings of scripture, and surely there are no 'innocent' formations of scripture . . . One way of recognizing that 'truth' is impacted by 'power' is to see that every text is a carrier of interest that voices truth from a certain perspective."[35]

Economic Survival

While it is true that the prophets generally do not spell out in detailed prescriptions how the various expressions of injustice are to be rectified and the precise manner in which justice and righteousness are to be crafted and meted out, they do on occasion give precise expression as to what has been done and what is needed to rectify the situation. Let me note two specific examples in this regard. Micah 6:8, encapsulates what God requires of the people, "walk humbly, do justice and love kindness." It is succinct, but imprecise in the sense that there are no specifics. But there are specifics that the prophet outlines elsewhere that give concreteness to the general admonitions. Later in Mic 6:11–12, YHWH inveighs against dishonest weights and measures; deceitful gains; violence used by the wealthy; deception. Here within these broad categories, there is unassailable evidence of the magnitude of the injustice, with a pointed economic factor that reaches into the very basic welfare of the poor, the undermining of basic security and sustenance. Second, Isa 5:7 pronounces the beautifully crafted and devastatingly poetic parallelism. "For the vineyard of the Lord of hosts is the house of Israel, and the people of Judah are his pleasant planting; he expected justice, but saw bloodshed; righteousness, but heard a cry!" God looked for justice but received bloodshed instead, sought righteousness and saw and heard cries instead. The fact that both justice and righteousness are fundamentally relational in nature and orientation, makes clear that at the very heart of the condemnation is the impoverishing and killing, perhaps literally, but most certainly figuratively of the weak and marginalized. Immediately following these general indictments, are the two specific expressions of the injustices. The wealthy have taken away from the poor the essentials of livelihood, namely means of sustenance and shelter. In doing so, they have taken away the basic security of the poor. In adding field to field, house to house, they are in the process of accumulating and expanding their holdings while further isolating the neighbor. In this case, among the many unconscionable expressions of injustice, is the somewhat invisible and deadening act of forced isolation. This isolation is not solitude but solitariness, with no place of belonging and place to call home.

35. O'Brien, *Challenging Prophetic Metaphor*, 7–8.

One might speak in generalities about justice and righteousness; poverty, hunger and homelessness, but what these circumstances all have in common is that of the particularities of violence. Though these acts might not necessarily conform to the conventional idea and definition of violence, the prophets knew that violence is the very notion of not having a place to call home, a sense of displacement; the reality of not having bread; the reality of being forced into debt then crushed for being unable to repay the loan tagged with exorbitant interest. This is violence and the prophets knew it. "The consequences of injustice manifest themselves in people as mortal and physical sickness, and in the land as destruction and loss of fertility. The punishment is not abstract; it is physical, affecting not just the people but the well-being of the land."[36] In similar fashion, one notes the complex and challenging text of Genesis 19. Both history and modern society have often concluded that this is primarily a text about homosexuality. One has to make something of an interpretive leap to arrive fully at this conclusion, but it is an interpretation that has come to be indelibly connected with this text and "Sodom and Gomorrah" have come to be synonymous with homosexuality. Yet, what is the nature of the "cry" in this text? What is the evil that God speaks about and is spoken of? One might point to the reference in Ezekiel, where Judah's sin is spoken of in the vein as Sodom's sin. This is also reminiscent of Isa 1:10–17, where indeed Judah is referred to as Sodom and Gomorrah, and the frenzy of cultic activity is outlined as meaningless in light of the many expressions of injustice. As we also note in Ezekiel 16:49, "she and her daughters had pride, excess of food, and prosperous ease, but did not aid the poor and needy." As one might surmise, the idea of "outcry" has a wide range of references and need not be reduced to a narrowly construed idea of sexual immorality.

It is impossible to speak of biblical principles in general and the Hebrew prophets in particular without focusing on, or at the very least exploring and discussing the socio-economic and political aspects. To overlook or cast aside these issues and themes within the body of prophetic literature is to nullify the message of the prophets. It is to gut the overall message of the prophets and transform the biblical mandate for justice and righteousness into a choice. When the prophet speaks about the people's relationship with God, it is impossible to do so without a natural and urgent connection with the cultural, economic, and socio-political framework in which he is located. There is no "middle ground," no "sort of just," no taking "baby steps" in these prophetic pronouncements. This is in part why the prophetic word

36. Marlow, "Justice for Whom," 107.

is so very painful for many to whom it is addressed. "The socioeconomic relations of ancient Israelites were egalitarian in the sense that the entire populace was assured of approximately equal access to resources by means of their organization into extended families."[37] The notion of egalitarianism was not some kind of utopian ideal but very much at the heart of the covenant community and not surprisingly those who were most opposed to it were those who were committed purely to their personal wealth and power, and saw the possibility of using others for their own gain.

> The socio-economic processes that are reflected in this characterization are common in agrarian societies. They point to the concentration of property through land foreclosure—which may be accompanied by eviction—and similar actions. Further the evaluation of these actions as akin to robbery (and the like), and in general as ungodly is both a recurrent feature in agrarian societies and a common literary and theological *topos*. References to this process in the Hebrew Bible is numerous, and they are certainly not restricted to a particular, putative time in the traditional history of Israel . . . The wrongdoers are constructed by the text as a timeless type of "landgrabbers." Such a characterization—and there is no reason to assume that it was accidental—surely allows the readers and rereaders of Micah 2 to identify the wrongdoers in vv. 1 and 2 with multiple referents, depending on their chosen approach to the text.[38]

It is impossible to speak of life in ancient Israel as a place apart from the economic welfare of the people, a place to live, land, and the resources essential for the production of daily sustenance. In the message of the Hebrew prophets is the fact that while they are hardly ever prescriptive, they are certainly not general and abstract.

> Woe to you who join house to house,
>   who add field to field,
> until there is room for no one but you,
>   and you are left to live alone
>   in the midst of the land![39]

But there are specifics to this generality, as pointedly spelled out in Isa 5:8, with direct reference to the economic factors that constitute everyday life. There is a fundamental inequity at play here and those who have much

37. Gottwald, *Hebrew Bible*, 285–86.

38. Ben Zvi, "Wrongdoers," 89.

39. Isa 5:8.

seek to garner more at the expense of those whose lives are defined not by excess but by that which is basic and necessary for belonging and daily sustenance.

Yet, "blood" is being shed in economic ways by taking away fields and homes, adding to the plenty of the wealthy and powerful and crushing the poor and powerless in order to do so. This is not only an "in-your-face" violation of the commandment not to covet, but it is a practical impossibility to add house to house and field to field and still claim to care, let alone actually care for the neighbor. Therein lies the root of the punishment that will be meted out against the perpetrators. Avarice itself will lead to poverty, though those who are indeed avaricious do not have the vision to see such, nor the memory to recall that the very architect of their existence is YHWH, who gives, but also expects, and when necessary, will take away and destroy. So instead of the yield that would be expected from the accumulation of fields, acres upon acres will yield little and the accumulation of houses will finally lie desolate.[40] Those whose lives are bracketed by mornings of yearning for drink and evenings of lavish music and intoxication are singled out; such is the lifestyle of those who have shown disdain for YHWH and the lives of their neighbors. In the midst of all this, the people indulge in sacrifices and offerings all of which have lost their rootedness, but in their prodigious quantity, the people have continued to believe that they are in proper standing with God. Yet how could this be even as they are systematically unraveling the neighborly fabric. What is particularly striking here is that the punishment and devastation are not abstract or hint at the supernatural, but rather, there is concreteness to it. The irony is not lost here as the very powers about which the people boasted, namely political and military, will be the instruments used to bring about their devastation.

In Isa 3:1–12 the prophet's systematic pronouncements that life as the people have come to construct it, life as they have come to imagine as being permanent, and the invincibility of the power grids that they have constructed will in fact be dismantled in a most devastating manner. Judah and Jerusalem are not entitled to continue with life as if it is the way things will always be. In particular here, there are two aspects to the prophet's response. Both the human generated expressions of power and those elements that are necessities for life will be taken away, not permanently, but for a while. Here too in the midst of judgment and punishment, there is an expression of grace-filled reprieve, "for now." The judgment and punishment, as widespread and pronounced as they are, will not be in perpetuity.

40. Isa 5:8–10.

53

All means of sustenance will be removed; the very basic means of sustenance for life, bread and water, will be taken away together with the human
generated military complex that might appear to guarantee invincibility.
Moreover, those prophets and diviners who have deceived the people into
believing that they are speaking on behalf of God when in fact they are
driven by their personal impulse for power, and in so doing make destructive pronouncements will be punished.

> For now the Sovereign, the LORD of hosts,
>   is taking away from Jerusalem and Judah
> support and staff—
>   all support of bread,
>   and all support of water—
> warrior and soldier,
>   judge and prophet,
>   diviner and elder,
> captain of fifty
>   and dignitary,
> counselor and skilled magician
>   and expert enchanter . . .[41]

It is never the case that the prophet relishes a message that brings destruction and punishment to the people. As devastating a message as one
is likely to find in the prophetic corpus is that of Isaiah's verdict in 6:9–13.

> And he said, "Go and say to this people:
> 'Keep listening, but do not comprehend;
> keep looking but do not understand.'
> Make the mind of this people dull
>   and stop their ears,
>   and shut their eyes,
> so that they may not look with their eyes,
>   and listen with their ears
> and comprehend with their minds,
>   and turn and be healed."
> Then I said, "How long O Lord?"
> And he said, "Until cities lie waste
>   without inhabitant,
> and houses without people,
>   and the land is utterly desolate;
> until the LORD sends everyone far away,
>   and vast is the emptiness in the midst of the land.

41. Isa 3:1–3.

> Even if a tenth part remain in it,
>   it will be burned again,
> like a terebinth or an oak
>   whose stump remains standing when it is felled."
> The holy seed is its stump.[42]

The prophet knows that he must deliver the message, but he also wants to know the degree and the length of the devastation; he takes no pleasure in witnessing what is to come. Taking joy in the suffering of the people and the devastation of the land, despite the ruinous behavior of the people, is not part of the prophet's constitution. The prophet's question to God, "How long O Lord," is not to seek a timeline or for that matter to question as it is to reflect on the nature of the punishment, almost to wonder if in fact the punishment is too excessive. This is a question born out of a wounded heart, one that clearly grieves for the people. While clearly not overlooking the need for judgment and punishment, it is one of personal grief. To place an exclamation to the annihilation, even a hint of life that might be left will be destroyed. It is noteworthy that the punishment is not only focused on the people and the need for healing that will not be afforded to them, but the ravishing of the land, erasing every sign of hope and life in the land. For the land itself, it will be a long time before healing will come, so complete will be the devastation. The land, and the houses and the cities will not be waiting for the people to inhabit again. Instead, everything will be crushed and there will be no joy and enjoyment of the wealth and power that had been gained at the expense of those members whose very lives have been crushed. The basic *need* of the poor has been cast aside to fulfill their *greed*. It would be tempting to take this text as something of an anomaly, and thus viewed more as an exception, but in fact it is no exception. Indeed seven centuries after the prophet spoke these words that hearken to a decimation of unprecedented proportions, the words would again be voiced, this time in connection with Jesus. When we become immune and numbed to the welfare of all people, to the well being of the weak, and the downtrodden, there will be the consequences. When the very elements of our ancient counterparts that seem to define life then, as well as life today, predicated on the belief that self determination in the narrowest and most self consumed way regardless of God, while simultaneously immersing ourselves in the liturgy of self–indulgence, then the devastation that is meted out will be no less severe. It was difficult to comprehend then, in the time of Jesus,

---

42. Isa 6:9–13

and equally today, but the truth of the prophetic words have withstood the test of time.

> Let me sing for my Beloved my love song concerning his vineyard:
> My Beloved had a vineyard on a very fertile hill.
> He dug it and cleared it of stones, and planted it with choice vines;
> He built a watchtower in the midst of it, and hewed out a wine vat in it;
> He expected it to yield grapes, but it yielded wild grapes.
> And now, inhabitants of Jerusalem and people of Judah
> judge between me and my vineyard.
> What more was there to do for my vineyard that I have not done in it?
> When I expected it to yield grapes, why did it yield wild grapes?
> And now I will tell you what I will do to my Vineyard.
> I will remove its hedge and it shall be devoured;
> I will break down its wall and it shall be trampled down.
> I will make it a waste; it shall not be pruned or hoed,
> And it shall be overgrown with briers and thorns;
> I will also command the clouds that they rain no rain upon it.
> For the vineyard of the LORD of host is the house of Israel,
> And the people of Judah are his pleasant planting;
> He expected justice but saw bloodshed;
> Righteousness but heard a cry!
> Ah, you who join house to house and add field to field,
> Until there is room for no one but you,
> And you are left to live alone in the midst of the land![43]

This song not only encapsulates something of the history of salvation by God for Israel, but notably the impeccable care that has been taken to "plant and nurture" a people with inherent expectations; expectations, neither presumptuous nor unreasonable, but ones that are dashed in the most egregious ways. Even as YHWH is conspicuously attentive to the needs of the people, those to whom such care has been given are remarkably inattentive to others who are poor and the powerless. Thus, where once YHWH was engaged with such preparatory, nurturing and expectant words as, "dug, cleared, planted, built, hewed," now abandonment of the vineyard will be reflected through being "devoured, trampled, not pruned, not hoed, overgrown." The "why" question must be reckoned with so as not to leave these prophetic words as simply a matter of reminiscence. The crime that brought such abandonment is that of the shedding of blood and the cry that is heard; these stand in sharp contrast to the expected justice and righteousness. "The 'bloodshed' that concerns the poet is not thuggery and

43. Isa 5:1–8.

murder, but the more subtle, slower, but equally decisive killing through economic policy against the vulnerable and resourceless."[44] Who are the people responsible—the nobility, the haughty, those entrusted with the execution of justice, those who are deceitful; those who have replaced divine wisdom with their own, indeed all the people, the throngs. Not only will those in power, but everyone will be held responsible.[45] Ultimately everyone is responsible for the welfare of the other. In the midst of all this, the people indulge in sacrifices and offerings that have lost their meaning, but in their prodigious quantity, the people have continued to believe that they are in proper standing with God. Yet how could this be even as they are systematically unraveling the fabric of neighborliness.

There will be no life without each other and without YHWH. These two categories are particularly significant in that they reflect positions of power. They simply and wantonly have abused their power for their gain and accumulation of wealth. It is instructive that the central issue of the prophets is not necessarily the matter of wealth, but rather that the wealth and land accumulation is done at the expense of the poor, at the expense of those who can least afford to lose their land, and the grounding of their identity. It is precisely this kind of self-indulgent behavior and unabashed greed that lead the prophets to make the pronouncements against the elders and princes.

> Hear this, you that trample on the needy,
>> and bring to ruin the poor of the land,
> saying, When will the new moon be over
>> so that we may sell grain;
> and the Sabbath, so that we may offer wheat for sale?
> We will make the ephah small and the shekel great,
>> and practice deceit with false balances,
> buying the poor for silver
>> and the needy for a pair of sandals,
>> and selling the sweeping of the wheat.[46]

Amos is very precise in his condemnation. The language in Amos 8:4–6 as in Micah 3:2b–3 is graphic and there is little possibility of misinterpretation or misappropriation of the prophets' words. It is the trampling of the needy and the ruination of the poor of the land that are at stake. These are the neighbors whose lives are lived on the edge of survival and whose

44. Brueggemann, *Isaiah 1–39*, 48.

45. Isa 5:11–25.

46. Amos 8:4–6.

lives depend on the land. It is against these indigent and most vulnerable members of the community that those with power and wealth plot. These actions are not simply a matter of initiative for one's economic wellbeing, but rather the very systematic proactive plan to crush the other for one's own gain. The particular image of the extent of the devastation of the poor is captured in the pronouncement, "ruin the poor of the land." Even before the devastation occurs, the people are already described as the "poor of the land." With the loss of the land, it will in fact be the end of the poor of the land. The proactive plans show a wanton disregard for both the ethics of economic activities and the essence of cultic activities. Cultic activity stands in the way of profiteering. It is not simply a matter of selling grain, but the inherent triple cheating. The balances are weighted in favor of the grain dealers, and so the poor receive less and they are charged more, and the cost is increased. Even the "sweepings" of the grain are sold as grain, where in fact there is no value to such "sweepings." Communal and covenantal commitments are of no account here. This rampant and unconscionable ruination of the neighbor is graphically underlined by the actions of the wealthy in Amos 2:7–8. Not only are the poor crushed and the afflicted cast aside, but the extravagant lives of the wealthy have taken on a new level of arrogance as they openly flaunt the fruits of their oppression in the "face of God." They openly prostitute themselves in the Temple where father and son consort with the same girl, and the very name of God is profaned. If there is to be a place for "profanity" it is to be outside of the Temple as the very word intimates, but the powerful flaunt such profanity in the face of God, and in so doing profaned the holiness of God's name. They have collapsed the wall that separates holiness from profanity and in so doing have trampled on the holiness of God. Very specifically, the wine that is drunk comes at the expense of those members of the community that they have crushed through the imposition of fines. In this instance, both the corruption and injustices against the poor members of the community are directly connected with the corruption and profaning of the Temple and God's name.

> Can I tolerate wicked scales
> and a bag of dishonest weights?
> Your wealthy are full of violence;
> your inhabitants speak lies,
> with tongues of deceit in their mouths.[47]

47. Mic 6:11–12.

Micah makes it clear that what transpires in the marketplace and the unquenchable appetite for profit and wealth at the expense of others is not a matter singularly of economics, but indeed it is most fundamentally relational. The wickedness of scales and the dishonesty of the weights are a violence against the people, and it is the wealthy who are singled out. Their "tongues of deceit" know no limits; such deceit is a part of who they are. This sense of utter disregard and disconnection from those who are the poor and vulnerable stands in sharp contrast to the opulent life of luxury lived by the wealthy; lives lived at the expense of the poor. The punishment and destruction that will come to those who are the principals of such injustice will be swift and complete. The very particular houses of luxury will all be torn down. Not only will the perpetrators not be allowed to live in them, but they will be destroyed. Winter houses and summer houses, and all sorts of houses that have been built on the oppression of others will be destroyed.[48] The image of "winter houses" and "summer houses" underline the extravagant life of luxury. The fact that they are cited alongside the crushing of the heads of the poor in the dust of the earth established the magnitude of the violence and the quality of the injustice and the utter lack of moral conscience.

Micah like his contemporaries is devastating in his indictment of both the religious and political leaders, in bringing about the catastrophe that is about to befall Judah.[49] In one of the most graphic images in the Hebrew prophets, Micah speaks of the leaders as cannibals. Micah is unequivocal about what will happen to those who claim to be prophets and speak on behalf of God for financial gain. This could not be a more pointed note for those who today do the same. The prophet says that "darkness and shame" will come upon those who are nothing short of prostitutes even as they claim to speak on behalf of God for financial gain.[50]

> Alas for those who lie on beds of ivory,
>   and loungee on their couches,
> and eat lambs from their flock
>   and calves from the stall;
> who sing idle songs to the sound of the harp,
>   and like David improvise on instruments of music;
> who drink wine from bowls,

48. Amos 3:15.

49. Mic 3:1–2a, 5, 9–12.

50. Mic 3:6–7.

> and anoint themselves with finest oils,
> but are not grieved over the ruin of Joseph.[51]

This "woe" oracle (Amos 6:4–6; Isa 5:22–23) is not a mere repetition of what has been said about the widespread injustices and what is repeated in a variety of ways by the various prophets. This particular oracle brings together the shocking contrast between those who live luxurious lives with the inherent idea that much of this lifestyle comes at the expense of those who are the impoverished and struggle for the basics of life. The affluent have redefined for themselves what is the "new normal." The language is pointed and generates the sharp heartbreaking contrast necessary to underline the prophetic indictment. The perpetrators "lie on beds of ivory," they "lounge on couches." These are not the ordinary modes of sleeping. This is opulence. Moreover, they eat "lambs and calves," because they have such luxuries at their disposal; they are able to go to the stall and have such exquisite meats for their meals. They are able to drink wine from bowls, and anoint themselves with the finest oils. Everything in their lives reflects a particular level of luxury, and so even as they recline and lounge and eat tender meats and drink wine in abundance, they idly play on their harps. In and of themselves these activities might point to a particularly extravagant lifestyle, but the prophet sets this lifestyle over and against the destitution of the impoverished. So it is with this life of woeful abundance, the prophet notes that there is no grief over those who are wanting and on the cusp of ruin.

> Hear this word, you cows of Bashan
> who are on Mount Samaria,
> who oppress the poor, who crush the needy,
> who say to their husbands,
> "Bring something to drink!"
> The Lord GOD has sworn by his holiness:
> the time is surely coming upon you,
> when they shall take you away with hooks,
> and the last of you with fishhooks.
> Through breaches in the wall you shall leave,
> each one straight ahead;
> and you shall be flung into Harmon says the LORD.
> Come to Bethel—and transgress;
> to Gilgal—and multiply transgression;
> bring your sacrifices every morning,

---

51. Amos 6:4–6.

your tithes every three days;
   bring a thankoffering of unleavened bread,
      and proclaim freewill offerings, publish them;
      for so you love to do, O people of Israel! says the Lord GOD.[52]

This text again underlines this extravagant luxurious lifestyle, one that even runs contrary to what is conventionally viewed as luxurious in the ancient Near Eastern context. In this context, wives are singled out for particular indictment and punishment. These women enjoy lives of leisure at the expense of the poor and needy who they have crushed and oppressed and there is not a modicum of remorse. Indeed the world has been turned upside down and the wives live such lives that they order their husbands to bring drink and replenish the supplies for their enjoyment. Amos views such a lifestyle at the expense of the poor, to be inseparable from the equally extravagant worship practices that have no redemptive value, except for external show. The trangressive social behavior parallels the transgressions of the excessive and meaningless proliferation of worship practices. Quantity of attendance and excessive sacrifices and offerings are of no value and without salvific value. The irony cannot be lost here, as tithes and offerings are offered to God even as the poor suffer precisely because the tithes and offering are generated by money taken from the poor. These exaggerated self-indulgent worship practices are for public viewing. The abuse of the Temples at Gilgal and Bethel only multiply the transgressions, as they are simply for the public display. The oppressors love this expression of public display as is expressed in Amos 4:5b. Indeed, Bethel is deemed the king's sanctuary and the temple of the kingdom, and the prophet is told not to ever prophesy there again. The king has usurped both the role of God and Temple. If indeed the people will live, then it will not be through a proliferation of sacrifices and offerings, but seeking YHWH (Amos 5:5). The oppressors are reminded that the God of the poor and oppressed, their God, is the God of the entire universe. There is the possibility for redemption, for new life even for those who have destroyed justice and righteousness and poisoned them. The utter stubbornness of the people is accentuated by God's reluctance to bring about a destruction that would be commensurate with the injustices. The "yet" refrain in Amos 4:6–11 on five occasions underline the various opportunities that have been given to the people to repent, to return to YHWH. The five *velo shabetem* "yet you did not return" parallel the five occasions that YHWH brought varying degrees of punishment to the people, so that they might repent, but in each instance,

52. Amos 4:1–5.

there is no repentance. Thus in v. 12, the text begins with *leken*. After the various opportunities granted by God comes a sense of *enough* and thus "therefore." This "therefore" brings a quality of finality to the punishment. Now the people will not be allowed to live, rather the time has come to face God, and there is finality to this moment, "prepare to meet your God." The vocabulary in the prophet's message paints the dramatic life of luxury: beds of ivory; lounging; eating lambs and calves; singing idle songs; music of the harp; drinking wine from bowls; anointing with the most expensive oils. The final line sharpens the extravagance and the wanton disregard of the poor. The wealthy live their lives in utter disregard of the ruin of Joseph.

> Be shocked, be utterly desolate, says the LORD,
> for My people have committed two evils:
>> they have forsaken Me,
> the fountain of living waters,
>> and hewed out cisterns for themselves,
> Broken cisterns,
>> that can hold no water.[53]

Jeremiah calls upon the heavens even as the earth seems incapable of being moved by the pervasive brokenness. In this regard, one is reminded of the opening verse of Micah 6, where the hills and mountains are called upon to adjudicate. The vocabulary is striking: appalled, shocked, desolate. These are the reactions that the heavens are called upon to have for such is the gravity of the offenses. They have rejected that which YHWH has done and have instead pursued their own course. The image of God as the source of "living waters" is rejected in lieu of a leaky human cistern! Not only is God's living water rejected, but what the people have created is incapable of holding water, let alone providing what is necessary for life. And as Isaiah announces dramatically, "tremble, shudder, strip" and be in a state of mourning, for they are complacent (Isa 32:11).

> Woe to him who heaps up what is not his own, . . .
> Woe to him who gets evil gain for his house, . . .
> For the stone cries out from the wall,
>> and the beam from the woodwork responds.
> Woe to him who builds a town with blood,
>> and found a city on iniquity![54]

---

53. Jer 2:12b–13.
54. Hab 2:6, 9, 11–12.

The economic emphasis is unmistakable, focusing on those who accumulate property upon property. It is the heaping of property that in the absence of any voice that would cry out about such injustice, the very stone and beams will cry out. In this text, the prophet combines both the personal and the corporate; the individual and those in positions of power to care for the larger community. For the corporate power that builds a city on the shoulders of those who are forced to do so, those enslaved and those whose blood has been shed, this indictment is squarely on their shoulders. Those who abuse their own will face devastating consequences. The focus here is on both the sacred and the secular institutions, individuals and communities. It is idolatry and a two part henotheistic expression of such idolatry, namely wealth and power, both of which have inherent possibilities of corruption and injustice.

ECONOMICS OF LIVELIHOOD

The notion of egalitarianism was not some kind of utopian ideal but very much at the heart of the covenant community. "Economics in ancient Israel has to do with the production and distribution of resources necessary to meet basic human needs. Naturally the land was fundamental to those needs, but covenant concern extended to the resources drawn from the land and the structures necessary to make those resources accessible to all."[55] This is the issue that goes to the heart of economics in ancient Israel. The etymology of the term economics from the Greek οἰκονόμος typically is rendered as "manager of the household." This term underlines all that is necessary for a household to sustain itself. When there is no house and there is no field, the conclusion is unencumbered by any complicated and challenging means of interpretation. If there is no field, then there are at least two factors that must be reckoned with. First, not to have a field means there is no fundamental source of food and thus the absence of bread and the means of the very basic quality of security in life. Second, in an agrarian society, it is *the* means of economic support for a family and the source of ongoing economic welfare. The purchasing, or more often than not, the seizing of the field through rent capitalism, undermines the fundamental idea of God as landowner and the prohibition against selling the land in perpetuity. The joining of house to house simply out of the quest to accumulate and build wealth means that members of the covenant community

55. Birch, *Let Justice Roll Down*, 180.

are left homeless and the other basic means of security is taken away. It would be enough of an issue if in fact members of the covenant community vied against each other at a level that only involved internal struggle among the "haves" but it is the utter disregard of the "other" who is simply viewed as property to be bought and sold, and when felt to be of no further use, discarded.

The economics of ancient Israel is clearly one of the areas that was very much a part of the focus of the prophetic invectives. There is the devastating indictment of those who destroy the economic life of covenant members and then proceed to use their gains in a lavish way within the Temple and flaunt what they have gotten through the most egregious of means in the presence of YHWH, thus underlining a sense of audacious entitlement and a total lack of fear and shame.

> Thus says the LORD:
> For three transgressions of Israel,
>   and for four I will not revoke the punishment;
> Because they sell the righteous for silver,
>   and the needy for a pair of sandals—
> They who trample the head of the poor in the dust of the earth,
>   and push the afflicted out of the way;
> father and son go in to the same girl,
>   so that my holy name is profaned;
> They lay themselves down besides every altar
>   on garments taken in pledge;
> And in the house of their God they drink
>   wines bough with fines they imposed[56]

There is an unavoidable connection between the abuse of the economics of everyday life and the cultic life that was being equally abused and made into a farce and a spectacle for the world to see, but with little just substance. It is at the very core an effrontery to YHWH. The economics of unfair and unscrupulous trading practices inevitably led to the crushing of the poor. The graphic image of "trampling the head of the poor in the dust of the earth" is such that no additional words need to be added for further elucidation. But what led to this imagery is of particular significance in understanding the collapse, ruination, and corruption of the economic system. Because of loans that were made to the poor landowners by their wealthier counterparts ostensibly to grant them aid in the face of failed crops and thus little to sustain themselves, and when they are unable to

56. Amos 2:6–8.

repay the loans, their land is seized. Instead of restoration, they are made destitute. On the basis of a transaction between covenant members, one loses everything to the other and economic greed trumps all other relational aspects. It is instructive that Jesus spoke of the need to care for the poor, and often when he spoke thus, the Greek terms used is *ptokos* and not *pene*.[57] Both of these terms are commonly translated "poor" but Jesus often spoke of the destitute, that is, not only of the basic poor, but those who live on the basis of the other's mercy and goodness for their welfare; the ones whose very lives are at stake as they teeter on the edge. In Amos 2:6–8, there are four words that capture the economic situation of those who are being crushed: righteous, needy, poor, and afflicted. To underline this rampant and shocking abuse, these wealthy purveyors of injustice demonstrate their vituperative effrontery by the utter desecration of the temple, and the very name of YHWH is profaned through their actions. They are not only satisfied with their utter disregard of the covenantal responsibilities, but do not evidence even a modicum of care and compassion. Rather they have taken the wine and the coats that they have seized from the poor and consort with temple prostitutes. It is not simply a lifestyle of extravagance, but a lifestyle that is built on the backs of their neighbors and is flaunted in the face of YHWH. The great commandment to love God and neighbor is dismantled in the most extraordinarily selfish way, and thus it is not predicated even on the love of self. It is wanton selfishness. A further element needs to be emphasized here in that it is "the house of their God" that they have chosen to display the baseness of their behavior, and the importance of this lies in the fact that they still believe that this is their God.

The prophets did not speak *their* personal message, or act on grudges that they bore. Not to listen to the prophets or tell them not to speak is to, in reality, say to YHWH we no longer wish to have you in our midst, as Jeremiah is told; do not prophesy to us, as Amos is told. Dramatically, Amos, the spokesperson for YHWH, is told that he must leave the king's temple and prophesy elsewhere, for the Temple is the king's sanctuary. Not only is he not welcome to prophesy at Bethel but in effect, the king has usurped the role of YHWH and taken over the Temple.[58]

> Ah, but I am rich,
>   I have gained wealth for myself;
> but all his riches can never offset
>   the guilt he has incurred . . .

---

57. Crossan, *Jesus: A Revolutionary Biography*, 60–62.

58. Amos 7:12.

> Because you have trusted in your chariots
> and in the multitude of your warriors,
> Therefore the tumult of war shall arise among your people,
> and all your fortresses shall be destroyed.[59]

The very idea of being "self made," "I am rich; I have made wealth by myself" underline not only a sense of individualism to the extreme, but an idea based on a premise that is fundamentally flawed. Howsoever one becomes wealthy and accumulates wealth, it is never done singularly and in isolation. Perhaps there was initiative and risk, but always community plays an essential role. Moreover as in the Habakkuk text cited earlier, the personal is connected with the corporate and personal accumulation of wealth is inextricably tied to military power and the level of trust that has been placed in a nation's military might.

> And on that day, says the Lord GOD,
> I will make the sun go down at noon,
> And darken the earth in broad daylight.
> I will turn your feasts into mourning,
> and all your songs into lamentation,
> I will bring sackcloth upon all loins,
> and baldness on every head
> I will make it like the mourning for an only son,
> and the end of it like a bitter day.[60]

Given the unquenchable greed of the powerful at the expense of the poor and those on the margins of society, and the hope for present and future power and safety predicated on the military, the punishment is direct. Not only will the fortresses be destroyed, but as a result of the tumult of war the people will also suffer as a consequence. As if to further emphasize the extent of the devastation, all of creation, both the guilty and the innocent will suffer the consequences. Those who are at ease will tremble at what is to come.

> There is no faithfulness or loyalty,
> or no knowledge of God in the land.
> Swearing, lying, and murder,
> and stealing and adultery break out;
> bloodshed follows bloodshed.[61]

59. Hos 12:8; 10:13–14a.
60. Amos 8:9–10.
61. Hos 4:1b–2.

There is an unceasing and seemingly perpetual shedding of blood, coming on the heels of a catalog of other expressions of the fractured relationships. The fact that murder is mentioned in the catalog of broken moments makes clear that "bloodshed follows bloodshed" is much more inclusive than murder and killing in a literal sense. Given that all of the issues at stake are relational in nature, the bloodshed that is ongoing reflects a brokenness that pervades all of life.

> For they have transgressed laws,
>   violated the statutes,
>   broken the everlasting covenant.
> Therefore a curse devours the earth,
>   and its inhabitants suffer for their guilt.[62]
>
> The end has come upon my people Israel;
>   I will never again pass them by.[63]

Indeed as Isaiah and Amos pronounce in these instances, the consequences of those who have transgressed laws, violated statutes, and broken the covenant have affected all of the earth. With a note that hearkens to the Exodus event, deliverance and salvation will be cast aside as well.

> Because you have said, "We have made a covenant with death,
>   and with Sheol we have an agreement;
> when the overwhelming scourge passes through
>   it will not come to us;
> for we have made lies our refuge,
>   and in falsehood we have taken shelter";
> Therefore thus says the Lord GOD . . .
> And I will make justice the line
>   and righteousness the plummet;
> hail will sweep away the refuge of lies,
>   and waters will overwhelm the shelter.
> Then your covenant with death will be annulled,
>   and your agreement with Sheol will not stand;
> when the overwhelming scourge passes through
>   you will be beaten down by it.[64]

For not only have the people abandoned and neglected the covenant with YHWH and the memory of what has been foundational, there is a flaunting of a replacement covenant, with death, with Sheol.

62. Isa 24:5b–6a.

63. Amos 8:2b.

64. Isa 28:15–18.

> Woe to those who hide deep from the LORD their counsel,
> > whose deeds are in the dark,
> > and who say, Who sees us? Who knows us?
> You turn things upside down!
> > Shall the potter be regarded as the clay;
> that the thing say of its maker,
> > he did not make me;
> or the thing formed say of him who formed it,
> > he has no understanding?[65]

In this regard, the choices are not encumbered with the grey areas or nuances; the choice is clear. The covenant with YHWH is about life and the people have chosen to ally themselves with death. The measure of the relationship with YHWH that would be foundational are justice and righteousness, and by these all will be gauged and judged. The response by YHWH is not only that the people will be allowed to continue in their relationship with Sheol, but further underlining the role of the YHWH as *the* architect of the covenant, the covenant with Sheol will be as if it never occurred, as the idea of nullification dictates. While the covenant with death will be nullified, it does not mean that there will be no punishment. The people will be *beaten down*!

> Alas for those who devise wickedness
> > and evil deeds on their beds!
> When the morning dawn, they perform it,
> > because it is in their power.
> They covet fields and seize them;
> > houses and take them away;
> they oppress householder and house,
> > people and their inheritance.[66]

As if to emphasize the extent of the greed of the indicted people, Micah paints a devastating portrait of the people. They use a time of rest in the dark of night to scheme ways of devising evil and wickedness against their covenantal kin. They do evil and plot and execute their plans because they can. They have the power to do so; it is the Promethean struggle between the powerful and the powerless. We are reminded repeatedly that the message of the prophets brims with seeming contradictions. Jeremiah is also told by YHWH that he has been sent "to pluck up and to break down, to

65. Isa 29:15–16.
66. Mic 2:1–2.

destroy and to overthrow, to build and to plant."[67] Amos after the devastating indictment and invectives pronounces the incongruous and seemingly impossible. But it is also exactly this kind of seeming contradiction that reminds the reader and interpreter that it is not so much the fact that these are words uttered by the prophets, but that the words reflect the character and being of the one who called the prophet, namely YHWH. This woe oracle utters a stark, devastating contrast between the lives of those who live in luxury as the normal and expected, and bear no grief or empathy for the suffering; a people without empathy is a people without moral mooring.

OUTLANDISH GREED

In ancient Israel it has always been about the land in shaping the identity of the people, and indeed it the case today that land is the defining quality that shapes most peoples. The people's identity is finally shaped by the land.

> Hear this, you that trample on the needy,
> and bring to ruin the poor of the land,
> saying, when will the new moon be over so that we may sell grain;
> and the Sabbath, so that we may offer wheat for sale?
> We will make the ephah small and the shekel great,
> and practice deceit with false balances,
> buying the poor for silver
> and the needy for a pair of sandals,
> and selling the sweeping of the wheat.[68]

Among the many prophetic texts, Amos 8:4–12 is particularly illustrative. "Like Micah and Isaiah, Amos draws a close link not only between worship of God and social structures, but also between the way society operates and the fruitlessness of the land."[69] As I have suggested elsewhere among the sharpest prophetic invectives are those against the disenfranchisement of the poor regarding land ownership.[70] The prophets are particularly pointed in their criticism of the dispossession of the land that the poor need for basic sustenance, and a livelihood. With regard to Amos 5, I have argued that: "Now, the "fruitful earth" is no longer providing for the poor, the "people of the land," but is taken over by the powerful . . .

67. Jer 1:10.

68. Amos 8:4–6.

69. Marlow, "Justice for Whom," 109.

70. See Gossai, *Social Critique by Israel's Eighth-Century Prophets.*

The land, as a gift from YHWH and as element which is the right of every Israelite, now becomes the exclusive property of the rich."[71] Perhaps the central issue of both bane and blessing was that of the land. It was in the first instance the land that was the governing promise, the gift that was granted and then taken away as the people entered into exile. But while we may speak of the land as a general matter, it is most often at the very particular and individual levels that issues of injustice and inequality most often transpired. It is the land that has generated the greatest economic injustice with its inextricable ties to the fracturing of YHWH's promise that the land is a gift to all and must not be taken and sold in perpetuity. By taking the land away from others and accruing at other's expense and indeed livelihood, the perpetrators were also usurping God as owner and giver of the land. This usurpation was arguably the most critical issue, but the land issue and its economic effect on the poor and disenfranchised have far reaching effects. Not to be a landowner meant that a person was made to dwell on the margins of society; beyond the punishment of excommunication, where one is made to be something of an outcast from the community.

> Woe to him who builds his house by unrighteousness,
>> and his upper rooms by injustice;
> who makes his neighbor serve him for nothing,
>> and does not give him wages;
> who says I will build myself a great house
>> with spacious upper rooms,
> and cuts out windows for it,
>> paneling it with cedar,
>> and painting it with vermilion.
> Do you think you are a king?
>> because you compete in cedar?
> Did not your father eat and drink
>> and do justice and righteousness?
>> Then it was well with him.
> He judged the cause of the poor and needy;
>> then it was well.
> Is not this to know ME?
>> says the Lord.
> But you have eyes and heart
>> only for your dishonest gain,
> for shedding innocent blood,
>> and for practicing oppression and violence.[72]

71. Ibid., 249.

72. Jer 22:13–18.

In ancient Israel, for all practical purposes landlessness was a loss of identity including a loss of community and belonging. Without the land, individuals and families were unable to participate in the life of the community, in assemblies, in cultic activities, and in the deliberations in the gate. It was the loss of a voice, without which, and lacking any discernible power, there was the inexorable spiraling into a vortex of nonentity. At this point, to whom would the oppressed and marginalized turn? The natural progression would be to take their claim to the judges, through the judicial process, but here too, the wealthy and the powerful deliver bribes, and justice is corrupted for the sake of a bribe, and the cycle of further injustices and oppression continues.[73] That which has been a source of protection and recourse for the poor became yet another tool to be used and abused by the wealthy and the powerful. With all the resources essentially usurped, those with no land became slaves and indebted to those who owned them. Thus began for many a cycle out of which there was seemingly no end. While the effect of being landless might not have the same overtones today as it did then, there are clearly still implications. "Land was the sign of God's salvation, the basis of participation in assemblies, cultic festival, mutual defense. It was the basis of freedom as members of God's people."[74] Rather than aiding the poor, the landless, and the disenfranchised, the judicial system served to aid the increasing dominance of the wealthy class and the powerful in society. So as the wealthy became wealthier, the poor became poorer and the divide expanded. Thus when the prophets hurled their invectives at the oppressing classes and groups, the pronouncements were sharp and unrelenting. What these oppressing groups would like most of all is to ensure that the *status quo* continue; however to allow that to happen is to allow injustice to further run a course of destruction. Mays speaks of this movement thus, "The shift of the primary social good, land, from the function of support to that of capital; the reorientation of social goals from personal values to economic profit; the subordination of judicial process to the interests of the entrepreneur."[75] It is precisely this kind of self indulgent behavior and unabashed greed that leads the prophets to make the pronouncements against the elders and princes. They simply and wantonly abuse their power for their gain and accumulation of wealth. In Mic 6:1–8, the overview of YHWH's history of salvation and deliverance of the people is countered by the human response that essentially predicates

---

73. See Isa 5:22–23; Amos 5:12.

74. Birch, *Let Justice Roll Down*, 262.

75. Mays, "Justice: Perspectives from the Prophetic Tradition," 146.

the covenantal relationship on offerings and sacrifices. And so, once again we are reminded that the injustices were simply more than the matter of ritual propriety and quantity of offerings. In this case there are three very particular and inseparable expressions of injustices that have brought about devastation to the people, namely, cheating in the marketplace, violence, and deceit in the spoken word. No longer can the spoken word have power and be expressed in truth and be taken as an event of goodness.

With a "bag of dishonest weights" used in the scales, we know that such dishonesty is premeditated, and clearly it is not a solitary accidental moment in time. Instead it is systemic and is designed to have dishonesty injustice and the ongoing crushing of the poor be a part of the landscape of life. The prophet pronounces that God would not be a part of such callousness and those who are the purveyors of violence and injustice are identified and punished. In having violent actions woven into everyday life, it is clear that those who are the perpetrators simply see their actions as part of life and thus it is accepted as the way things are and the way things will be. What makes these actions even more egregious is the fact that those with a voice to speak have remained silent, and not surprisingly when the prophets speak, their words are not welcome.

The prophet's life is such that his identification with his people, (and one thinks most notably about Jeremiah in this regard) his loyalty and deep compassion, only made his message so much more unbearable and difficult to pronounce. Indeed Jeremiah grieved and was pained for his people, the people whom he loved and with whom his life was deeply invested. But it is precisely a prophet such as Jeremiah that reminds us that as much as he cared deeply for his people, he could not casually approach the message nor was he anxious to deliver it; yet, his principal and first loyalty was to God. The people's pain would be his pain and in this respect, his words first pierced his heart along with the people. The prophet is not only God's megaphone as he/she has been called, but there are moments when the prophet has to interpret for the people who have faced the judgment of God, when it feels as if God has abandoned them. In this regard, the prophet, not only pronounces judgment but is also the one who brings hope. She/he walks a difficult line, where integrity and credibility are at stake. Can the prophet convince the people that the very God who punishes is also the God who delivers and saves? One might say then that memory is essential, for the history of God is such that one who delivers and redeems must be remembered precisely in time where it seems as if God has abandoned, times when abandonment and silence are equated with absence. This is arguably the time when the prophet takes on the most challenging role, and not only pronounces the message of judgment and gives assurance and reassurance, but accompanies the people on their journey through the night, and lives out with them the pain of punishment. Not every prophetic circumstance presents this scenario, but the prophet must be one who embodies this when necessary.

Two prophets in particular come to mind in this regard. First, Hosea's married life mirrored his prophetic message. The infidelity and disloyalty of Israel's relationship with God is lived out by Hosea in his relationship with Gomer.[76] Foundational in the relationship between Hosea and Gomer is that the infidelity did not emerge surprisingly, but in fact the very call by God to Hosea to seek out and marry Gomer was predicated on the fact that the marriage would have to be lived out as a living example of what has transpired in the relationship between Israel and God, including the birth and naming of the three children. What he does, who he is, and his decisions are all significant in the context of what he proclaims. But simply living out the moments of the prophecies does not mean that the prophet will be embraced by everyone. Jeremiah had his loyal supporters and he also had his fierce critics, many with power, such as Jehoiakim. Second, Jeremiah had that unusual and challenging situation of having to compete with another prophet, Hananiah, whose message was the opposite of his, and whose message with its sublimely positive trajectory was clearly preferable to those who simply did not wish to hear a message about punishment and exile. There are moments when certain realities are so palpable in their prospects for pain and suffering that many of us would prefer not to face the harsh truths, but in the face of such inescapable devastation, we are sometimes willing to cast our lot with a superficial hope that is without foundation. Many in Jeremiah's day chose to believe in Hananiah who for a while until his own demise, had a throng of believers. The situation had become so extreme that Jeremiah had one final admonition from God that appears counter intuitive to us. "As for you, do not pray for this people, do not raise a cry or prayer on their behalf, and do not intercede with me, for I will not hear you."[77] This is the extent to which the situation had deteriorated; the opportunity for repentance is long gone; the time for turning back is lost. How recalcitrant are the people? Even the Ninevites were given an opportunity, and they repented and God relented. The people of Judah in Jeremiah's time had long foregone that moment and there is no

---

76. Hosea 1–2.

77. Jer 7:16; 11:14.

longer a moment to stem the tide of the impending doom. So what must the prophet do when God will no longer listen to his intercessions? He laments. Lament, like prayer, is not to be seen as a last resort, and a matter of "throwing one's hands in the air" in an act of desperation. Rather, lament is an act of faith in itself. Lament is not a matter of sitting back and waiting. So in the Babylonian Exile, surrounded by despair, darkness, taunted by the captors, and an ever present fear of the absence of God, there is lament, deep, soulful, painful lament. And what is the prophet to do, but to join the laments and give an essential quality of sacredness to lament. God will be reminded unceasingly that the people, wounded as they are together with the prophet, wounded as he is, will not forget that God is a God of justice.

One thinks of Elie Wiesel's account in *Night* where he tells of the miraculous return of Moshe the Beadle from what seemed like certain death at the hands of the Nazis, to warn the remnant in Sighet of what was happening in the world beyond Sighet. He went from house to house to tell of what he had seen and to warn the people of what awaited them, to prepare them if possible, but they refused to imagine that any such horror could befall them. Wiesel had seen the change in Moshe even as he carried the weight of a knowledge that for a while only he believed. And how did the people respond? "He's just trying to make us pity him. What an imagination he has!" they said. Or even: "Poor fellow. He's gone mad." And as for Moshe, he wept.[78]

Proclaiming the prophetic word in a society that is steeped in human power where the people might be led to believe that the manner in which people lived can only be shaped by the people themselves, and given that those with power and wealth are the one who give shape to society, they come to believe that the ways things are, is the way things will always be. While God does not function with human constructed time frames, and thus what will unfold might not be what we are able to see or for that matter envision, often the alternative is to embrace what can been seen and what is tangible. When nations stand at the crossroads and the prospects of war are on the immediate horizon, it is tempting to imagine and believe that military might and human generated and powered institutions are the only necessary resources. Here the prophet reminds us that these are the moments that become defining moments. Trust is defined precisely in those times when it appears that one or a people is surrounded by hopelessness and facing mighty enemy powers, and the natural impulse is to rely entirely on human powers.

78. Wiesel, *Night*, 4–5.

When Jerusalem is facing the unlikely alliance of Syria and Israel, the prophet tells the king that this is a time for faith in YHWH.[79] The admonitions to the king are unequivocal, though challenging when faced with the prospects of threats from without. It is a reminder that it is much easier to trust and have faith when little, or that which is of small account is at stake. But for the king, much is at stake and thus the prophet's admonitions take on a particularly great effect. There are four admonitions; two positive and two negative. "Take heed, be quiet, do not fear; do not let your heart be faint."[80] The moment is not only for the present, but for the long term future; thus the admonition is to have a faith that extends beyond. What happens to Jerusalem is not simply for the immediate assurance, but to ensure that which is immediately before us, the ongoing House of David.[81] This is a time to trust and not take matters into one's own hand and depend on military, political and economic might, and their respective institutions. The choice without equivocation is encapsulated in Isa 3:9: "If you do not stand firm in faith, you shall not stand at all." This is the standard and on it rests not the king's personal inclination, but the Davidic dynasty.

In this regard, the people are always given a choice. Isaiah 36 stands as one great example, among many, of the choice that the prophet places before the people. The choice to listen to the other voices is invariably tempting. It would always be something tempting that captures the imagination of the people. There are two extraordinary and often intertwined narratives that have King Hezekiah at the center forming brackets of personal and communal challenges. In Isaiah 36, the powerful Assyrian army confronts Judah in what can only be described as an audacious moment based on military might, where the Rabshakeh of Assyria flexes his muscles on behalf of the Assyrian king. On this confrontation one could focus on any number of themes that emerge, but there are two questions that are immediately asked by the Rabshakeh. On what do you base this confidence of yours? Do you think that mere words are strategy and power for war? These are meant to be "fighting words," and they are certainly taunting words. Yet, these are exactly two of the most important questions that one must ask. We ask these questions not as taunting questions but as reflecting precisely the foundation of the prophetic word. And the answer is that those who pronounce the prophetic word do so on the basis of God and divine power, the Holy One. And, therein lies our confidence and not in weapons of war

---

79. Isa 7:1–9.

80. Isa 7:4.

81. Isa 3:2.

or the military industrial complex. Further, it is exactly the word that is essential for contemporary society. Not because it might be cast aside derisively as "mere words" but because there is active power in the word. It has always been the way for the people of God. Divine words are a strategy but only for those who believe that the divine promise, will in fact come to fruition whether it is in states of barrenness or states of powerlessness. Perhaps for a while the inhabitants of Jerusalem would be paralyzed by what they perceive to be a particular truth, but the paralysis is only temporary, and indeed as the manner of how God functions in the world is viewed more clearly, the paralysis dissipates. Hezekiah prays to God and miraculously, the powerful Assyrians are crushed by the "Angel of the LORD" and so ends the taunting; the LORD's people prevail. Or, in the instance where Hezekiah struggles with a serious illness and he faces the real possibility of death, he once again prays to God and he is healed and lives for another fifteen years.

So one could take these stories as they are, truly extraordinary, and simply let them stand. But beyond the natural impulse to shout out joyfully for what happens, such joy should be made, knowing that the confidence in God should not be restrained. But these stories also have a cautionary quality to them. Is this the way life happens on every occasion? Is this the way that nations who look to God prevail against other taunting power nations? The answer is self evident and easily forthcoming, "No." What could possibly be the message here, the word of hope here to be pronounced to people of every generation? So what might one take away from these two instances with Hezekiah? God is active in all of life and nothing is outside of God's dominion and purview, from the wide sweep of politics, war and military might, to *the* very personal quest for healing and restoration. So perhaps it is the case that if we should place all our confidence and hope in human institutions for even the powerful military might will not necessarily have the last word, and perhaps even the medical establishment might not have the last word. In the midst of the victories we also know that this is not always the way it happens, and so hope in God will not be predicated on the basis that we can dictate what God does!

Prophecy and Political Ideology

As long as inequity and oppression are present, alongside the promise of freedom and equality grounded in the biblical principles that all human beings are created equal, there will be a need for the voice of the prophet. As long as there is a radical imbalance of power that manifests itself in economic, political and social inequities, there will be a relevant and prominent place for the prophetic voice. It should not be surprising that those in power, in whatever capacity, and who have determined that the power distribution as it presently exists is just right, are typically resistant to the prophetic message. Historically the prophet has not been aligned with any ideology or movement, and the prophetic voices of today must do likewise. Moreover, while there are unmistakable trajectories of justice in the message of the prophets, there is no political agenda and certainly no "chip on the shoulder." Indeed the prophet does not fit and must not be forced to fit within one's particular agenda or ideological framework. Political affiliation is simply counter to the role of the prophet. While the well known maxim "we all breathe the same air" underlines our equality and that which fundamentally unites us, there is nonetheless structural and institutional inequalities that separate and divide us. True, the same air has been provided for all of us to breathe, but literally and figuratively, we do not all have access to the same air. The air for some is in fact poisoned, and what is inherently free and life giving for some is death for others. Whatever specifics the prophets espoused, they were never in the business of making specific policy suggestions or mandates. The prophets never dictated a particular form of government. Indeed while all of the prophetic words within the Hebrew Bible are pronounced in the context of the monarchy, they were not in opposition to the monarchy per se. Theirs was not a message that called for a particular government though their words can certainly be understood as advocating an ideal government. To use language familiar to most of us, they were seeking a "more perfect union." This was a fundamental right that was born out of a relationship with God and each other. Thus, whether it was a monarchy then or a democracy now, the essence of the message is unaltered. The prophets' message transcends time and place, governments and systems.

The prophets' pronouncements and invectives are invariably directed against those in power, in whom political and economic capital are vested. As was the case in ancient Israel, it is the role of the prophets' message today to stir up, to pain us, and to sharpen our social, political, and economic consciousness. The prophets themselves came from all walks of life and they felt the pain of the circumstances in which they found themselves, and the pain of the message that they bore. One might say the prophets became one with the message, for they were not objective messengers, but there was a personal, inextricable investment on their part. Regardless of the identity of the leaders and powerbrokers, the voice of the prophet carried the same tone, and the essence of the message was the same. They challenged and took to task those who would divide, cast aside, oppress and marginalize, particularly structurally in terms of the State. While those who hear the prophetic word might have questions, or might be surprised or even shocked, the word itself cannot be embraced only in part, and surely must not be negotiated away. "For them to be alive and present to us we must think not about, but in the prophets with their concern and their heart. Their existence involves us. Unless their concern strikes us, pains us, exalts us, we do not really sense it. Such involvement requires accord, receptivity, hearing, sheer surrender to their impact."[82] Heschel insightfully insists that before we ask the quite pertinent question, "what do the prophets mean to us?" we must place it in a larger framework. "The only sensible way of asking the personal question is to be guided by another more audacious question. What do the prophets mean to God. All other questions are absurd unless this one question is meaningful."[83]

Within the Bible there is no one political system that is given a privileged position. Some might imagine that it is theocracy, and while theocracy was a ruling system, it was not the only one. There are two inter-related issues at stake here. First, it is clearly the case that the Hebrew Prophets did not only shape their message to one particular political system; the prophetic words are addressed to whatever human institution and the human condition that are in place, and those who rule regardless of the political system are held responsible for the welfare for its citizens. Given that the only authority to whom the prophet is responsible is God, it finally does not matter who the human authority is or what the nature of the system is. The prophet's role was not necessarily to aid in overthrowing a governing power, though that occurred as well (Elisha) but to bring the word truthfully and without guile or personal ideological bias. Second, the United States, with its particular emphasis on Democracy, has been known to seek this form of government as the ideal for all countries. Not infrequently, it has set out during wartime in particular to establish democracies, under the assumption that this form of government is such that it will certainly provide the best possible option for governing, regardless of geography, culture, religion or history.

82. Heschel, *Prophets*, xiii.
83. Ibid., xiv.

Historically the prophet has not been aligned with any ideology or movement, and the prophetic voices of today must do likewise. Whatever particularities the prophets espoused, they were never in the business of making specific policy suggestions or mandates. The prophets never proposed a particular form of government. Thus, whether it was a monarchy then, or a democracy now, the essence of the message is unaltered. The prophet's message transcends time and place, governments and systems. Moreover, it is entirely contrary to the biblical tradition of the prophet to be aligned or associated with institutions. The prophet did not regard himself ultimately as a spokesperson for the people howsoever noble or significant their cause or circumstances were. It is far too simplistic to conclude that matters of social justice generated by biblical tenets and civil laws are items that are only to be espoused by liberals. Perhaps this is what traditions that are perpetuated do, but finally social justice is not about religious or political left or right, but about relationships, and what it takes to sustain a healthy relationship with God and each other. It is impossible for one to say that he or she takes the Bible seriously and not be actively involved in social justice. Fretheim insightfully and straightforwardly concludes that "to be concerned about social justice in this way is basically, a conservative agenda. It could be said that anyone who does not attend carefully and explicitly and publicly to issues of social justice in our life together betrays the cause of conservatism."[84]

Many today who seek and title of prophet (though often coyly declining such a designation) are invariably aligned with institutions. The Hebrew prophet stood to gain nothing from his role as prophet, and on a purely personal level they lost much; indeed the prophet was neither in the business of self promotion nor for that matter the promotion of a cause. While there are intentional and unmistakable trajectories of justice in the message of the prophets, there is no political agenda; howsoever conservatives or progressives think about the prophets, the latter should not be forced to fit within one's particular agenda or ideological framework. The words of the prophet invite both the people and their leaders to think of the world as dynamic, a world that was ever changing and one that must ultimately and unwaveringly move towards justice. This vision for then, and now, ensures that one must never be in a state of perpetual hopelessness on the one hand, nor arrogance or robed in the vestment of power on the other. The prophets' message might thus be bracketed by two general principles. Neither those who are oppressed or the disenfranchised nor the leaders are

84. Fretheim, "Interpreting the Prophets," 97.

to settle for what is, believing that the way things are, will always be, the way things will be. Rather, one must imagine a just and equitable world. Then, as now, the prophetic words insist on calling the leaders to believe, embrace and actively pursue justice for everyone. The imperative here is that the prophets are unwavering in their pronouncement that the way things are, cannot, and must not be the way life will be. Moreover even though the prophets appeal to history, the message is not to be construed as a return to a "golden era." For the powerless the future is not only a re-imagining of the present, but rather a time and place of hope predicated on a God of hope and transformation. For the powerful and those who make and shape policy, a blind sense of ownership of the present and arrogant rejection of hope is a distinct path to peril. The prophetic word is ultimately a word of hope, and if the leaders cannot envision a future of justice and equality, then perhaps they cannot envision a future where their present reality will lead to exile and punishment. Imagination in a most concrete way is what is called for and sought.

The significant encounter/experience between Elisha and Naaman the Syrian General is illustrative of this principle. In 2 Kgs 8:46, Naaman the General, questions Elisha's aide, Gehazi about his boss: "Tell me about Elisha." Clearly, something is of great significance when a General wants to know about a prophet. Tell me a couple of stories about him. One certainly wonders why this interest and what could possibly generate such attention. Gehazi chooses to tell the king about the resurrection of the dead boy; the one story that emerges as most significant and dramatic is one of life and healing at the highest order. And it is this healing story in particular that gets the attention of the Syrian General. Here is someone with military power and the power and capacity to declare war, but here seems clearly interested in healing. This is not something within the parameters of conventional power constructs. One thinks of the story of Simon Magus (Acts 8) in this regard, a known magician who witnesses what Peter's healing power does, and wants to have such power.

> Now a certain man named Simon had previously practised magic in the city and amazed the people of Samaria, saying that he was someone great. All of them, from the least to the greatest, listened to him eagerly, saying, "This man is the power of God that is called Great." And they listened eagerly to him because for a long time he had amazed them with his magic. But when they believed Philip, who was proclaiming the good news about the kingdom of God and the name of Jesus Christ, they were

baptized, both men and women. Even Simon himself believed. After being baptized, he stayed constantly with Philip and was amazed when he saw the signs and great miracles that took place . . . Now when Simon saw that the Spirit was given through the laying on of the apostles' hands, he offered them money, saying, "Give me also this power so that anyone on whom I lay my hands may receive the Holy Spirit." But Peter said to him, "May your silver perish with you, because you thought you could obtain God's gift with money! You have no part or share in this, for your heart is not right before God." (Acts 8:9–13, 18–21)

The only way that Simon Magus knows how to gain this power is to pay for it. That is, he assumes that it must be for sale. But of course such healing power does not have a monetary price, and one cannot buy healing regardless of how much power or wealth one has. Neither Simon Magus nor anyone else can do this. And he is rebuked. Indeed his name would live on in infamy in the term *simony*! But there is another aspect of this kind of healing that is a divine gift. Gehazi too later discovers tragically that one cannot put up for sale the capacity to heal, in an instance that serves as a stark reminder to those who are self promoting "healers" and prey on the illnesses and fears of those who desperately want to be healed. They "heal" for a price and those who seek healing also must know in the midst of their desperation that healing does not come with a monetary price. Naaman goes to the Syrian king for healing though this is neither the role nor the protocol of kings. Despite all their conventional power, the king cannot heal. One of the ironies in the juxtaposition of the king and the General is that they are both decorated personnel and held in high regard in the public eye. At least in the case of Naaman the General, his military decorated uniform with all of its stars of distinction serves to veil the true General, namely, the General with leprosy. If this is known publicly, he will be seen as a leper and no level of distinction will hide this socially outcast person; decorated General or not. When finally Naaman agrees to go and seek healing from Elisha he comes prepared as befits a General, armed with extravagant gifts and money for Elisha. But such is not the nature of healing. Perhaps Naaman wanted to be gracious and generous, or perhaps he did not wish to be beholden to a foreigner. Regardless, healing is not for sale.

The drama of healing lies not in the extravagant gestures but in the very simplicity that is the act of surprising grace. Naaman wondered how it could be possible that he could be healed without the kind of fanfare that befits a General. Once again prophets do not function within the constraints and confines of societal expectations, and in a way healing is in the category of the Sabbath, a time set apart from all of the busyness of life, an act that does not fit in the confines of constructed human norms. It is not about monetary and commercial transaction, but rather it is about gift and grace. Those who embody conventional power and are shaped by such power have a difficult time acknowledging, let alone accepting this kind of power. There is a sense that when Naaman the General inquires about Elisha, one is reminded that finally we do bring who we are to the text. A message might strike a national or even universal chord, but finally it all comes down to what affects us, and the manner in which one's life is affected.

EXCEPTIONALISM

"In both ancient Israel and the current sense of self in the United States, there is a theologically rooted *exceptionalism* that images privilege and entitlement of idolatrous proportion."[85] Exceptionalism is a term and ideology that is fraught with challenges, and brings with it all sorts of presuppositions and implications. Yet, even so, it must be discussed, clarified in order to generate a clearer sense of what this term spoke to in the context of ancient Israel, the Hebrew prophets, and what the implications are for contemporary society. While the idea of Israel being "chosen" is well known and generally accepted among both Jews and Christians, what is less clear and certain is the understanding of "chosen." The concept of "chosenness" like exceptionalism with all of its challenges is not given widespread attention in scholarship. When used in reference to the United States as is frequently done in some religious and political quarters, exceptionalism is almost always viewed as something of a privilege. But biblically speaking such a view is not entirely tenable. Two things to note in this regard. First, "chosenness" always comes with an inherent sense of responsibility and it is never simply an honorific title that stands above responsibility. Second, the title of "chosen" is one that comes only from the one who has the power and authority to do so, and that is God. Far too often when this title is used it is self-proclaimed and the irony is that this *self-anointing* does by default usurp God's role, and in so doing clothes itself with a divine mantle.

---

85. Brueggemann, *Word Militant*, 18.

With this view and mentality embedded within the collective psyche from generation to generation, it was apparent that the agency of YHWH as the architect of the relationship with Israel was all but neglected, perhaps in some instances forgotten. What happens when there is public claim to allegiance and faith in God, but in practical reality, God is all but a reminiscence of a time gone by, and not acted as relevance anymore? An essential component of the idea of American exceptionalism is the notion that as a nation the United States has been set apart from other nations for a purpose, which is to say the biblical definition of "holy." Given this self-designation, it also means that the United States is not subject to the standards of the rest of the world, and indeed such a designation also means that the United States is granted the freedom to impose on others what it deems proper and right. There is a more insidious issue at stake here. Exceptionalism not only has the real prospect of silencing those who raise questions about the "above reproach" but that is silencing God as well. That is to say, if those who still believe in the active agency of God are not allowed to speak, then such ideological constraints extend to God as well, for God refuses to be bound by ideological constraints, progressive or conservative. One of the inherent effects of this exceptionalism is the insistence that such a position must be maintained, and if need be, it will be done so by invoking God. "This ideology of privilege sustained by power is so pervasive that it is the air we breathe and the water in which we swim. It is beyond question or criticism."[86]

There is yet another serious setback to the idea of chosenness with all of the benefits that seem to accrue from such a designation. With the power of the State, there is the capacity to hide and allow members and sections of society to remain hidden. Hiddenness is an inherent part of those vested with the "chosenness ideology" because in hiddenness one is able to live in a state of denial, and the challenges, injustices, fears, and inequities do not have to be faced and reckoned with. But that can only last for a while. If a nation or a people will take on the mantle of exceptionalism, then this designation not only needs definition but clarity in terms of source. For Jews and Christians, there is the biblical idea of exceptionalism with regard to ancient Israel, and with this designation comes not only a sense of particularity, but the remarkable responsibility and the concurrent judgment. We are reminded repeatedly that exceptionalism does not mean that God does not attend to the needs, interests and injustices of other nations

---

86. Brueggemann, "Prophetic Leadership," 4.

and peoples including those who might have other worldviews. Again, the prophet Amos' words are instructive.

> Are you not like Ethiopians to me,
>   O people of Israel? says the LORD.
> Did I not bring Israel up from the land of Egypt?
>   And the Philistines from Capthor and the Arameans from Kir?
> The eyes of the Lord GOD are upon the sinful kingdom,
>   and I will destroy it from the face of the earth—
> Except that I will not utterly destroy the house of Jacob, says the LORD.[87]

> Hear this word that the LORD has spoken against you, O people of Israel,
> against the whole family which I brought up out of the land of Egypt:
> You only have I known
>   of all the families of the earth;
> therefore I will punish you
>   for all your iniquities.[88]

In other words, this kind of "set apartness" comes with a particular worldview based on the God who is the architect, and whose actions are such that they have to be followed. In reference to being chosen or set apart, Williams notes, "in its witness to the God of the oppressed it could never be at ease with sacred structures of violence. In Israel's tradition of the exodus a community does not converge upon a victim, but God guides the victim away from the collective structures that marginalize, exclude, or slay the victim."[89]

If YHWH's expectation of justice for all of God's creation is absent, withheld or abused, then there is redress, and not only a spoken word, as powerful and generative as this is, but there will be practical redress. The quest to domesticate God is neither a new nor a novel idea, and has been very well documented in ancient Israel. Inherent in the biblical text is the idea that seeking to domesticate God and unilaterally decide that God belongs to one people or one nation, or even more radically one group, has dangerous and destructive implications. If nothing else, interpreters and practitioners alike are reminded that before God was God of a people set apart, God was the God of all creation, where all peoples and persons were created and sustained by the creator God. Where groups have determined

87. Amos 9:7–8.
88. Amos 3:1–2.
89. Williams, *Bible, Violence and the Sacred*, 148.

that God is on their side or that they have a corner on the truth about God, and that it is on their behalf that God will act, then they are in fact approaching a dangerous precipice. This position however seeks to veil the idea that not only do they have God on their side, but in so doing gets perilously close to the very groups that Amos spoke about regarding the Day of the Lord.[90] As a self-proclaimed newly minted "chosen people" or "chosen group," they might very well see themselves as beyond reproach, for after all there is the inherent claim that they speak on behalf of God, and by default they are the voice of God. With this perspective comes an unparalleled degree of power, and with this power comes the potential of abuse. With God therefore securely ensconced in their belief system, a type of henotheism gradually develops. "Idolatry always helps out the promise of manipulating the divine to one's own favor and advantage. The radical freedom of an undepicted God is not a comfortable prospect for kings. Why not box the presence of that God in a royal temple and surround it with other idols?"[91] This is precisely the temptation, and indeed the reality of domesticating God, for it is ownership and entitlement of sorts, and thus one may choose to worship other gods while maintaining that God sanctions the behavior. We see this today not in golden calves, but in wealth, power and privilege. The domestication of the radically free God of covenant is also accomplished through the creation of a nationalized religion where the interests of God are considered inseparable from the interests of the king. The people were to be different from their neighbors and this difference was meant to accentuate particular qualities such as justice and equality, and care for the other, including not only members of the covenantal community but others as well. The difference however posed an evident challenge. To be different is to not so much to be separate with the moniker of "chosen" without purpose. The difference needed to reflect the character of God and have a particular purpose; this purpose was often lost amid the quest for, and abuse of power and perpetration of injustice and violence. The special or more specifically, the covenant relationship was predicated on certain non-negotiable qualities. Justice, righteousness, mercy and compassion were to be lived out in concrete ways, and it is precisely these qualities absent or corrupted in a variety of ways that led to the prophetic pronouncements, all of which are born out of the foundational covenantal expectations.

90. Amos 5:18.

91. Birch, *Let Justice Roll Down*, 226.

Covenant faithfulness required of Israel the effort to embody justice, righteousness, and steadfast love in systemic social structures and practices, and could not be left to abstract or episodic concern.

> The social reality of Israel was an attempt to embody an alternative model of community consistent with the alternative Yahweh represented over against the gods of the ancient world . . . In contrast to the hierarchically constructed political systems of the surrounding ancient world, Israel constructed a social system that was to a considerable extent "grass roots up" rather than "top down." Much of this seems due to a valuing of every member of the community, even the weakest or the poorest, and thus, to an effort to remove severe class distinctions.[92]

At the Republican National Convention in 1992, former President Ronald Reagan spoke of the United States as being an "Empire of Ideals" and principal among those ideals are the "ideals of Democracy." The question is not whether a nation should have ideologies that might come to define the identity of the nation. Ideals by definition mean that one is constantly in pursuit of them, and in the case of Democracy it is a pursuit that moves beyond the boundaries of the nation to others. One of the challenges of ancient Israel is that of people and nation being chosen and chosenness that became a point of departure for the misguided belief that not only are they beyond reproach, but in fact they will be protected from all harm. In ancient Israel the powerful came to believe that such an ideology meant they were entitled to YHWH's protection, without question. The social ills and injustices became simply a part of the natural landscape.

Senator Albert Beveridge's speech in the US Senate regarding the annexation of the Philippines is germane here. "[God] has made us the master organizers of the world to establish a system where chaos reigns . . . And of all our race, He has marked the American people as His chosen nation to finally lead in the regeneration of the world."[93] It is precisely this current of privileged power to which all others must bow, if in fact the reality of false and expanding division and entitlement would become normative as viewed as part of the "chosenness." Moreover there must be a voice that is generated by the agency of God that challenges on behalf of those who have been made voiceless as a casualty of *such* exceptionalism. The natural impulse by many who know otherwise is in fact to "drift along" by the tide

92. Ibid., 178.

93. Delivered January 9, 1900.

fearing that to do otherwise is to face a challenge that might lead to death or at the very least lost in the force of the current and its machinery. For far too many who know they must, they simply drift with an ideology that God's role is that of a "rubber stamp." Some prominent scholars over the years have argued that it was precisely the prophets' patriotism and their sense of moral purpose, and in recent times, particularly in the United States, American exceptionalism that is central.[94] In this regard, where patriotism carries a privileged position as motivation, God is simply viewed as the judge and executioner and the concern centers around the protection of the country. While it is certainly true that the prophets spoke to their respective communities, it was never simply a matter of bringing attention to injustices or outlining the issues that need to be rectified. That is to say, these are not simply pronouncements, but rather there is an inherent quality that is designed to compel those with power to change the system, and the manner in which the society and all the various groups function. The particularities of change are not typically spelled out, and in this regard, the prophets are not narrowly prescriptive in their pronouncements. Whatever dominant ideology is in place by its very orientation expects that citizens will accept things the way they are, and believe that it is the way things will be. The dominant ideologues instill within the consciousness of the citizens that inequities are simply an avoidable part of life's landscape. But this is precisely one of the points where the prophets launch their challenge.

Samuel was well aware of this when told by God to find a new king from among the sons of Jesse. One might be called to go to places of such uncertainty and fear that awareness is not a sign of weakness. But both Samuel and Elijah establish what must be done; go to God and listen intently and carefully. Listening to the voice of God is critical not least of all because frequently the voice of God is overshadowed by many other voices, including one's own. But there is another moment in both the experiences of Samuel and Elijah that is instructive here. Both of these prophets had predetermined ideas that stood in the way of hearing the divine voice. This is not unlike David, who sought to build a house for God, more accurately a place that would house God, but God would not be domesticated, and so the Temple was not allowed to be built by David. The voice of God, or the manner in which God might be expressed or heard, cannot be restricted.

94. See inter alia, J. G. Herder, "Ueber Begeisterung, Erleuchtung, Offenbarung," in *Werke XI*, Stuttgart, 1852; and N. Schmidt, ed., *Die Schriften des Alten Testaments in Auswahl*, Göttingen, 1910.

Samuel concluded on seeing the first born son of Jesse, Eliab, that surely this must be God's Anointed, and without further ado decided that Eliab was going to be the new king. Samuel based his determination on the fact that Eliab was physically attractive and he was the first born of Jesse. Except, Samuel got it wrong as did Elijah as did Nathan when he first told David that building a house for God in Jerusalem was acceptable. None of these moments however suggest that these men could not be worthy prophets, but these instances do make clear that the prophets were complex human vessels, "flawed crystals." Thus, those who would bring the prophetic message of justice in contemporary society cannot and must not place themselves on the pedestal of virtue of such a grand scale that the message is obscured by self-promotion. Despite the great roles that the messengers of God played in biblical times, finally it is the message that is primary, and if this is lost in the process, then all is lost.

It would be easy to conclude that the prophets in their relentless attack against the injustices in society are focused on a particular group. And certainly while there are certain groups that are particularly excoriated in large part because of their systemic abuse and intransigence, there is no privileged group that is beyond or above the prophets' invectives. In fact the religious establishment is equally under condemnation by the Prophets. Perhaps the religious leaders are even more so condemned because they purport to bring the "good news" to the people, but in fact they too sustain the status quo and align themselves with institutions of power. However this prophetic proclamation is not an invitation for a leader to use his/her position merely for shock and ridicule, self-promotion, and self-aggrandizement. Those who are in positions of power to ensure the care and welfare of the poor and disenfranchised have used their position to further abuse the very people who have been placed under their care and they purport to help. Certainly there is something particularly egregious about abusing the very people who are the centerpiece of their rhetoric of care. For those who today might prey on the disenfranchised, the voiceless, the marginalized, and the deeply wounded are set apart for a particular level of indictment.

When we think of the prophets and prophetic speech today, invariably one gets the impression that they are really deeply patriotic and that is their principal motivation. That is, the prophetic word is cast in patriotic terms; the prophets deeply love their country and so they feel compelled to proclaim a word of condemnation and punishment that would be meted out by God. The primary issue here is to save the nation though patriotic fervor. This is not a new idea about the role of the prophet. This position is most notably occupied by many conservatives and evangelicals and it is the preservation of the moral fabric of the society that is the main concern. A more cynical interpretation of this motivation would be the maintaining of a particular ideology and doing so under the guise of divine guidance. But there is also another aspect to the role and motivation of the prophet. Many who are called social activists and speak and pronounce with a prophetic voice might give the impression that they speak on behalf of those who are disenfranchised, the poor, the oppressed, those who have been cast aside by society, but here too this is not entirely resonant with the biblical prophet.

WORSHIP WITHOUT JUSTICE

The covenant people of ancient Israel had arrived at a point where the security of YHWH and the promises made were taken for granted. There was a sense of entitlement that intimated that regardless of what transpired by way of injustice and oppression, God would still act on behalf of those in power, even those who have blood on their hands. It is entitlement of the highest order, entitlement that suggests that YHWH is at their disposal, and they respond with disdain to the covenantal responsibilities. Such wild arrogance propels one to conclude that if the powerful saw YHWH, the architect of the covenant in this manner, then surely those who were poor and powerless had little chance to receive justice and mercy at the hands of the powerful. What is even more troubling according to Micah is that the perpetrators are not the commonly assumed "evil" of society or the vagrants of society but those in positions who are there precisely to ensure that justice is upheld, and to ensure that the fulcrum of the society pivots on justice and equality. What is even more troubling is that those who have been placed in positions to aid others are now controlling access to God, and evidently the only way to gain access, both by listening and speaking, come with a price. That which was granted as a gift is being abused for the sake of building additional wealth. Thus, some of the priests and prophets do not only sin by the schemes that they have conjured up by themselves, but they have in effect taken what God has granted onto themselves, and use for their own gain at the expense of precisely those who need it most of all. With this in mind, how would one discern and know who to trust, and which priest or prophet might be true? The "prophets and priests for hire" create a system of distrust and an unraveling of all that is meant to be trusted and held above reproach. "Sacrificial forms, with their inherent and partially concealed victimization mechanism, express themselves through many different avenues. As we see here the sacrificial substitutions are supplemented with further substitutions through bribes and irregular payments for services. All three of the offices represent means of access to the sacred in the sense of the bounty and means of life given by God."[95]

A principal and unequivocal issue here is that while an individual might be so moved or inclined to show kindness or compassion, admirable as it is, it was ultimately not the focus of the prophets' pronouncements. It was more of the systemic injustice and oppression. As laudable as the individual acts of kindness were, finally the leaders were the ones held accountable, namely the ones with power to seize land and charge exorbitant interest rates, the kings who enslaved their people for their personal propensity for building and the expansion of the infra structure. To employ a grammar metaphor, the people are deeply entrenched in the use of *subjunctives*, while God employs *imperatives*. The issue with the people (Isaiah 58) is not that they were not religious. Indeed in a clinical sense they were very religious, and that was exactly a major part of the problem. They have kept all of the observances and performed all of the rituals exceeding the expectations, and so naturally one is left to wonder and what the issue was that brought about the prophets' indictment. "They were hyper correct in their religious observances and delighted to exhibit their piety, but in their very exercise of religion, they miss the essential point, God's order of compassionate justice."[96] Isaiah 58:3 captures the reality of the disconnect that clearly the people do not comprehend, namely, that justice cannot be satisfied through rituals alone, howsoever elaborate they may be. "Look, you serve your own interest on your fast day, and oppress all your workers."[97]

> Look you fast only to quarrel and to fight
>   and to strike with a wicked fist.
> Such fasting as you do today
>   will not make your voice heard on high.
> Is such the fast that I choose,
>   a day to humble oneself?

---

95. Williams, *Bible, Violence and the Sacred*, 152.

96. Hanson, *Isaiah 40–66*, 204.

97. Isa 58:4–5.

> Is it to bow down the head like a bulrush,
>   and to lie in sack cloth and ashes?
> Will you call this a fast,
>   a day acceptable to the LORD?[98]

The people are doing all of the "right" things, religiously, so to speak, as the world sees by these external expressions, in particular by those who see from afar. But of course, the one who is the architect of the universe, and by whose initiative these people have been set apart, knows and is not fooled. Indeed YHWH is incensed even as the people proceed to promulgate their prolific but empty rituals. Much has been said and written about the prophets' perspective on the role of Temple and Cult. We think of such devastating words in Amos 5:21–24, Isa 1:10–17 or Jer 7:4 among many others, and it would of course be easy to conclude that the preoccupation with Temple and the extensive cultic activities was really at the heart of what the prophets were concerned about. Indeed some have argued that it is the abolition of the cult that was the ultimate issue for the prophets. But there is finally no evidence that this is really the ultimate issue. In the words of the prophets what we witness is the very common feature that has crept in practically every aspect of life, namely, *means* have become *ends* in and of themselves. As is the case with signs, rituals and cultic activities they must lead and point to destination, to what is ultimate. As important and proper as they might be, rituals are not ultimate, perhaps sacred, but not ultimate; they are *means*, not *ends*.

For example in the case of fasting one may have all of the external expressions of religious piety with all of the trappings to show the world; sackcloth and ashes; bowed head and demonstration of humility. On the surface, this all appears to be proper, but such religious piety is of no account when simultaneously the practitioners quarrel and fight with hands "full of blood" (Isa 1:15). Can fasting ever be reconciled with selfishness and oppression; quarreling and fighting; with violence and wickedness? They are irreconcilable. Indeed, on the day of fasting, the people bury themselves in a state of conventional grieving, except that here too, they are doing all the right things, but the grief is void of heart and feelings. One might very well ask, for what are the people expressing such external *mea culpa*? It is noteworthy the people's mode of fasting are all expressed in facing the ground and not looking upward into the eyes of those they oppress, but this looking away will not satisfy YHWH. Thus, humility, bowing, and lying down, all suggest a mode of grief, but there is no grief for

---

98. Isa 58:3–4.

what is occurring, for the actions against the weak and marginalized among them, and for whose state they are responsible. Instead there is a sense that all of the expressions are perfectly in keeping with the convention, except, that they are void of meaning. Instead what is required is captured in the deeply emotive rhetorical questions, questions which presuppose a prior knowledge (Isa 58:4–5).

> Hear the word of the Lord,
>> you rulers of Sodom!
> Listen to the teaching of our God,
>> you people of Gomorrah!
> What to me is the multitude of your sacrifices?
>> says the Lord;
> I have had enough of burnt-offerings of rams,
>> and the fat of fed beasts;
> I do not delight in the blood of bulls,
>> or of lambs, or of goats.
> When you come to appear before me,
>> who asked this from your hand?
> Trample my courts no more;
>> bringing offerings is futile;
>> incense is an abomination to me.
> New moon and sabbath and calling of convocation—
>> I cannot endure solemn assemblies with iniquity.
> Your new moons and your appointed festivals—
>> my soul hates;
> they have become a burden to me,
>> I am weary of bearing them.
> When you stretch out your hands,
>> I will hide my eyes from you;
> even though you make many prayers
>> I will not listen;
>> your hands are full of blood.
> Wash yourselves; make yourselves clean;
>> remove the evil of your doings
>> from before my eyes;
>> cease to do evil,
>>> learn to do good;
>> seek justice,
>>> rescue the oppressed,
>> defend the orphan,
>>> plead for the widow.[99]

99. Isa 1:10–17.

In Isa 1:10–17 the prophet begins by drawing a comparison between Israel and two of the more notorious cities, Sodom and Gomorrah, known then and infamously known throughout history for the sin that led to their destruction. The prophet enumerates in particular detail the various elements of worship what had erstwhile been foundational, are now not only empty and void, but utterly unacceptable. As we read the catalogue of cultic activities, it is tempting, as has been the case by some, to cast blame and derision upon those Judeo-Christian communities that historically have had "high" liturgical practices. To draw this conclusion as the central issue in this text is to miss the principal matter that the prophet addresses. Indeed those who today might view themselves as beyond reproach in this matter are precisely the ones in danger of missing the prophetic implications. In referring to Israel and Judah as Sodom and Gomorrah, the prophet has established a new level of "sin" in the community, and in this instance the "outcry" is that of the hypocrisy and shame that are the cultic practices. There is simply no way to avoid the devastating indictment of YHWH's rejection in these verses. There is the blatant and shocking disconnect between the personal and communal piety of the people in the context of worship, and the manner in which they live and relate with each other. The ritual propriety is odious even as those with the greatest need languish on the margins of society, and are left without voice. There is no more painful evidence of this disregard than the prophet's despair that the very hands that are stained with the blood of the people are the hands that reach out to God in prayer. This is so egregious that God will disconnect as well, as God will neither see nor hear the people, the two essential components of prayer, and that which is necessary to be in relationship with God. When the "soul" of God hates, this must be an indication of the depth of divine grief and pain. Yet, there is hope, and the prophet's imperative all point to "doing." Indeed before the people can begin to act justly on behalf of others, a necessary quality to bring meaning to rituals of worship, they must first cleanse themselves, and this is integral to acting justly. Beyond the prophet's general admonition to act justly, and cease to do evil and learn to do good, the people must have within them that which is necessary as a foundation before good could be done for others. This is not entirely different from the "Love the Lord with all your heart, soul, mind and strength and your neighbor as yourself." The love of neighbor cannot be apart from love of God and love of self. It is incumbent for a personal and communal self-awareness as a prerequisite.

The ideas expressed in Isa 58:6–7 are clearly ones that the people have heard before and must now know.

Is not this the fast that I choose:
to loose the bonds of injustice,
to undo the thongs of yoke,
to let the oppressed go free,
and to break every yoke?
Is it not to share your bread with the hungry,
and bring the homeless poor into your house;
When you see the naked, to cover them,
and not to hide yourself from your own kin?
Then your light shall break forth like the dawn,
and your healing shall spring up quickly;
Your vindicator shall go before you,
the glory of the LORD shall be your rear guard.
Then you shall call and the LORD will answer;
you shall cry for help, and he will say, Here I am.
If you remove the yoke from among you,
the pointing of the finger, the speaking of evil,
If you offer your food to the hungry and satisfy the needs of the afflicted,
then your light shall rise in the darkness
and your gloom will be like the noonday.
The LORD will guide you continually,
and satisfy your needs in parched places,
and make your bones strong;
and you shall be like a watered garden,
like a spring of water, whose water never fail.
Your ancient ruins shall be rebuilt;
you shall raise up the foundations of many generations;
You shall be called the repairer of the breach,
the restorer of the streets to live in.[100]

This text speaks pointedly to some of the gravest human issues both in the time of Isaiah and in our time. So as we read the text we become immediately aware that the prophet speaks to matters of hunger, shelter, freedom, belonging, care, compassion, and the fundamental reality of what it means to be in relationship. This is about belonging, and about security. It is finally impossible to speak of covenantal relationship with all people without the active acknowledgment of basic necessities of all people and particularly for those who are perched precariously on the edges on society. Gray has suggested that "it may also be a text for our times in offering challenging and costly dimensions of justice with reconciliation."[101] Such expressions

100. Isa 58:6–12.
101. Gray, "Justice with Reconciliation," 176.

of belonging and ordinary sustenance cannot be done at a distance and in the abstract. The prophet is as pointed in the particularities of the relationship as is present in any of the prophetic texts. It is personal and face to face. When one chooses to fast, certainly an intensely personal matter, even here, fasting must be connected to the community, to those who are on the margins of society. Fasting without attention to the welfare of those who are oppressed, poor, and starving is unacceptable to God. Indeed Isaiah makes clear that fasting should be expressed through the feeding of the hungry. The juxtaposition of those who choose not to eat as a religious commitment, because one can, is in sharp relief alongside those who do not eat because they have no food, and thus not a matter of choice. Those who fast must feed the hungry. The personal commitment and investment is further accentuated in v. 7b. One cannot care by proxy and have caring become the responsibility of deputies. Instead, the prophetic word is such that the homeless poor must be invited into *your* house. Those who are naked must be personally clothed. This is a direct challenge to any convention that cares from a distance or in an unattached way. Such is the radical and essential nature of fasting as a matter of sacrifice. Indeed the very well-being of the people will depend on the restoration of the personal relationship, for only then will light overcome darkness and only then will the people's call to God be answered. We may not be able to see God face to face and live, but we have a mandate to see each other face to face, in the eyes, speak and listen, feed and clothe, shelter and care, and thereby live and bring life to each other. It is incumbent upon us to move away from the place in which we find ourselves deeply entrenched and perhaps entirely too comfortable and protected. It is for those who would take these texts seriously and apply the admonitions and mandates to our lives, and thereby become vulnerable.

Thus the prophet takes fasting out of the very private and makes it into a moment that is inseparable from living justly in the context of community and the needs of community. One cannot hide behind the privatization of religion and in the process neglect the care and compassion of others. Religion in other words cannot be a private matter and those who seek to do so, with its myriad practices, will be taken to task by YHWH and made to face the hypocrisy of their behavior.

> In a community where those who regarded themselves as the most religious had converted religion into private acts of study and ritual, thereby leaving the private realm of social relations and commerce under the dominion of ruthless, self-serving exploitation, the prophet reaffirms . . . the experience of God's liberating

slaves from their bondage, feeding them in the wilderness, and giving them a homeland of their own. It is a rigorously moral understanding that places the one who would be true to God on the side of the same ones whom God reached out to help and empower, those suffering injustice at the hands of the authorities, those imprisoned for acts of conscience, those denied their fair share of the land's produce, those denied housing and proper clothing, those turned even by their own relatives.[102]

102. Hanson, *Isaiah 40–66*, 205–6.

3

Food and Power

Some time later King Ben-hadad mustered his entire army; he marched against Samaria and laid siege to it. As the siege continued, famine in Samaria became so great that a donkey's head was sold for eighty shekels of silver and one fourth of a kab of dove's dung for five shekels of silver. Now as the king of Israel was walking on the city wall, a woman cried out to him, "Help, my lord, king!" He said, "No! Let the Lord help you. How can I help you? From the threshing floor or from the wine press?" But then the king asked her, "What is your complaint?" She answered, "This woman said to me, 'Give up your son; we will eat him today, and we will eat my son tomorrow.' So we cooked my son and ate him. The next day I said to her, "Give up your son and we will eat him. 'But she has hidden her son.' When the king heard the words of the woman, he tore his clothes—now since he was walking on the city wall, the people could see that he had sackcloth on his body underneath—and he said, "So may God do to me, and more, if the head of Elisha son of Shaphat stays on his shoulders today." So he dispatched a man from his presence. Now Elisha was sitting in his house, and the elders were sitting with him. Before the messenger arrived, Elisha said to the elders, "Are you aware that this murderer has sent someone to take off my head? When the messenger comes, see that you shut the door and hold it closed against him. Is not the sound of his feet behind him?" While he was still speaking with them, the king came down to him and said, "This trouble is from the LORD! Why should I hope in the LORD any longer?"[1]

---

1. 2 Kgs 6:24–33.

This text strikes a searing juxtaposition between hunger and the military. In 2 Kgs 6:26–33, it is the voice of a woman who speaks, and she becomes the voice of all who were hungry. There is a stark contrast between this poor woman and the king, whose life and rule is one of abundance; while she struggles for bread he inspects the military, the two within earshot of each other, living in the same society, and yet worlds apart. With this Promethean struggle, this woman has no realistic chance of speaking with the king, and in fact all she has is a voice. While the king inspects the security of the military believing that it is underpowered, the very basic essentials that are necessary for fundamental daily sustenance, namely bread, is unavailable to those who need it most. The irony is clearly lost here on the king. He is either unaware of the desperate woman or he simply disregards her. In giving her attention, and taking note of her, he might very well have to attend to these most basic of needs. "She has no right to speak. Except that the desperately hungry do not wait for a right to speak. She will not wait for royal protocol. The one who is most hungry voices her desperate stomach to the one who presides over the food monopoly. If anyone has food, it is the king . . . The king is the only one who stands between her and starvation.[2] That is to say, it is the one with the convention who has the capacity to determine life and death. His silence means death. There are two ideas that are inextricably connected in this text. Firstly, the only "power" that the woman has, such as it is, is her voice. Though perhaps weak because of lack of sustenance and daily bread, she nonetheless speaks. There is the issue of basic welfare, where the one with conventional power who does not know what it means to be without food, to be without daily sustenance, but is concerned about military security and is deaf and blind to the issue of hunger and starvation, even though he is in proximity to hear the voice of the other. Second, the woman insists on letting her voice be heard. She does not have the capacity, time or the energy to spell out the disgrace over hunger and starvation when there is plenty, or the irony of "security" when "insecurity" at its most basic level silently screams in every direction for the king to hear. She is neither interested nor equipped to make policy statements. This is a fundamental human impulse. In one defining moment she says, "Save me." Both of these examples have extraordinary and pointed relevance for contemporary society. Hunger, as a matter of life and death is juxtaposed with the military and establishment power. There is the shallow and cynical answer that is all too present today, and more widespread than

2. Brueggemann, *Testimony to Otherwise*, 67.

even the text testifies. When the king finally answers the woman's command to save her, he tells her to let God save her. This is the kind of devastating and cynical platitude that in some quarters is altogether axiomatic. What makes this statement under these circumstances particularly egregious and unconscionable is that the truth of such a statement is being abused, and crudely silences the suffering person. Unlike the king in 2 Kgs 6:24–25, whose needs are always fulfilled, the woman's imperative to save herself from starvation, is turned into a religious cliché.

After he dismisses the hungry woman with the all too familiar, "Let the LORD save you" the king seemingly is still bothered about the woman's situation. The most positive and decent interpretation that one might put to this unexpected interest in the woman's problem might be that his conscience has somehow been touched and he is moved to compassion. Perhaps it is because he has been shamed in public; perhaps it is an indication of his disconnect from, or his disregard for the very people over whom he rules. He is clearly unaware of what the lives of the people are like, the definition of basic sustenance, and what they are enduring; his situation is markedly different from theirs. To be sure, the king knows that the issue is food, but he is woefully unaware of the extent and the depth of the despair; he does not understand that this is systemic and that it is a matter of life and death. Under no circumstances is the king able to say, "I know how you feel." The king comes to the conclusion that something mysterious has brought this about, and it is not a matter of economics. This is a curse and the person to be blamed is the prophet! Instead of seizing the moment as a defining one, he instead casts blame on the prophet and sees the incident as a mysterious aberration. When one has both power and freedom to draw conclusions that are baseless, it also means that ultimately the king will not take responsibility, and instead he decides that killing the prophet Elisha would somehow resolve the bread issue. That is to say in killing the messenger the message will also disappear as would the existential issue of hunger. Elisha knows that he is a marked man; he knows that there is a bounty on his head, and he has the king's attention in a way that he needs protection. Here we have one of several examples in the Bible that pits prophet against king; conventional power against prophetic power. The problem that divinely generated famine brings is that it does not necessarily punish the king and those in power, but most often the powerless and the marginalized are the first to suffer. As in war, it is typically the foot soldiers and not the Generals who first face the danger and are the first to die. This is a moment that something drastic must be done; the woman must leave the land and go, simply go. The fact that 2 Kgs 6:21–23 immediately precedes this text is enormously revealing.

> When the king of Israel saw them he said to Elisha, "Father, shall I kill them? Shall I kill them?" He answered, "No! Did you capture with your sword and your bow those whom you want to kill? Set food and water before them so that they may eat and drink; and let them go to their master." So he prepared for them a great feast; after they ate and drank, he sent them on their way, and they went to their master. And the Arameans no longer came raiding into the land of Israel.[3]

Even though the narrative extends beyond these verses, nonetheless, the essence of this text reflects a very particular message. The invitation to hospitality in the form of a shared meal does establish the distinct possibility of staving off warring tendencies. In the midst of the ongoing and seemingly never ending war between Israel and Syria, the prophet has a proposal and intervene. The king of Israel suggests killing the Syrian prisoners of war, but the prophet suggests otherwise. Instead of an early iteration of "death to the enemy," the prophet suggests granting food and drink. And this evidently makes the world of difference. The Arameans no longer came raiding, at least for a while.

Freedom and Daily Bread

One of the cornerstone responsibilities for a leader, any leader, is to ensure that the citizens over whom he/she rules or governs are safe and have a quality of security. So what happens when the king is unable to respond to the demand "save me" for what he considers lack of resources?[4] After the encounter with the woman who is without bread and facing starvation, clearly an unwelcomed encounter, the king cannot quite say that "I feel your pain," for not only does he live a life of plenty but he is in fact unaware of the emptiness in the lives of the people.

> Their land is filled with silver and gold,
> there is no end to their treasures,
> there land is filled with horses,
> there is no end to their chariots.[5]

---

3. 2 Kgs 6:21–23.
4. 2 Kgs 6:26–31.
5. Isa 2:7.

And here, in this verse the prophet Isaiah encapsulates what the two foci are: wealth and military power. This surely must not come as a novel revelation in today's society. Then, as now, people have come to believe that finally what defines success and glory, prosperity and goodness, are wealth and power and the military industrial complex. But these would be the very elements that will bring the prophet's relentlessly sharp pronouncements, divine sorrow, and anger, and ultimately the nation's downfall. One of the questions that must be reckoned with in the exploration of the prophets' message and the denunciations of injustices is the theme of freedom. What does it mean to be free? Assuredly it is a term that it is ubiquitous, employed in a variety of circumstances, and by various sources including those who might consider themselves free and claim to have an understanding of the importance of freedom, but also hold others in bondage. It is not enough to simply speak of freedom, and there is no correlation between the repetition of the word with the corresponding action. What should be a basic and non-negotiable standard for the care of the other? Share a meal as an act of simplicity and one of shared intimacy. To share a meal then is seen as collapsing a social, class, economic barrier that for many is the final line of defense.

The Hebrew verb *srp* (to break) is germane to the discussion here. While this verb is not uncommon in the Hebrew Bible, two instances of its use in Isa 58:7 and Jer 16:7 are particularly instructive in our discussion. In both of these instances *srp* refers to the breaking of bread. It is the foundation of social unity, and gives definition to what it means to be in relationship with, and care for each other. There is hardly a more profound moment of engagement with the other than a shared meal. In this case it is not a shared meal with those who are loved, the cadre of friends, the community to which you feel a sense of belonging. Instead, it is a shared meal with the one who has been on the margin with whom perhaps there is no social or familial connection, except that is a human bond.

> In Jeremiah 16:7, the author pictures a context of social disintegration in which "no one will break *(srp)* bread" with those in distress, whereas, in what might be taken as a reversal of that text, Isa. 58:7 strongly suggests that, in such conditions, it is precisely in acts of solidarity such as the breaking *(srp)* of bread with the oppressed that social cohesion will begin to be established . . . In the development of thought in Isa. 58:6–7, the inference is that all manifestations of breaking in v. 6 should properly lead to the breaking of bread and all that follows in v. 7. So the struggle towards freedom

properly entails feeding the hungry, sheltering the homeless, clothing the naked, and being available to those in need—that is, addressing primal hungers for food and community.[6]

The idea of a shared meal is not one that is central to the prophets' message and yet there are both allusions and indeed references to such a moment of significant connection.

> Is not this the fast that I choose:
>   to loose the bonds of injustice,
>   to undo the thongs of the yoke.
> To let the oppressed go free
>   and to break every yoke?
> Is it not to share bread with the hungry,
>   and bring the homeless poor into your house;
> When you see the naked, to cover them,
>   and to hide yourself from own kin.[7]

Isaiah 58: 6–7 underlines one of the critical factors in the prophets' message regarding what it means to be free. Clearly the message of the prophets, at its core often cited in the New Testament regarding freedom reflects what it means for all people to be free, for the inextricable connection to justice. If a person is trapped in the cycle of injustice or for that matter imprisoned by a system that focuses on the promotion and interests of the select, where wealth and power are the henotheistic ideals, then there must be a loosening of the shackles, for the enslavement or imprisonment run radically counter to the divine intention. Freedom must never be in the abstract; it must never be enough that one is only interested in the *idea* of freedom significant as this may be. Freedom must be concrete, and for those who have been freed, there must be the commensurate actions that accompany such freedom. In Isa 58:6–7, we have a glimpse of the requisite qualitative actions.

> Whereas [Isa. 58] v. 6 focuses on the actions that precede and eventuate in liberation (loosening, undoing, letting go, breaking), v. 7 concentrates on what it is necessary to do in order to sustain life for those who have been released (sharing bread, housing, clothing). Liberating the oppressed without also providing resources

---

6. Gray, "Justice with Reconciliation," 165.

7. Isa 58:6–7.

for life (Exod. 3:21–22) is an incomplete exercise likely to lead to
little long term substantive change in the conditions of the poor.[8]

Thus for example an unavoidable feature of the ministry of Jesus is
that he never collapsed and discussed the human condition in generalities. He not only speaks of love of neighbor but indeed lived out such love
with remarkable specifics in what it means to love the neighbor. One of
the ways in which he demonstrated such neighborliness was through the
very act of eating, and eating with anyone, and particularly those who
were on the margins. The issue here is complex and there are likely several
components to be reckoned with. Certainly there are persons who seek to
express their care through monetary aid, and while this is an essential way
of combating injustice and creating freedom, it seems equally important
that when it is possible, personal relationships need to be forged, restored
and reconstituted.

Isaiah 58 focuses on the essential importance of justice that is indelibly connected with reconciliation. While this is often construed as justice
to those in the covenantal community, to be reconciled to each other, the
text intimates that in fact this reconciliation must also be meted out to all,
including the Egyptians and even the Assyrians. One focused issue underlined here is that of nakedness, both literally and figuratively. For there to
be reconciliation, all people must be clothed; the nakedness of all people
must be covered and thus a people, regardless of their identity, cannot be allowed, or for that matter be made to live lives of shame. This is an essential
question that must be asked when one nation or people seek to make another take on a different identity. In 1989, the Berlin wall, which had hith-
erto divided Germany into East and West, fell, and on November 9, East
Germans crossed freely into the West. More recently, we have witnessed
such re-awakenings with all of the inherent complications in nations such
as Egypt and Libya, along with others who were involved in the dramatic
Arab Spring. What all of these nations have in common is not simply the
quest for freedom, a new reality, but also the convivial spirit of hope that
was generated around the world, and the quality of excitement that en-
gulfed the world. But one of the immediate and now persistent questions
that must be reckoned with, is that of, now what? What happens after the
euphoria? What happens after the bright lights of the world have departed
and the dictators, and even tyrants removed? Now what? There must be a
follow up of concreteness that follows freedom, the practice of justice and

8. Gray, "Justice with Reconciliation," 164.

the establishment of a sense of belonging, a sense of goodness, the basic requisites for security, such as food and shelter among others.

> So when the prophet urges those he addresses, "not to conceal themselves from their own flesh and blood," the implication of the rhetorical development of 58.6 and 58.7 taken together is that anyone hungry or poor or naked or in need is to be considered as kin, even if they belong to a broader grouping that would be regarded as the enemy. The vision is of reconciliation emerging as the poor, and those prepared to stand in solidarity with the poor, reach across traditional lines of enmity, exclusion and suspicion in a common search for justice.[9]

There is yet a further note in Isa 58:6–7 that creates a view of reconciliation that must be reckoned with. How does one break the yoke of oppression? There are two distinct and perhaps diametrically opposing alternatives. The call of the prophet is a radical kind of solidarity over and against a radical violence. In this case, Isaiah resonates with his earlier counterpart Jeremiah who even more strikingly in his "Letter to the Exiles" calls for peace, for the very radical idea of seeking the *shalom* of the captors and in so doing secure their own welfare, a radical counterintuitive notion of reconciliation and belonging if ever there is one in the biblical text. A further sense that the identity of the people will be different from the others is that relationships will be forged and restored not on the shoulders of military might and violent acts but through solidarity and shalom.

It would be easy and even tempting to imagine and place the prophetic message of justice into a time and space so distant and in the far future as to cast the fulfillment into the next world. This runs contrary to the prophetic word, and this perspective would essentially seek to maintain the status quo, inequality, power and injustice with hackneyed words of hope and patience pronouncing that justice will come in the next life. What the prophets proclaim will transpire in the world in which the oppression and injustices are present, and while all of the prophecies will not eventuate in the prophets' lifetime, they will nonetheless transpire in this world, and thus it is not a kind of "utopian ideal" (in a place of *nowhere*) that most will find impossible to grasp and equally impossible to place any hope in.

Moreover, the prophets have not called for separation from the society or any kind of division or the kind of sectarian disconnect that we sometimes witness within certain religious groups. There is no such idea within

9. Ibid., 168.

the prophets as a sectarian justice. Perhaps the most profound expression of this idea is found in Jeremiah's "Letter to the Exiles." If any place, this would have been the place where the exiles might have been told to live a life of separation and disengagement, or adamantly refrain from assimilating into the Babylonian idea of justice and peace. But instead, they are told the opposite. There is no "separate peace" for exiles, no private deals with God, no permitted withdrawal from affairs of the Empire. The only *shalom* these troubled Jews would know is the *shalom* wrought for Babylon. The letter implies that that the exiled community of Jews can indeed impact Babylon with the *shalom* through its active concern and prayer.[10] The peoples' lives are placed in the context of all of creation. We see that when punishment is meted out, the innocent are punished along with the guilty, but also, when there is restoration, it is done within the context of the created order. We see this most notably in Hos 2:18–20. Restoration, will be within the context of creation, and so, now as then, the neighbor is not only the one whose face we see and with whom we have the proximity of village, home, school, work, Temple or Church, but those who dot the landscape of the world, and whose lives are inextricably connected with ours. Often we think that we are somehow autonomous, and society seems bent on ensuring that this is the message that we hear and embrace. This in turn creates a chasm of enormous proportions that gives privileged places to accumulation and greed, and those who pay are the ones who are pushed further and further to the margins. Moreover, if we are shaped into believing that we are autonomous, then ultimately we will come to believe that we not only deserve the most, but have an inherent sense of entitlement to accumulate by whatever means. This leads inexorably to actions that crush those who are the least and who in fact see their lives as interwoven with others and are interdependent; it is not however a mutually shared value.

Those who listen to the prophets' words and the prophetic word of today and conclude that the prophets words might unreasonably be directed at them, might openly disparage the prophet and cast him aside as simply *mad*. It would not be the first occasion to vilify the one who pronounces a challenging message as *mad*. Of course this is not to say that all so-called "madmen" are prophetic. But even those who might know better and believe the truth of the message, might not be willing to accept or imagine that what is being said could be true, and as such conclude that the prophet must be *out of his mind* or *mad*. Perhaps it is the case that if one does not

10. Brueggemann, *Word Militant*, 145.

wish to face the truth of the message, then vilifying the messenger and relegating her/him as being *mad*, is one way to avoid the painful reality of the message. *Mad* is a common moniker used by those who are the subject of the prophets' invectives, and so Elisha among others is designated *mad* and the authorities conveniently place them more in the category of nuisance, persons who are tolerated, and even humored, rather than those whose message must be reckoned with. Maimonides encapsulates with appropriate hyperbolic emphasis when he says, "The world could not exist without madmen." Perhaps Maimonides might have been thinking of the Hebrew term *nabi* which has etymological connections with insanity and madness. Thus, there is a sense that the one who speaks prophetically must be possessed with something of a supernatural force. Of course this is not to say that so-called *madmen* are inherently prophetic.

4

Eminent Domain

Emerging from the shadows of prophetic discourse with resonance and particular significance for us is the issue of eminent domain. This issue which has been redesigned and reconstituted in our time continues to function on the same basic pretext of its ancient counterpart. It is typically one sided as well, where one's land, one's domain, is sought after and often seized by those in positions of power. Conversely the person who might be in desperate need for a place to call home, to build a house, to plant a necessary garden for food, is never able to cite and employ "eminent domain" for his or her use. Eminent domain belongs to the powerful, the wealthy and those who are deeply ensconced in positions of authority and power. Under the pretext of necessity that is more significant than what the land is being used for, the property is essentially taken without the owner's freedom of refusal. In this regard, one with power and authority is able to exercise such, being shielded by the law, and simply employ the power to make the issue a matter of public or national interest.

> Later the following events took place: Naboth the Jezreelite had a vineyard in Jezreel, beside the palace of King Ahab of Samaria. And Ahab said to Naboth, "Give me your vineyard, so I may have it for a vegetable garden, because it is near my house; I will give you a better vineyard for it, or, if it seems good to you, I will give you its value in money." But Naboth said to Ahab, "The Lord forbid that I should give you my ancestral inheritance." Ahab went home resentful and sullen because of what Naboth the Jezreelite had said to him; for he had said, "I will not give you my ancestral inheritance." He lay down on his bed, turned away his face, and

would not eat. His wife Jezebel came to him and said, "Why are you so depressed that you will not eat?" He said to her, "Because I spoke with Naboth the Jezreelite and said to him, 'Give me your vineyard for money, or else, if you prefer, I will give you another vineyard for it'; but he answered, 'I will not give you my vineyard.'" His wife Jezebel said to him, "Do you now govern Israel? Get up, eat some food, and be cheerful; I will give you the vineyard of Naboth the Jezreelite."[1]

The biblical story that most powerfully underlines the challenge and indeed injustice of this system is that of the encounter between Ahab/Jezebel and Naboth.[2] The king, the one with central power, simply tells Naboth that he needs the latter's vineyard so that he might have a vegetable garden. We do not have to delve deep into unknown details about the size of the garden etc., but what is known from the narrative is more than enough to establish what is at stake, and the arguments that are used to frame the quest for Naboth's vineyard. Naboth's vineyard is in proximity to the king's palace, and that in itself appears to be reason enough to seize it. It is not in Ahab's interest to worry about Naboth's life and livelihood; power and convenience for him trumps all else. Naboth frames his response succinctly with two pillars, namely God and tradition. Perhaps there might have been other economic, personal and family factors to be reckoned with, but Naboth simply says that this land cannot be sold into perpetuity as is forbidden by God. So goes the tradition in ancient Israel, and it is the case that clearly Ahab knows this, and perhaps this straightforward answer from Naboth is what sends Ahab to his bedroom sulking. On seeing her husband's deflated look and realizing that he has not eaten and that he seems depressed, Jezebel, the very resourceful Queen, asserts her royal initiative. She demonstrates already to the very unscrupulous king exactly how to use and abuse his power to ensure that he gets what he wants. Somewhat disdainfully, she reminds Ahab that he is the one in, and with power, and with authority, and the one who governs. Given the fact that Naboth's ideas cannot be disputed legitimately, Jezebel proposes an alternative that is sure to generate the desired result. What is critical here is the fact that in the pursuit of a piece of land that belongs to the other, one who needs it for livelihood, the king and queen are relentless in their pursuit, exerting their imperial power and crushing the other in the process. The Naboth episode certainly intensifies

1. 1 Kgs 21:1–7.
2. 1 Kings 21.

the level of Ahab's selfishness and abuse of power. Even if the 1 Kings 21 and 1 Kings 22 stories were not consecutive, the juxtaposition is striking. In 1 Kings 22, when Ahab seeks the partnership and support of Jehoshaphat, it is not in any real way to seek his advice or his wisdom but to support a decision that is already made and now it is a matter of bolstering what has already been decided. But Jehoshaphat knows that something is awry—and this could have been generated by any number of reasons, not least being the very notion of 400 prophets giving unanimous assent to Ahab!

Naboth is instead framed for the most blasphemous crime by "two scoundrels" and is stoned to death. There is no concern or care for Naboth, and for what has transpired. Rather the report is to the point: Naboth has been stoned: he is dead."[3] So take the vineyard! That's it. But that is never the end of such stories. This should not be the end of such stories or variations of such stories today. When Elijah confronts Ahab, Ahab's greeting to the prophet is: "Have you found me, O my enemy?" Yes, that will always be the perception, for those in power and authority will view the prophet as the enemy, personal enemy and enemy of the State. And those who are purveyors of injustice and oppression, crushing the poor and taking what they wish, at all costs, including innocent life, will be exposed. Perhaps one discovers in contemporary society, this might happen immediately, but those who crush the poor and further disenfranchise them will have to face the consequences of their actions, and at some point divine justice will be executed in God's timeline. As devastatingly violent and unconscionable as Naboth's death was, it is the action against God that is most egregious. The rulers are aware that cursing God is such that it results in death. It is a direct affront to God, and Ahab and Jezebel through their actions would lead some to believe that they cannot be touched, that they are above reproach and that there would be no punitive measures against them!

The implications of the Naboth narrative at one level seems self evidently clear, but here too there are complexities. Acutely noticeable in our society is the unabashed invocation of God on behalf of a nation and people, that seeks to give sanction and credence to some actions which might ordinarily be viewed as utterly void of the quality of *humanitas*. In today's society, some who are leaders in Church and Society eagerly identify with Ancient Israel as a people oppressed and in bondage and view Egypt as the enemy. But this association may be misplaced and the identification perhaps needs to be reversed. We are uncomfortably reminded that Jezebel

3. 1 Kgs 21:14.

pivots God at the very heart of her scheme. The simple recitation of religious rhetoric that is nothing more than a pious veil ultimately will not shield one from the punishment that will inevitably be meted out for acts of injustice, regardless of the persistent expressions of justification that one posits. Nelson has noted sharply:

> The community which accepts this story as scripture must read its newspapers and then ask itself hard questions. Who are the Ahabs and Jezebels? Who are the Naboths? . . . Piety often cloaks oppression. The invocation of God is the center of Jezebel's scheme (v. 10). The community of faith must always ask if it is functioning as Elijah, bearing the Word of God to governments and corporations. Or is it playing Ahab's role, sharing in Jezebel's responsibility by permissive silence and quietism?[4]

Isaiah is pointed in his denouncement.

> The LORD enters into judgment
>> with the elders and princes of his people;
> It is *you* who have devoured the vineyard;
>> the spoil of the poor is *your* houses.
> What do you mean by crushing *my* people,
>> by grinding the face of the poor? Says the Lord GOD of hosts . . .
> In that day the Lord will take away the finery of the anklets, the headbands, and the crescents; the pendants, the bracelets, and the scarfs; the head-dresses, the armlets, the sashlets, the perfume boxes, and the amulets; the signet rings and the nose rings; the festal robes, the mantles, the cloaks, and the handbags; the garments of gauze, the linen garments, the turbans, and the veils.
> Instead of perfume there will be a stench;
>> and instead of a sash, a rope;
> and instead of well-set hair, baldness;
>> and instead of a rich robe, a binding of sackcloth;
>> instead of beauty, shame.
> Your men shall fall by the sword
>> and your warriors in battle.
> And her gates shall lament and mourn;
>> ravaged, she shall sit upon the ground.[5]

The prophet is sharp in casting the distinction between those who are the perpetrators and those who are the victims, and makes it clear that in this regard God takes sides. Mentioning God as part of one's elaborate piety

---

4. Nelson, *I & II Kings*, 145.

5. Isa 3:14–15, 18–26, my italics.

is particularly repugnant. This is often a challenging issue and to make such a claim about God and the partiality of God; however in Isaiah 3, it is clear. There will be a dramatic reorientation of life and what was once taken for granted, a lifestyle of wealth and opulence will be dismantled and there will be palpable loss of all that was seen to be an essential part of life. The indictment in this text is pointed against those with particular positions of power, religious (elders) and political (princes) leaders. They are the ones who have devoured the vineyards and have lavished their homes with the spoils that have been taken from the poor, and in this case, the language is also stark. It is "you" versus "my people," where "my people" are the poor. Howsoever one might think of the general impartiality of God, it is clear in this context and instance, God is inextricably yoked with the poor. The princes and elders have confiscated vineyards and houses, arguably those that have to do with survival, sustenance, and belonging. There is little doubt that this accumulation is underlined by unbridled power and greed, and it hints at a sense of entitlement born out of power. That is to say, those with power may take from you they desire even if what you need it for sustenance, because they can do so with impunity. Such is the arrogance and the belief that those with power who might parade with fineries, and who wield their power in utterly unconscionable ways are beyond reproach or more troubling, beyond the reach of God.

Part of the unavoidable challenge for interpreters is the fact that the "justice of God" frequently arches towards a "preferential option for the poor" an idea that has legitimate currency in biblical scholarship. However it is not nearly this clear cut in the overall biblical text. There is a conflation in the text that poses a serious problem for those who would like to see a monolithic understanding of divine justice. So, for example we have an act that would provide a land for people, but in so doing, there will by necessity be displacement for others and in fact create something of a genocide for others who have already established the place as home and belonging. One could of course argue that in fact these events are not rooted in historical reality and therefore cannot be used as such to make arguments against genocide, displacement or even complicity in such acts. But, whether or not this is historically the case, it does remain the case that it is part of the biblical text, and for religious leaders and institutions, along with those who use the Bible as the basis for theological development of ethical guidelines, and the granting of moral agency, these texts have to be taken seriously with all of the inherent complexities.

Part of the challenge in seeking a monolithic understanding of divine justice is the fact that invariably to ensure the welfare of a particular group, and certainly for a *chosen* group is that others might be oppressed in the process. The interpreter knowing that each of us brings a point of view to the text shaped by a variety of factors, must recognize this. None of us is without a point of view. Simply repeating that one reads the text objectively does not make this possible, let alone true. Indeed, such a quest may not ever be possible or for that matter advisable. Some who lay claim to objectivity often do so to provide a justification as to why God might have acted in a certain way. Yet, the reality is that God's justice has a quality of complexity, perhaps a divine inscrutability, and mystery to it, to the point that for human endeavor, full understanding is ultimately not possible. There are certainly a number of examples to underline the claim that God shows preference for the poor, but demonstrably it is also the case that God acts on behalf of a chosen people and fulfills the promise of land and people at all cost. Apart from seizing the land, all of the inhabitants are destroyed and while one might not wish to use language of genocide with all of the evil associated with it, it is in reality precisely genocide.[6] What is further challenging about this reference is the justification that is given, namely that the people were wicked! Not to justify wicked, but genocide? A further interpretive issue surfaces here. If one is to follow the idea of having been created in the image of God and should strive to be like God as is the ideal, then does this action give permission to act likewise, where people on the basis of what might be viewed as "wicked" or "evil" be destroyed and disposed, under the guise of doing what God's expects? There is to be sure a distinction to be made between *eminent domain* and possessing a land to fulfill a promise when it is necessary for one's personal use. However, what these two ideas have in common is the fact that the one who does the possessing is always then one with power, and then perhaps it is the one with even more power who takes ownership and the cycle continues. Inevitably the one with lesser power is forced to relinquish one's land even if the land provides one's livelihood. So one must pose the question: what are the guiding principles that would lead one to the conclusion that taking a land, disposing of a people, even genocidal acts are acceptable simply because one has been granted the divine *imprimatur*? "The relation of YHWH to his people in many parts of the Old Testament is governed by a concept of justice which is properly ethical, but because of its partiality is not the same

6. See Josh 10:40; 11:11, 14.

as the concept of impartial world justice found in some other places, and is potential tension with it."[7] Almost two hundred and fifty years ago, Oliver Goldsmith's poem "The Deserted Village" (1770) spoke to the demolition of a small village to make way for a wealthy man's estate. Several cottages in his neighborhood were destroyed, to give way to progress and commerce. The following lines are strikingly poignant.

> Along the lawn, where scattered hamlets rose;
> Unwieldy wealth and cumbrous pomp repose.

The rights of the peasantry were crushed and the people either drifed away or were made to dwell alone in the midst of the "progress."

---

7. Houston, *Contending for Justice*, 213.

5

Trust and Trauma

Some religious communities have an aversion to the notion of overt grief and certainly a palpable resistance to grieving over what might be perceived to be a punishment from God. Yet, finally, grief like other essential human expressions cannot be avoided. To avoid grief is to destroy oneself from within and unwittingly create something of a landscape of denial for those who are inheritors of one's beliefs. Whether the Bible is viewed as sacred scripture or a body of significant literature, it is simply impossible to overlook the countless moments where there is grief and the poignancy and depth of emotion with which such grief is voiced. To neglect such an essential component of faithful representation is indeed to cast away an essential component of what it means to be human and divine. Not only our humanity, but it would be to silence those whose lives have been deeply pained by whatever experience, justified or not. In a disturbing way it would silence the voice of the broken and wounded to appeal, and the freedom and capacity to address God in their most vulnerable and devastating state of being. There is certainly considerable truth to Hillers' observation that "People live on best after calamity, not by utterly repressing their grief and shock, but by facing it, and by measuring its dimensions."[1] To avoid grief either through community coercion or a personal disinclination based on one's particular beliefs, is to invite deep unraveling of oneself, as finally grief cannot simply be cast aside. Even those who make such a claim carry within them grief that has deep and abiding importance. Indeed as counter-intuitive as it might appear, grief is essential for our health and

1. Hillers, *Micah*, 4.

well-being. "Grief and the need to grieve is a part of our creaturely makeup, and like other human emotions embodies in holistic fashion (kinetically and cognitively) a powerful way of knowing . . . Indeed as psychiatric and medical professions know all too well, grief ignored or too quickly bypassed potentially can fester and grow into harmful pathologies that ultimately distort and deform our creaturely makeup."[2]

There is a sense that the human being in grief has power not only to express grief and complaint, but in so doing the one who has expressed grief is also demonstrating that or she has a certain level of power beyond the imperial or conventional power. In their powerless state of being, wounded or being in exile, the exiles still have power. "Such modeling of anger in prayer to God is critical, for it shows that our most damning and hurtful thoughts and feelings may be brought before God."[3] In so doing, there is a particular demonstration of confidence in God that one will not be neglected or abandoned. There is little that is abstract about suffering and grief in the Bible, in both the Hebrew Bible and the New Testament. From Amos "The heads of the poor being crushed in the dust of the earth" to *Lamentations'* description of a rape of a woman, a child starving, a man being pursued by a lion, and old people abused, the reality is that suffering is very personal, and happens in the context of community.

> [T]his profusion of images constructs a richly and finely con-
> toured topography of pain and suffering, eerily mirroring the
> shattered and fractured reality of post-destruction Jerusalem. The
> sheer number and diversity of these evocations . . . gestures ef-
> fectively toward the vastness and incomparability of a suffering in
> which no one is left untouched . . . God is encountered in the face
> of the suffering other and our relationship to God, then, is to be
> worked out through our engagement with the other, through our
> care for the other. From the point of view of biblical faith, the God
> of Israel . . . is made known and always encountered through the
> fragmentation and brokenness of created historical existence.[4]

As the people are led into exile, and God is the one who had made the decision, even though the people's actions have brought them to this precipice,
there surely must be grief and trauma, and such grief and trauma must
be expressed. The psychological trauma of keeping such pain within, and

2. Dobbo Alloopp, *Lamentations*, 36–37,

3. Ibid., 39.

4. Ibid., 41–44.

simply assert that this is a matter of faith will lead to disastrous results. As Caruth et al., have argued, events such as the exile have an extraordinarily traumatic effect.

> Trauma unsettles and forces us to rethink our notions of experience, and of communication, in therapy, in the classroom, and in literature . . . To be traumatized is precisely to be possessed by an image or event. And thus the traumatic symptom cannot be interpreted, simply, as a distortion of reality, nor as the lending of unconscious meaning to a reality it wishes to ignore, nor as the repression of what was once wished . . . The traumatized, we might say, carry an impossible history within them, or they become themselves the symptom of a history that they cannot entirely possess.[5]

As one continues to reflect on the potential and arguably likely effects of divine judgment for whatever reason or in whatever circumstances, it becomes clear that simply having a kind of amnesia of the event, or keeping the experience locked away, and veiling or protecting the one responsible for the event, one lives a life of debilitating disorientation and self deception. This is all by way of arguing that events such as exile and Shoah or loss of Temple and land cannot be dismissed simply as acts of punishment without any kind of deep psychological and traumatic effects, scars that remain even after homecoming. For example, those who were sent into exile because of the injustices that they had perpetuated, together with many innocents, are told that God has a plan for them and there will come a time to plant and build, a time of restoration. In fact those who are so traumatized surely must find it difficult or even impossible to believe such prophetic words on behalf of God, the very one who gifted them the land into perpetuity, and who just as easily cast them into exile. Even more dramatic in modernity is the trauma of those who have been victims of the Shoah who cannot be said to have sinned so egregiously as to be deserving of such evil. So can one recover from such trauma, when much of what one holds to be true and trusting are from God? This idea is certainly seen in some of the Hebrew prophets. In Hosea, it is almost universally assumed that in fact Gomer/Israel is to be blamed for the predicament in which they find themselves and as always Hosea/YHWH are the ones who suffer on occasion for their behavior. Sweeney's analogue in this regard places the narrative firmly within the framework of domestic abuse. While this perspective is

---

5. Caruth, *Trauma and Experience*, 4–5.

not likely to generate universal acclaim, there are aspects that surely must be reckoned with.

> Gomer never speaks, and never has the opportunity to present her view in the relationship in which she might defend herself or challenge her husband's portrayal of her as a harlot. Readers do not know if Hosea's charges are true, or if he has somehow maligned his wife and children. Readers must bear in mind that it is not unusual for a philandering husband to accuse his wife of adultery to cover his own fidelity of neglect . . . In the face of overwhelming Assyrian power, however, YHWH's failure to protect Israel produces a charge of Israel's infidelity to YHWH. Such a charge protects YHWH's reputation, power and righteousness in the face of charges that YHWH was unwilling, unable, or negligent in seeing to the protection of the nation. Of course we will never know if Gomer is a Harlot or not, but the uncritical acceptance of this charge on the part of interpreters has resulted in interpretation of the book that accepts Hosea's portrayal of her infidelity and thereby charges that the victim of evil, whether Gomer or Israel, are responsible for their suffering. In the aftermath of the Shoah, the uncritical acceptance of such a charge is unconscionable.[6]

When translated into the context of the Shoah, and indeed in contexts such as Darfur, Rwanda, and Kosovo, and certainly in the context of domestic abuse, the truth of Sweeney's observation is much more striking and certainly cannot be dismissed casually or uncritically. The voice of the victim cannot be silenced and be blamed for his or her suffering. This is not to say that there are no consequences to one's actions, but the one with power cannot be protected routinely and the powerless who is victimized be blamed and silenced. One of the major issues with the perspectives that many interpreters hold regarding Gomer/Israel as the one whose actions have brought on their suffering, and the textual silence, is that since this is a biblical portrayal, then it must also be acceptable in everyday life. Since it is evident in God's relationship with a people who invariably bring such punishment upon themselves, they do not in fact deserve to have a voice. How then does one explain, or worse even, justify the Shoah with this kind of sentiment?

Yet, in this same vein, who will ultimately make the decision as to who receives mercy and what might be the guiding principles in making this determination. For example the narrative in Jonah refuses a pathway that

6. Sweeney, *Reading the Hebrew Bible after the Shoah*, 154–55.

draws a simplistic distinction between Jews and Gentiles. So, one might ask whether prophetic pronouncement of judgment is the final word or if it is typically intended to lead to repentance? Or is the prophetic pronouncement penultimate and a reminder that YHWH has ultimate power and may make a determination be it punishment or redemption? If the latter is the case then two additional issues arise. It might very well be the case that Jonah's awareness is not so much as one who seeks to place blinders on God's mercy and obstruct the mercy of God to be played out for all people, but perhaps his role and voice as one that might not finally matter. What one might legitimately conclude is that a relationship with God is not one sided but does have human responsibility.

We might very well discern from Job an essential lesson in terms of how humans might relate to God, and not only in times of one's personal pain and suffering but particularly in times when one is not personally involved. Of further significance here is the fact that one who takes the relationship with God seriously, must in fact have the level of confidence and trust to ask personal and existential questions. In matters of gravity, one should have to face the devastating statement, "you should have asked." Job asked, and after the "God speeches" in which Job seems to be taken to task, God then extols the sustained righteousness of Job. One of the qualities that one might determine from the "God Speeches" is not so much that Job should not have asked questions as is so commonly concluded by some interpreters, but that the questions of Job are not encompassing enough, not existential and universal enough in nature. It is not that Job should not be concerned about himself, but God invites Job to think of all of creation. In this regard, Job invites all interpreters to pose significant and large questions to God not only about oneself or for that matter one's community or nation, but for all people wherever there might be evidence of injustice and in particular circumstances where God might be held accountable. It is precisely God's encounter with Job at the end of the book that suggests something of a divine mandate to question in a wide-ranging way. Among the many pertinent questions that we are compelled to raise include perhaps the most challenging, namely the issue of God bringing suffering on the innocent for reasons that only God knows, reasons that are never told to the suffering, and to those who wonder and question. Thus, it is that the prophetic voice today must not focus narrowly but be attentive and accountable to the entire world where there is injustice and oppression in whatever way.

In being traumatized, one is not only affected by the particular circumstances or events that brought about the trauma in the first place but any or everything that one perceives to have the potential to recreate, recall, or further accentuate the trauma. Thus one who has a traumatized memory of the sounds of war might very well react dramatically to the sound of an automobile "backfiring" until such sounds are contextualized differently for the person. Trauma also has the effect of losing one's capacity for rational thought and reasoning that might ordinarily be expected in particular circumstances. One thinks of Psalm 137 and the last verse that surely is born out of the exilic experience. We are never told what the Babylonians might have done to the children and the infants of the exiles, but we do know that the exiles are traumatized by the act of being dispossessed of their land and Temple, home and community regardless of what they might have done. So, when it is believed that God is responsible for the suffering and the associated trauma, and one feels even more helpless given that one cannot with impunity retaliate against God, then how does one trust again? Events that lead to trauma redefine *normal* and whatever else normal might be, it is never the same again. Thus, interpreters must be attentive to the casual reordering of society by saying in passing that the exiles returned to Jerusalem and the Temple was rebuilt. Certainly, the survivors of the Shoah could not go home again, literally, even if they wanted to do so. Even in the wildest of dreams this would not be possible, as the entire landscape of life has been altered.

> Trauma has the quality of converting that one sharp stab . . . into an enduring state of mind. A chronicler of passing events may report that the episode itself lasted no more than an instant—a gunshot, say—but the traumatized mind holds on to that moment preventing it from slipping back into its proper chronological place in the past, and relives it over and over again in the compulsive musings . . . The moment becomes a season, the event becomes a condition.[7]

When one is traumatized either as an individual, a group, or a community, life is seen differently, and one might very well find that the rest of the world, and certainly those generations who come after, might not only be unable to identify, but might even develop a sense of disbelief, and the need to forget that such events or circumstances ever happened. Those who are witnesses to the Shoah will undoubtedly see life and the world differently.

7. Erikson, "Notes on Trauma," 185.

For some, the difference is so dramatic, and the very act of remembering is so extraordinarily painful, that they can only appeal to silence as the quality that best serves their experience. Elie Wiesel notably committed himself to remain silent for ten years after the Shoah, not because of the unimportance of words, but precisely because there were no words and only silence could speak. Some who have been traumatized by such horror might wonder if their story might find disbelief in listeners and thus undermine and diminish the drama of their experience. One of the challenges in this regard is that the stories of such evil, such violence must be told, and as such the witnesses must tell their stories to those who will form a memory from which the stories will be told.

> Traumatized people calculate life's chances differently. They look out at the world through a different lens. And in that sense they can be said to have experienced not only a *changed sense of self* and *changed way of relating to others* but a changed *worldview*. Traumatized people often come to feel that they have lost an important measure of control over the circumstances of their lives and are thus very vulnerable . . . the hardest earned and most fragile accomplishment of childhood, basic trust, can be damaged beyond repair by trauma. Human beings are surrounded by layers of trust, radiating out in concentric circles like the ripples in a pond. The experience of trauma, at its worst, can mean not only a loss of confidence in self, but a loss in the surrounding tissue of family and community, in the structures of human government, in the larger logics by which humankind lives, in the ways of nature itself, and often . . . in God.[8]

It is precisely this last point that needs to be reckoned with regarding the prophets and the role of God, focusing on the punishments that have been meted out, punishments that are typically seen as the consequences of the people's actions. How the punished people survived, how their lives are lived, and the trauma they most certainly would experience are never really explored. Only that there are promises for redemption and the promise by which they will have to live. The assumption is always that naturally the people will come home again to Jerusalem after having been told to make Babylon their home in every meaningful way of belonging. Of course not everyone returned, and indeed the post exilic world continued to wonder how it is that the behavior of the people could be so pre-exilic in its worldview. But in fact the people's experiences were never really talked about. In

8. Erikson, "Notes on Trauma," 194–98.

the BBC production entitled, *God on Trial*, there is an extraordinarily moving and challenging dramatization of placing God on trial by a group of Jewish prisoners, representing a wide spectrum of religious, political, intellectual positions, the charge being that God had broken the covenant that God had made with the people. Jewish prisoners at Auschwitz made their arguments, prosecutorial, and in defense of God, and the heart wrenching closing arguments suggest that God had indeed broken his covenant with the people, the very people that he had set apart for a purpose. This perhaps is one of the dramatic expressions of what trauma does. What was once beyond question, and a God who was beyond reproach can no longer be the case as the layers of trust begin to unravel, and there is no conceivable way to return to the way things were, and certainly not without sacrificing integrity. One cannot overlook the issue of the trauma of the exile. Jeremiah's *Lamentations* underlines a fear that can only be seen as real; a sense of total divine abandonment. The pleading wonderment centers around the large existential themes of being remembered, being forsaken, restoration, renewal, anger and rejection. Any of these would be devastating for the exile, but this outpouring of the heart carries with it a fear that seems beyond the ordinary.

Writing about Jeremiah's message in the context of the world and circumstances in which he made his pronouncements, Kathleen O' Connor employs a "trauma and disaster" method as a way of expanding the angle through which the prophet's message might be interpreted and applied to today's society. In her essay "Teaching Jeremiah," one is struck by two particularly significant qualities. First, as interpreters, within or outside the academy, ecclesiastical or otherwise the hermeneutical possibilities of the biblical text are not nearly exhausted. Certainly there are those who look to the biblical text as "answer book" or "lexicon" of answers, and once read "faithfully," the answers emerge. But surely this cannot be the case, and even as we bring who we are to the reading of the text, we are reminded that the breadth and depth of the text are such that always there will be more. One must have the courage to plummet the depth and the courage to return when nothing or little might be immediately forthcoming. Second, to speak of the prophetic message with language of trauma also invites us to enter the narrative in a way that cannot be abstract or for that matter theoretical, but personally be invested in the story. One of the forces of trauma is the fact that it is rooted in a reality that eschews the abstract and theoretical. It is concrete. As one thinks of the trauma of exile, and the concrete reality of displacement, it is not a stretch of the imagination to move to the place of slavery and indentured servanthood, when those who have been taken away against their will, have also been made to serve their captors for survival and welfare. Jeremiah's admonition (Jeremiah 29) to the exiles to seek the *shalom* of their captors certainly has a powerful resonance for those who have experienced and witnessed such moments in their lives, and the lives of their ancestors; they see themselves as inheritors of such an admonition. Displacement, diaspora, loss between place of promise and origin, home, and that of a place with no sense of connection, and being made to serve those who have taken you into a foreign place is the definition of trauma. Land, a place of belonging is the centerpiece of one's existence. Indeed one might argue that it is precisely the loss of the land, that traumatized a people, and not only for a generation, but also for the inheritors of the experience.

There is even the fear/trauma of the very presence of a prophet in the midst of a people. Given that the Hebrew prophet never comes into a community to sanction the status quo, there is also a fear and anxiety about his/her presence. One thinks of Samuel in this regard being sent to Jesse's house to choose God's newly anointed one to be king. Samuel knows the inherent danger, and not only is there fear on his part, but he understands that his presence in the midst of this people will bring about angst and suspicion on the part of community members. Knowing that invariably the message of the prophet means that the present reality cannot continue; the fact that the prophet has come into their midst means that life will not continue in its current state. Not surprising, there is no prophet who is embraced by those who are deeply committed to continuing the status quo. The prophets invariably are asked to leave, cast out, threatened, vilified or killed.

Many seek to will the traumatized to seek hope, renewed faith, redemption, finding meaning out of their trauma, but this often has the troubling effect of forced silence and taking away the voice of the traumatized. One cannot place prescriptive guidelines for how one should, and must grieve within a particular timeline. Many who survived the Shoah have not been able to speak of their experience and some needed years of silence before they write or speak about the experience. The time will come, but not at another's insistence. "According to Bakhtin, we are all co-authors of one another's identities. In other words, the whole story about us cannot be told by us alone . . . Part of the job of authoring others involves listening to them as responsibly as we can, listening and responding fairly."[9]

9. Mandolfo, "Perseverance," 53.

6

Challenging Imperial Militarism

While there is much that we can point to in Isaiah regarding foreign policy issues, such as the Assyrian/Egyptian alliances and Rabshakeh/Hezekiah exchanges, finally the domestic issues are the ones that bear heavily on the mind and heart of the prophets. One thinks of Thoreau's idea of the "far off foe" in his essay, "On Civil Disobedience," in which he cautions against always looking for the "far off foe" in the sense that it is a veil that we have used to deflect attention away from what transpires domestically. In many respects the point here is to galvanize a collective voice against the enemy that is not us, and in so doing not be compelled to face the realities that divide and destroy us from within. But there comes a time, that will draw us back to face ourselves and therein lies the painful encounter, the honest and unfiltered facing of ourselves. This is not to say that foreign affairs in ancient Israel were not important for the prophets. Indeed, the prophets were deeply embroiled in foreign issues, and not only narrowly construed with respect to Israel, but as nations relate with each other.[1] However, finally foreign policy will only matter if internal issues or actions are addressed in all of their potential pain and self-transformation. As we have seen in Isaiah, the prophet's principal concern is not for foreign policy, but for the internal unraveling, divisiveness, and the widespread injustices. Moreover, one of the striking paradoxes of Israel's reality in the eighth century BCE is the fact that while the nation prospered for the world to see, it is impoverished internally in terms of the covenant relationship. What is clear is that prosperity that glitters for the world to see is not a mark

1. Amos 1–2.

of harmony and goodness, virtue and justice. If anything, it might be an expression of the problem.

> For you have forsaken the ways of your people,
>   O house of Jacob.
> Indeed they are full of diviners from the east
>   and of soothsayers like the Philistines,
>   and they clasp hands with foreigners.
> Their land is filled with silver and gold,
>   and there is no end to their treasures;
> their land is filled with horses,
>   and there is no end to their chariots.
> Their land is filled with idols;
>   they bow down to the work of their hands,
>   to what their own fingers have made.
> And so people are humbled,
>   and everyone is brought low—
>   do not forgive them!
> Enter into the rock,
>   and hide in the dust
> from the terror of the LORD,
>   and from the glory of his majesty.
> The haughty eyes of people shall be brought low,
>   and the pride of everyone shall be humbled;
> and the LORD alone will be exalted on that day.
> For the LORD of hosts has a day
>   against all that is proud and lofty,
>   against all that is lifted up and high;
> against all the cedars of Lebanon,
>   lofty and lifted up;
>   and against all the oaks of Bashan;
> against all the high mountains,
>   and against all the lofty hills;
> against every high tower,
>   and against every fortified wall;
> against all the ships of Tarshish,
>   and against all the beautiful craft.
> The haughtiness of people shall be humbled,
>   and the pride of everyone shall be brought low;
>   and the Lord alone will be exalted on that day.
> The idols shall utterly pass away.
> Enter the caves of the rocks
>   and the holes of the ground,

from the terror of the LORD,
    and from the glory of his majesty,
    when he rises to terrify the earth.
On that day people will throw away
    to the moles and to the bats
their idols of silver and their idols of gold,
    which they made for themselves to worship,
to enter the caverns of the rocks
    and the clefts in the crags,
from the terror of the LORD,
    and from the glory of his majesty,
    when he rises to terrify the earth.
Turn away from mortals,
    who have only breath in their nostrils,
    for of what account are they?[2]

In this Isaiah text the vision of the indictment and the divinely instituted violence is again predicated on the basis of military might, accumulation of wealth, and the compromising of fundamental ideals of relationship with God. The "emptiness" of the society is set in sharp relief with the striking repetition of "fullness" in Isa 2:6–8 and this sets the basis for all that has come to constitute what is central to the society. Thus, "the land is filled with silver and gold, and there is no end to their treasures; the land is filled with horses and there is no end to their chariots. Their land is filled with idols; they bow down to the work of their hands to what their own fingers have made."[3] Over against such haughtiness, the prophet makes it clear and pronounced with ten refrains of "against" reflecting the manner in which God will severely punish the people. Such refrain pivots on particulars, not generalities or abstracts. It is the loftiness, the haughtiness, the pride that have come to define the people and these are precisely the qualities that will be dismantled. The two elements that have come to define Judah, namely military might and wealth, that have in turn led to pride and haughtiness have striking implications for contemporary society. It is not simply a question of having *enough wealth*, necessary for a society to exist, but rather being "full"; it is not simply a matter of having *enough weapons* of war to defend oneself, but in fact "the land is full of horses and chariots." With this kind of self designed level of military might, and the power of self indulgent consumerism born out of the accumulation of wealth, it is not surprising that Judah filled the land with idols of their own making, reflecting what

2. Isa 2:6–22.

3. Isa 2:6–8.

Brueggemann coins as "projections of self-achievement, self-security, and self-congratulations."[4] One cannot miss the irony here as in fact Judah with all of its self generated power will not be able to defend itself against the force that is YHWH, the architect of its existence.

> He shall judge between the nations,
>   and shall arbitrate for many people;
> They shall beat their swords into plowshares,
>   and their spears into pruning hooks;
> Nation shall not lift up sword against nation,
>   neither shall they learn war anymore.[5]

There will come a time as the words of these prophets testify, where wars will cease. The very weapons of war will be transformed into instruments of life, not in any abstract way, but instruments that will bring sustenance, and thus by definition, peace. The weapons will not be stockpiled and stored but transformed. There will be no evidence of war, but in this instance, future generations will not have a memory of weapons, but rather the landscape of their lives will be based on things that make for peace and this will be the new norm. Second, war will not be an inherited mode of settling differences or relating with each other. War will not be taught as the principal point of departure for the manner in which one is protected.

Empire is one set of lenses through which the Hebrew prophets made pronouncements about injustice and oppression; judgment and redemption. The lens of empire continues to be one that is pertinent through which to view contemporary ethical issues and the moral dilemmas that are posed by war, and the imperial edicts woven with religious triumphalism. What is finally at work here is the prophet's unencumbered and unequivocal reminder that all of the human institutions and forces that have been built will not last into perpetuity. Perhaps for a while, it might appear that such military and financial power will endure forever, but such forces by themselves are not infinite. "Turn away from mortals, who only have breath in their nostrils, for of what account are they?"[6] This remarkable concluding statement by Isaiah is a stark warning that "breath" is only within the nostrils and will not compete with "divine breath," and thus will not last. In this regard, human seduction is tempting, as one sees what appears as

4. Brueggemann, *Isaiah 1–39*, 29.

5. Isa 2:4; Mic 4:3.

6. Isa 2:22.

permanent and invincible. Yet, such seeming invincibility is rooted only in what is immediately apparent and very "human generated." This reality has significant implications for contemporary society as the propensity for self-aggrandizement and self-promotion, becomes the definition of the society's core. The challenge for contemporary church and society is complex; there is an even more noticeable clutching to YHWH and the outward expansion of the rhetoric and acts of liturgical moments, while merging the seduction of power and might into what God has gifted. Seduction had generated an element of blindness among the people; the vision is myopic and the history of the relationship with YHWH is relegated to that which can only be seen immediately.

> Their land is filled with silver and gold,
>   there is no end to their treasures,
> their land is filled with horses,
>   there is no end to their chariots.[7]

As elsewhere, the rulers who are rooted in injustice and sow injustice, reap and live with lies. It is not to be treated as accidental that the injustice and lies are unavoidably connected with the emphasis on military prowess, where the stark contrast is between trust in military might, and in so doing displacing the trust in God. Thus action by the leaders will not only prove devastating for the leaders, but the result will be war against the people; the people are the ones who will suffer. Moreover Isaiah's reliance on military alliance will be of no avail, and once again the choice is between dependency on strength and quantity in the military or seeking YHWH. The choice will determine life or death.

> You have ploughed wickedness,
>   you have reaped injustice,
>   you have eaten the fruit of lies.
> Because you have trusted in your power
>   and in the multitude of your warriors,
> therefore the tumult of war shall rise against your people.[8]

> Woe to those who go down to Egypt for help
>   and who rely on horses,
> who trust in chariots because they are many
>   and in horsemen because they are very strong,

---

7. Isa 2:7.

8. Hos 10:13–14.

> But do not look to the Holy One of Israel
> or consult the LORD![9]

In these verses the prophet encapsulates what the two foci are, namely, wealth and military power. This surely must not come as a novel or surprising revelation to today's society. Then as now, far too many have come to believe that finally what defines success and glory, prosperity and goodness are wealth and power. But these would be the very elements that will bring the prophet's relentless pronouncements about God's sorrow and even anger, and ultimately the nation's downfall. As horrific as it is to see the injustices that tear apart a people, it is even worse when the people and the leaders have become so accustomed to such injustices and oppression that they simply see it as a part of the landscape; as such no longer are the leaders and the wealthy and powerful shocked and shamed let alone repentant by injustices. When a people are no longer aggrieved by the sunken eyes of the hungry and the baked and soaked realities of the homeless, and the nihilism of those who cannot see or believe beyond the stretch of darkness in which they find themselves, then no longer can the ordinary solutions suffice. In our society, we have "landmark" cases and moments that have sought to alter the landscape; women's rights, civil rights, integration in education, etc., but what happens when it takes more than a landmark, as the landmarks are swallowed up or neglected? The leaders of Israel have closed their eyes to what Heschel referred to the "normal crimes."[10] So what must be done when injustices, bribery, plotting for material gains even on the Sabbath; when poor farmers lose their land to wealthy land brokers, who in turn celebrate in the Temple before the altar; when exorbitant interest rates crush the poor and these become "normal crimes"; when people have lost their shame and no one raises a voice? Such normalcy calls for extraordinary measures. It is under such circumstances the prophets hurl invectives that cast a sweeping punishment.

Assyria boasts:

> By the strength of my hand I have done it,
> and by my wisdom, for I have understanding:
> I have removed the boundaries of peoples,
> and have plundered their treasures;
> like a bull I have brought down those who sit on the throne.

9. Isa 31:1.

10. Heschel, *Prophets*, 78.

My hand has found like a nest
    the wealth of peoples;
And as men gather eggs that have been forsaken
    so I have gathered all the earth;
And there was none that moved a wing,
    or opened the mouth or chirped.[11]

But then YHWH's response with universal claim comes.

Shall the ax boast over him who hews with it,
    or the saw magnify itself against him who wields it?
As if the rod should swing him who lifts it,
    or as if the staff should lift him who is not wood![12]

This kind of arrogance not only suggests that Assyria and other lesser power equipped nations, such as Moab (Isa 15:6), have the final word, but that their power will continue unabated. They were wrong on both counts, and herein lies one of the unavoidable lessons for contemporary society. Repeatedly one notes that when humans determine that they have ultimate power, and they believe that they are only held accountable to God or gods through their abundant external ritual proprieties, then their world will inexorably disintegrate and collapse. It is precisely this false sense of both sovereignty, and by extension security, and belief that they are invincible and above reproach, with vituperative recalcitrance and chutzpah that will in fact be the basis for their ultimate downfall. Heschel speaks to these very issues in reference to Assyria and notes qualities such as "pride, arrogance and presumption."[13] At the zenith of their power, rare is it that empires imagine that they will decline or disintegrate, and collapse under the weight of their perceived invincibility. This might be attributed to qualities that seem to underline most of these empires, namely a vision that looks only narrowly into the future, where tomorrow seems a distant future and yesterday does not appear to have any serious reckoning. But empires rise and fall and those who are inattentive to such historical realties are doomed to live through such rise and fall.

The prophets, questioning man's infatuation with might, insisted not on the immorality but also on the futility and absurdity of war . . . Yet, the most astonishing thing in the world is the perennial disregard of the impotence of force. What is the ultimate profit of

11. Isa 10:13–14.

12. Isa 10:15.

13. Heschel, *Prophets*, 165.

> all the arms, alliances, and victories? Destruction, agony, death. As
> it was in the age of the prophets, so it is in nearly every age: we all
> go mad, not only individually, but also nationally. We check man-
> slaughter and isolated murders; we wage wars and slaughter whole
> peoples. Ferocity appears natural; generosity superimposed . . . We
> measure manhood by the sword and are convinced that history is
> ultimately determined on the field of battle.[14]

How far have the people gone? It has pierced the heart of God and the depth of sorrow resides there, and the prophets express the divine pathos and sorrow that are enough to pierce the human heart. The sorrow of God is born out of a divine weariness.[15] It would be painful enough for the people to have totally abandoned God, but instead, they have continued to give the external expressions of worship, with all of the propriety associated with worship. Finally, this is even more egregious for it is a farce and in some strange way they hope that their ritual activity will create enough of a veil for them; but God sees clearly and purely through the flimsy veil and renounces all ritual activity void of justice and righteousness. The sorrow of God has arrived at such a depth that Isaiah and Jeremiah were faced with such irreconcilable challenges in their calling. They are to bring the news to the people, pronouncements of the people's rejection of Torah, the living with injustices that have become normal, punishment for their crimes and redemption. But Jeremiah is told that God will not listen to his prayers on behalf of the people; he cannot be an advocate for them, nor intercede on their behalf, and Isaiah is told to stand on his head and face the people. So, even the role of the prophet is unimaginable as it is to moderns; it was such that the prophet was told to do the impossible, not as a figurative issue, but literally in most instances. So, "Go ahead and pray and I will not listen."

But the people are incalcitrant and there is a quality of intransigence by those who have a stake in the maintenance of the status quo. They are confident that their actions will not have consequences and nothing untoward will befall them. It is not merely a false sense of security, but an arrogance that suggests that they cannot be touched, and God would not punish them. Looking at their present situation, they find it inconceivable that any evil or punishment would or could befall them. This sense of false security points to at least two troubling issues. First, one is left to wonder whether the arrogance of the people had reached such heights that they saw

14. Ibid., 161.
15. Isa 7:13.

themselves as beyond reproach or untouchable. When the determination is made that one's reality, be it barrenness or hopelessness or oppression of such a magnitude on the one hand, or one's position of power or wealth on the other reflects one's status into perpetuity, then that implies that God is powerless to transform life. This perspective in effect seeks to limit God. Second, the people already have had a history of knowing how God has acted in their lives and in the lives of their ancestors; yet, they have somehow forgotten or in fact flagrantly disregarded what they surely must know is the truth. But the kind of power and injustice that they thrived on blinded them to the fact that finally they are accountable to God. So they are able to boast, "Evil shall not overtake or meet us."[16] Perhaps God's admonition to Cain regarding the Bible's first human criminal activity should be heeded. "If you do well will you not be accepted? If you do not do well, sin is lurking at the door."[17]

THE SHALOM IMPERATIVE

Jeremiah's *Letter to the Exiles* (Jeremiah 29) has justifiably generated significant attention over the years, with both scholars and laity alike exploring the many themes, their layers of meaning, and their implications particularly within the historical setting. It was the lack of justice, the living of injustice, that in large part led to the catastrophic circumstances in which Judah found itself. The lack of justice will result in the loss of the land; as has been seen elsewhere in Jeremiah, for the sake of the land the people are admonished to obey the Babylonian powers. Jeremiah's "Temple Sermon" makes clear that the very survival of Judah as a people is connected to justice in all the land (7:7). Within the larger context of Jeremiah's *Letter to the Exiles*, justice certainly parallels *shalom* in that the very identity, existence, and survival of the exiles will depend on *shalom* for all. The admonitions in Jeremiah 29, challenging as they are, and directed to the exiles in Babylon in the first instance, cannot remain as a point of reminiscence with little or no relevance for contemporary society. Indeed some of the themes, particularly ones that challenge some of today's conventions have remarkable relevance and implications for contemporary society. Birch suggests that the radical admonitions contained in the letter are there more for the sake

---

16. Amos 9:10.

17. Gen 4:7.

of the empire than for the exiles. That they are commanded to seek the welfare of their captors sets the stage for a greater purpose, argues Birch, namely spreading the word about their covenant God. This position, while having some merit also poses serious and potentially troubling implications in a post-Shoah world where many continue to look to the Bible to shape their worldview.

> In the place of vengeance many would desire (see Ps. 137:8–9) the prophet sees the task not only of becoming community in the midst of the empire but of learning to live there for the sake of the welfare (*shalom*) of the empire. The prophet suggests a vocation of creative minority in the larger social realities of the world that remains pertinent through the remainder of the biblical period . . . for seldom after the period of exile was the Jewish community of the early church able to live a political existence apart from the political reality of a larger political empire. Such a model is, of course, suggestive for modern Christian life in the midst of larger sociocultural realities. The role of intentional creative minority is an option open to those who feel that the church is endangered by more accomodationist models of community; but Jeremiah's words stand as a warning that such community in the midst of empire (majority culture) must be for the sake of that majority culture.[18]

While I believe that there is an important place for the essential role of the creative minority, I am not persuaded that the central role of the exiles is to live lives that were principally meant to shape the lives of the captors.

The manner in which *shalom* is employed in Jeremiah's *Letter to the Exiles* serves as a foundation for a new and transformative understanding of *shalom* and that stands in sharp distinction to the established and conventional understanding of *shalom* as espoused by Hananiah, and to imperial militarism. *Shalom* in Jeremiah 29 is not generic and instead challenges dialectical binaries such as good and evil; light and darkness; war and peace among others. Between these significant divides often lies truth enveloped in chasms of grey that cannot be negotiated away or skipped over for the sake of convenience. Thus *shalom* as delivered by the prophets Jeremiah and Hananiah is notably different in its implications. *Shalom* is neither monolithic nor one dimensional in its meaning and application. The manner in which *shalom* is outlined in Jer 29 is not only important for an understanding of Israelite life and indeed survival in Babylon in the

18. Birch, *Let Justice Roll Down*, 304.

sixth century BCE, but for an urgent understanding and application for contemporary societies' bondage to militaristic impulses in national relationships, and indeed for survival in general. In Jer 9:22–23 (ET 23–24), the prophetic pronouncement establishes that human wisdom, might, (military and otherwise), wealth will not finally be what defines the world and the relationships among persons, communities and nations but rather just love, righteousness and justice.

The hortatory language in Jer 29:5–7 makes clear that the exiles must live in Babylon not on a temporary basis but for generations. Indeed they are to become so much a part of the Babylonian society that they will have to be a source of goodness for their captors. This mandate further makes clear that the exiles' lives will be inextricably connected with the larger community, notably their captors. This certainly expands the angle in which the concept of community might be understood. What is equally notable is that many Jews remained in Babylon even after others were returning to Jerusalem. The people are told that the time to return is now as promised, but some choose not to do so. Is this because they have lost confidence or are they so deeply rooted that uprooting oneself and one's family is an option worse than remaining in the land of the captors. So many remained in Babylon. It is certainly not easy to uproot and many chose not to do so even as YHWH recalls and promises. The exiles were admonished to actively seek the welfare of the people. "The effects of this combination of work and prayers on the part of the exiles would affect their own lives in a positive way, but they would also reverberate out to contribute to the welfare of the Babylonians and all those with whom they came into contact."[19]

That is to say, with the combination of work and prayer, all of life must be attended to, and the effect is likely to have wide ranging implications. What therefore will begin understandably and justifiably with great reluctance will become part of the fabric of the exiles' life; in any event, it was never the case that the exiles were to do this only for themselves. Their actions would have ripple effects on generations to come. This too would be one of the reasons why the "good news" of the false prophets is not true. That the news of the false prophets in Babylon is significantly more palatable to the exiles does not make it true. If there was any universal claim to this idea it is certainly the idea that "good news" is not always true. The natural inclination of the exiles is to believe that the exile will end soon and they will not have to be in captivity for the measure of time pronounced.

19. Brueggemann, *I & II Kings*, 403.

This is precisely the sort of occurrence that has implications for contemporary society. Here too is a two-part warning. First, to those who are seeking "good news" about both the present and the promise of a future of hope and restoration, from whatever exile in which they find themselves, must be aware of charlatans who indeed will prey upon their vulnerabilities. This invites discernment and an almost counter-intuitive response, a challenge to be sure when the news seems to be resonant with their own hopes. Second, to those who are purveyors of false prophecy in the name of God, this is also a strict warning, for they are called "liars and deceivers" and they will face the punishment. This might be the most daring move by the false prophets in that they are speaking on behalf of God, except that God has not spoken to them.

While the expectation of justice is rooted in conventional promise, there is also a clear movement from God's actions to what the people must do, and do so in the midst of their own suffering. Deut 10:17–19 establishes the wide ranging expectations of justice for "widows and orphans" and "love of foreigners" in concrete ways. This expectation is rooted in the memory of the Hebrew experience in Egypt, for what has been afforded a people as members of the covenant community must now be afforded to all people. The particular experience of justice must have universal claim and application.

> Thus says the LORD of hosts, the God of Israel: Amend your ways and your doings, And let me dwell with you in this place. Do not trust in these deceptive words, "This is the temple of the LORD, the temple of the LORD, the temple of the LORD."[20]

Jeremiah iterates and reiterates sharply that the people no longer can hide behind religious platitudes and ritual propriety rigorously and even flawlessly performed. Religious language and piety in and of themselves will not suffice without the corresponding acts of justice. The walls of the temple cannot be merely protectionist in nature, and most certainly cannot serve as a barricade. Rather than fading in exile, perhaps the more *à propos* argument is that the exilic community will have their identity redefined and expanded; the identity of the people will be relational and not separatist. Israel through its covenant with God is bound to be in relation to all other nations. The concept of being "blessed through you" is deeply embedded in the covenant, and must be inscribed on the identity of the people.

20. Jer 7:3–4.

Cochran suggests that "the scholar cannot be neutral to the essential truth of scripture, its correspondence to and insights into the human condition and the human experience of transcendent meaning. Such neutrality would cut off the interpreter's access to deep levels of political teaching."[21] Indeed such neutrality is simply impossible. Finding the balance and tension between these essential components remains a persistent challenge. Levenson underlines this complexity in his response to Brueggemann's "irreducible claim." He notes, "The idea that one can cite the biblical demands for justice and then fill the word in with content from one's own personal values is highly problematic as a mode of application of biblical teaching. The dubious notion that justice is 'irreducible' serves to disguise the problem posed by the diversity and plurality of ideas of justice in all periods, our own certainly included."[22] Levenson argues with a substantial cautionary note that "cultures and traditions, when they are living and lived are irreducibly different, and no amount of similarity, common derivation, goodwill, mutual respect and communication can change this."[23] Perhaps adding to this note in a very particular way is Robert Carroll, who cautions against the use of Jeremiah's letter as a contemporary mandate for pacifism. Such modernizing, he argues, would be simplistic.[24]

One is well advised to reckon seriously with the perspectives of Levenson and Carroll, among others, that the hermeneutical task at hand is not, and must not be reduced to, a superficial and simplistic form. If Brueggemann's assertion of the "irreducible claim" of justice has merit, as I believe it does, such a claim must not lead to a simplistic reduction where the text is employed simply to undergird and support one's theology or ideology. T. S. Eliot observed a generation ago, "It is not enough to see the evil and injustice and suffering in this world, and precipitate oneself into action. We must know . . . why these things are wrong. Otherwise we may right some wrongs at the cost of creating new ones."[25] Hauerwas proposes that "the ethics of analogy may be easier to pursue because it calls for a sharper focus on particular events, issues and sets of relationships and this is less susceptible to a transformation of the story into what one can (or wants

21. Cochran, "Political Science Confronts the Book," 230.

22. Levenson, "Is Brueggemann Really a Pluralist?," 269.

23. Ibid., 288.

24. Carroll, *Chaos*, 275.

25. Broadcast talk, delivered on February 1937 in a series on "Church, Community and State."

to) hear."[26] The caution against simplistic modernizing while striving for serious engagement must not be construed as an invitation to pre-empt an essential consideration of Jeremiah's *Letter to the Exiles* in terms of its implications for a universal "peace ethic."

Even as one embraces Brueggemann's "irreducible" claims of justice there remains inherent hurdles, if not hermeneutical bridges to cross. The question or issue is not whether truth is to be told. Indeed one must force oneself and tell the truth, for truth cannot be stumbled upon.[27] This bridging of the creative, interpretive vision takes more than a casual approach or a hackneyed or conventional mode of interpretation. This observation and caution is *à propos* in that whatever hermeneutical principle is applied as ancient texts and themes are cited and appealed to, the interpreter must be aware that there always is a gap of significant proportions. This is not a point of discouragement, but an invitation to circumspection and attentiveness and a caution against making interpretive leaps that are impossible to span. With all of the background and historical and conceptual considerations it is still finally the case that the text must speak, and who we are cannot but come into play.

Among the prophets, Jeremiah stands apart as a particularly distinct and extraordinary example of a prophet whose very life came to exemplify and reflect the complexity and even dissonance of "plucking up" and "building up." While Jeremiah is often referred to as the "wrathful prophet" and the "weeping prophet," one might also propose the moniker "prophet of peace." At first sight, this might not immediately strike a chord either in terms of what the text says, or in terms of what the tradition has generated. In taking on the title "wrath of God," perhaps he is then associated as the "prophet of wrath." Yet, as one reads Jeremiah, it is abundantly clear that Jeremiah has a deeply irenic nature. Indeed, in a series of dramatic personal attestations, Jeremiah's rhetoric is nothing short of explosive in reaction to what God has called him to do. He describes such a divine apocalypse as "something like a burning fire shut up in my bones."[28] Complaining to YHWH, Jeremiah's words reveal the further depth of his misery. "I have become a laughingstock all day long; everyone mocks me" and "Denounce him! Let us denounce him! All my close friends are watching for me to

26. Hauerwas, *Community of Character*, 25.

27. Isa 59:14–16.

28. Jer 20:9.

stumble."[29] Indeed Heschel describes the prophet's condition as "inner misery."[30] The depth of the prophet's pathos cannot be underestimated.

Jeremiah's vocation required him to embrace and possess a pathos that seemed to lie beyond his capacity, beyond human capacity, where the central tenet and aim of his vocation was the establishment and pursuit of a particular idea of *shalom*. Jeremiah does not begin his letter with the conventional opening greeting of *shalom*. In fact, one could surmise that his opening was entirely unexpected and even offensive to those receiving the words. But the letter was not without *shalom*. Peace is there and conspicuously so, though not in the way the people expected or imagined or perhaps wanted. This new *shalom*, will take imagination, and what Jeremiah was mandated to pronounce, and the people to do, appear to transcend their imagination. A lack of imagination, or perhaps a reluctance to imagine, would also lead the people to believe only that which they knew or could see. Hananiah's over simplistic and misguided representation of peace, and his public proclamation in the presence of the king, "Thus says the Lord of the Hosts the Lord of Israel. I have broken the yolk of the king of Babylon. Within two years I will bring back to this place" maintains the *status quo* and lacks imagination.[31] The people, including Jeremiah indeed wanted to believe the truth of Hananiah's vision. Jeremiah desperately wanted the *shalom* the other prophets proclaimed to be true: "May the Lord do so; may the Lord fulfill the words you have prophesied."[32] But it was a vision that was no more than a momentary hiatus. But the exile would be more than a brief hiatus. The time in exile would not be a temporary change of reality; life would be irreversibly transformed.

A substantial challenge that seems counter productive was the very idea of pronouncing *shalom* in a context where the people had already heard such pronouncements from other prophets. How does he distinguish himself and the message from others when the title and core message on the surface appears identical? Yet, this peace for which he and others longed was not to be the peace that would be realized, neither was it what the *shalom* mandated. In this peace was no peace at all and the human perception on which it was based would be thoroughly recast in terms of a new worldview. Edwin Searcy observes:

29. Jer 20:7b, 10.
30. Heschel, *Prophets*, 119.
31. Jer 28:11.
32. Jer 28:1.

> At the temple, heart and soul of the nation's existence Jeremiah
> expresses the charade of the nation's misplaced trust. Judah is
> squeezed by the great powers. Its elite grow frantic; its public
> senses the impending terror. The people flock to join the great
> congregation singing the national song of assurance: This is the
> temple of the Lord, the temple of the Lord, the temple of the Lord.
> (7:4) They are like a frightened nation that ceaselessly reminds
> itself: God bless America, God bless America . . . Standing in the
> doorway of Judah's beloved symbol of national security and moral
> purity, Jeremiah dares to preach against patriotic fervor, saying,
> "Do not trust in these deceptive words" (7:4).[33]

As important and central as the temple was, indeed as *shalom* was
to the people, both came to be employed merely as ritual and political
veils. Jeremiah's *shalom* will not be hollow and shallow, that is, *shalom* that
peddled simply in words without substance. The hollowness of repeating
"peace" "peace" has been exposed for what it is. Jeremiah is painfully aware
that his message of *shalom* will be difficult to embrace and will in all likeli-
hood be rejected by the people. Heschel asserts insightfully: "A man whose
message is doom for the people he loves, not only forfeits his own capacity
for joy, but also provokes the hostility and outrage of his contemporaries.
The sights of war, the anticipation of disaster nearly crush his soul."[34]

While the truth of Heschel's assertion will justifiably and fittingly
find widespread resonance, there is another truth that is equally clear and
unequivocal. To be sure Jer 29:1 pronounces at the outset that this is Jeremiah's letter to the exiles, but ultimately, and indeed in the first instance,
these are God's words. The letter is bracketed both by God's stamp, "Thus
says the LORD of Hosts, the God of Israel, to all the exiles whom I have
sent into exile from Jerusalem to Babylon" and God as counter-signatory
with the statement, "'I am witness.'"[35] God reminds Jeremiah, "Do not . . .
bemoan them; for I have taken my peace from this people."[36] Perhaps the
conventional, comfortable reality of Israel, the quest and insistence of a
shalom that reinforces the status quo, believing that it is the way things will
always be, was reflected in their resistance. The re-casting of *shalom* will in
no way be cosmetic or superficial. The foundational developments in this
regard are dramatic. First, God designates King Nebuchadnezzar as "my

33. Searcy, "People," 334.
34. Heschel, *Prophets*, 114.
35. Jer 29:4, 23.
36. Jer 16:5.

servant"; shocking by any measure not least being the fact that Nebuchadnezzar was the principal architect of both the annexation and exile of Israel. The "plucking up and breaking down; the destroying and overthrowing" attest to the degree to which the Lord will go in identifying with a suitable imperial destroyer. God employs the enemy as his servant, and not for the first time in Hebrew scripture, but here Nebuchadnezzar will "ravish" the people. Before the new world of *shalom* comes, the military will ravish the people, the temple, the land. That is the key note, namely, the ravishing of a people and land by God's designee. The leader who is unquestionably and undeniably the one who tears down and destroys the people is unwittingly the one who will be the conduit, and not the purveyor of peace.

Second, what Jeremiah came to know, the people could not begin to understand. Perhaps it is because Jeremiah also described himself as being ravished by God. He understands the despair the people felt and their natural gravitation towards embracing the *shalom* of the false prophets, a *shalom* that, in part, refused to imagine that it could ever be possible that God would ravish them. But Jeremiah knew. Jer 20:7 is pivotal in this regard. The NRSV renders this verse, "Oh Lord, you have enticed me; . . . you have overpowered one." This, by and large, has been the conventional rendering; yet, as Heschel has elucidated, this verse is intensely brutal when appropriately and contextually translated as, "O Lord, Thou has seduced me and I am seduced; you have raped me and I am overcome." The image here, in the most understated way, is remarkably violent and brutal, but it is precisely this brutal language that reflects the devastation of the impending destruction. God's vocation for Jeremiah is such that Jeremiah is entirely overpowered and despite his protestations, he is unable to escape the divine possession. This overpowering ravishing is also precisely what will happen to the people who, like Jeremiah, will be unable to escape. Even the imperial power of Babylon will finally not escape divine overpowering, except that Nebuchadnezzar is unaware of being used as God's servant. Even as the prophet feels powerless and without recourse, he pours his heart out, "I must cry out; I must shout."[37] The words of poet John Donne captures the paradox of both the prophet and the people "Except you enthrall me never shall I be free. Nor ever chaste, except you ravish me."[38]

Brueggemann notes that in Deutero-Isaiah the prophet spoke of *baśor*, "good tidings" (52:7) in the context of exile. "The prophet intends

37. Jer 20:8a.
38. Donne, "Holy Sonnet 14."

that the views of God's fresh initiative should break the despair and shatter the ideological grip of the empire so as to free Jews for free subversive self confident activity of a new kind, powered by a peculiar, celebrated identity. Exile evokes gospel."[39] While Deutero-Isaiah's and indeed Jeremiah's bookends might be bracketed as "exile and homecoming," conceptually very much at the heart of these prophets, nonetheless, the issue before us is not one of homecoming, but what eventuates in the context of exile, and the manner in which exilic existence shapes life in freedom. *Shalom* as Jeremiah pronounces it cannot mean business as usual, for previously as a divine initiative it became routine, whereas Hananiah iterated and reiterated, "peace, peace," but now there is a new idea of *shalom* that is anything but routine and ordinary. David Aberbach sees the exilic experience and the relationship with empire differently. He argues that following the Assyrian defeat of Israel in 721 BCE:

> Israel's identity faded in exile and Hebrew as well as monotheism survived only in Judah. By the end of the prophetic era two centuries later, the Jews were broken by imperial crisis, defeat and exile. They responded by totally breaking with Near Eastern religion through the acceptance of an exclusive abstract monotheism . . . The dynamics of the biblical world seems to have the pattern for later Jewish relationships with empires: assimilation and the neglect of Hebrew in normal conditions, and separation, Jewish nationalism and Hebrew creativity in crisis.[40]

Acknowledging the merit of aspects of Aberbach's assessment, there remains nonetheless a serious challenge to his general assertion. First, while there is undeniable truth to the statement, "The Jews were broken by imperial crisis, defeat and exile," it is certainly not the whole truth. The exilic experience was not the last word; neither was it the end of their identity. Rather, the experience radically shaped their identity, one now inextricably connected with the captors. This exilic experience brought different levels of pain including singularly the pain of being sent into exile by God, where the gifts and promises of land, people and temple, were all destroyed or in the process of unraveling. This arguably is the most devastating existential issue for the exiles, where the very active presence of God comes into question. Second, "creativity in crisis" indeed might be construed as a radical and creative interpretation and employment of *shalom*. However, while

39. Brueggemann, *Deep Memory*, 37.
40. Aberbach, "Revolutionary Hebrew," 135.

the creativity will come, it will have to be construed within the prescribed parameters of seeking and sustaining the *shalom* of all citizens. Moreover while the new reality in captivity need not be one of total assimilation, neither will it be one of separation. Life will be defined by forging a unique relationship.

Frederick Niedner has noted that "the brutality of exile finds expressions in the Hebrew word [*galah*] which means literally 'to go naked.' The expression derives from the Assyrian practice of stripping captives before driving them on forced marches to other regions."[41] We might note the importance of "naked" in general in the prophets, and particularly in Isaiah. While it is often the case the readers are aware of the fact the prophet Isaiah walks around naked (Isa 20:2–3) and maybe this moment is a cautionary one that warns some contemporaries who might proclaim themselves as prophets to be aware of what might be required. But beyond this, this text is best understood in the larger context of the concept of nakedness and what this meant for the people in the process of being reconciled not only to each other, but to the *other*, the enemy of the people. In Isaiah 20, we are told that Egypt will be led away by Assyria in the most humiliating and publicly shameful manner, naked and barefooted and paraded so that all might witness. "The real focus of the text, however, is not Egypt. As Isa 20:6 makes clear, the sight of naked Egyptians is supposed to force the Israelites to ask themselves, 'how then can we escape?' That is, in the flight of the Egyptians, the Israelites are to see their own future condition as they are led into captivity . . . The implication of the verse is that as a community refined in the crucible of captivity, into which, presumably, many people had been introduced naked, it is no longer to countenance the degradation of that condition."[42]

The exiles will be stripped bare, and if not literally in this instance, certainly in other ways as they seek to live out a new identity. Judah's belief in its own military powers was in part responsible for the immediate consequence of being crushed and taken into exile. Whatever militaristic inclinations or impulses they might have had, ultimately would not be the quality that would define them. Instead, as an exiled community without a time line for leaving the land of captivity, the people have been given a new philosophy of life. The pointed choice is between a new radical *shalom* and military powers. Daniel Smith suggests that Jeremiah's letter to the exiles

41. Niedner, "Rachel's Lament," 408.

42. Gray, "Justice with Reconciliation," 167.

gives us insights into the social psychology of a group under stress.[43] None of this stress should have come as a surprise or strike a dissonant chord in any way.

How does one reach into history and embrace those moments that have come to define human existence, moments that shape and guide each generation, not only to continue a particular trajectory, but to create a new direction? In this regard, certainly memory is essential. There is often the more illusory notion of nostalgia, as was the case when the Hebrew slaves were freed from bondage in Egypt and began a period of life in the wilderness. It was not long before the memory of enslavement gave way to nostalgia where a painful reality was revised and recast into a time of plenty and acceptance, "a memory" of abundance in Egypt and even a place of rest in death. But this was not memory, but nostalgia, or at best faulty memory. The biblical text calls for such applications; and, indeed, over time within the biblical text itself, circumstances and situations have led to reinterpretations and new hermeneutical directions. Neglecting to constantly engage the text in such a manner means to lose memory, and thereby, lose an essential component in shaping the future. In the case of imperialism, it would be tempting to begin with contemporary ideologies and conventions on imperialism and its challenges, and bring these lenses to bear forcefully on the text. Rather, while one must not seek to escape one's experience under imperialism of whatever sort, in the case of biblical hermeneutics, one must reach to the biblical sources, to memory, and to history as the principal points of departure for interpretation and application.

ASHOKA'S SHALOM VISION

It is certainly possible to alter a worldview and set about embodying and implementing it. An example from a different historic time and place is illustrative here. Some three centuries after the time of Jeremiah, Prince Ashoka of India began an experiment that dramatically re-cast the landscape of Indian society, culture and life. It has been noted that the early part of Prince Ashoka's rule was dominated by the use of military force. It is recorded that after he walked through the battlefield of his last battle, instead of feeling euphoria on the victory, having vanquished the enemy, rather, in witnessing the carnage of 100,000 men killed, the victory was transformed

---

43. Smith, *Jeremiah as Prophet*, 103.

into a sense of depravity and revulsion for him. Nothing, except that which was within him became the point of transformation, and for the next thirty plus years, after converting to Buddhism he instituted a compassionate, non-violent form of government. Duane Elgin has noted that "Ashoka's political administration was marked by the end of war and an emphasis on peace."[44] Ashoka planted orchards and trees lining the streets to provide shade, encouraged the Arts, built houses for travelers and sojourners, water sheds for animals, and provided resources for the poor and infirmed. With an eye to the future, beyond his time, he placed markers across India inscribed with his vision for the society. Of particular note here is that "peace" was not merely a rhetorical device but an idea that became a part of the fabric of life and sought to transform all aspects of life. Yet, beyond the extraordinary parallels that exist between Jeremiah and Ashoka is the fact that Ashoka chose to convert to Buddhism. One is certainly left with a number of questions including whether Ashoka felt that the religion that he embraced at the time before his conversion was incapable of accommodating the kind of political policy that was predicated on peace, the common good and welfare for all. Jeremiah redefined the manner in which *shalom* is to be understood in the context of Jewish life and religion. He not only did not change or abandon his religion, but saw God as the chief architect of the new *shalom* worldview. If a particular religion does not lend itself to a policy of *shalom*, then surely that religion must be seriously examined.

The Babylonian Empire as has been the case with most empires since, functioned on the principle, "si vís pacem para bellum," that is, "if you wish peace, prepare for war." However, Jeremiah's admonition to the exiles might best be captured by the axiom "si vís pacem, para pacem." The simple, yet radical basis of this axiom lies in the active, vigilant and ongoing living out of *shalom*. Like Ashoka's policy Jeremiah's admonition of *shalom* cannot merely be spoken and repeated, but must be lived out and govern all of life. Jeremiah did not spend his time willing for the Babylonian Empire to be defeated by Egypt or Persia or collapse under its own weight. Instead, at the zenith of its power, God gives Jeremiah a radical message of how one relates to each other, and how inextricably our lives are woven together. It is a bond of such proportions that whatever happens to one is indelibly connected to the other. The society will be transformed over a period of time and the intent, as was the case with Ashoka, was not only for the present, and the immediate, but for generations to come. Like Ashoka's vision and

44. Elgin, *Promise Ahead*, 117.

imagination, where a private persona and a public declaration merge, there will be an embracing of a new vision of the world where personal acts of *shalom* will be transformed even as public policy is being formed. Elgin has observed that this *shalom* is "not speaking about an internal, spiritual peace of soul as subsequent centuries of Jewish and Christians would rather have it . . . [The writers] are neck high in politics and economics."[45]

Babylon's imperialism and nationalism shaped the identity of a nation and people, where its world was defined by military power, its own overpowering force, and the self proclaimed quasi-divine status of Nebuchadnezzar. Certainly in the manner in which the Babylonian Empire functioned, there was no need for partnership or any inherent need of the *other* for one's survival, life or identity. With the death of Ashurbanipal, there was in the scheme of things a remarkably dramatic collapse of the once dominant Assyrian Empire. At the zenith of power, the Assyrian Empire dominated the geographical landscape and contiguous nations, including the Babylonians. With the newly acquired freedom and imperial power, Babylonia spared no time in flexing its political and military muscles. The imperial interest as far as relationships are concerned is in domination. And thus the cycle of power proceeds: one is dominated by force, and violence, and in turn if it eventuates that they gain power, the cycle continues, not only in retaliatory measures, but also in crushing and dominating seemingly weaker nations.

Jeremiah's word to the exiles seeks to break this cycle. As such, Jeremiah's admonition to seek *shalom*, the welfare of the captors and the people of Babylon, not only runs counter to Babylonian protocol, but stands as a direct affront to Babylonian imperial prowess and military powers. What is not spelled out is the nature of the *shalom*. What is it that constitutes such a *shalom* and is it the same for both captors and captives? As is typically the case with the Hebrew prophets, Jeremiah's message is not one of policy or details or for that matter one that is narrowly prescriptive. Rather, the people must find their particular ways in defining and fulfilling the radical idea of peace. What we do know is that Jeremiah's admonition to live a life of *shalom* is certainly not an invitation for separation, but neither is it a summons to assimilate. A proactive *shalom* cannot separate the reality of the captors from that of the exiles. The radicalism of this *shalom* shines clearly as it is contextualized in the midst of oppression, exile, and war. Indeed this *shalom* might most profoundly be understood and defined in times of oppression, captivity and hopelessness. It was being instituted at a

45. Elgin, *Promise Ahead*, 116.

time of Babylonian military might and prowess and not when power was at a low ebb.

Moreover, the worldview of *shalom* is not predicated on the Babylonians acting in like manner, though the desired effect is that *shalom* generates *shalom* even from enemies. But in no instance does Jeremiah intimate this in his admonition. Sisson has suggested that "In demanding that the exiles pray for the land of their captivity, and seek *shalom* in its home, Jeremiah was saying in effect that Babylon had replaced Zion as the center of the order of creation."[46] Sisson has further argued regarding prophetic intercession, that Jeremiah would not intercede on behalf of the people unless they sought the welfare of the Babylonians.[47] This kind of *quid pro quo* is entirely absent from Jeremiah's admonition. Not only does Babylon not replace Zion or the new *shalom* but in no way is Israel being subordinate to Babylon, or as he suggests, "Israel's *shalom* is subordinate to the *shalom* of a foreign power . . . Divine judgment had subordinated the welfare of the community in exile to the welfare of Babylon, the vehicle of that judgment."[48] It is undermining the radicalism of the message of Jeremiah to conclude that his admonition of *shalom* is a matter of acquiescence to the Babylonian hegemonic pursuits. Jeremiah's *shalom* is not simply to appease, acquiesce, or sustain a worldview where military might and power are the generative factors that define a people and nation.

Furthermore, Jeremiah's *Letter to the Exiles* is neither abstract nor theoretical. At its very basis lies a practical component that will mean life or death for the exiles. There are no illusions regarding the potential pain and the unprecedented difficulty of this new *shalom*. The bar for exilic life has been set at a remarkably elevated level. This new worldview might have added to the belief of divine abandonment and punishment without redemptive quality to it, particularly given the longevity announced by Jeremiah. This too would call for both memory and vision on the part of the people. We witness in 9:9 (English v. 10) God weeping for the suffering that has been meted out to the neighbors. Scalise suggests that "God mourns for the people who suffer at their neighbors' hands and for the creation that will be destroyed because of this sin."[49]

---

46. Sisson, *Jeremiah and the Jerusalem*, 440.

47. Ibid.

48. Ibid.

49. Scalise, "Way of Weeping," 418.

Rare it is that one finds the grief of God so clearly and poignantly expressed, and here God weeps and wails for the land. To be sure, the emphasis is on the people, but it is not only about the people, it is the manner in which the people's actions have affected all of the created order. "Sharing God's grief over Judah's failure sharpens one's awareness of the enormous harm done to neighbors and events to the land itself by people who reject God's way of righteousness, justice, and faithfulness."[50] Catherine Keller, in exploring the role of Empire and postcolonialism, argues that:

> Empire indicates an organizational illness of history, clearly but not necessarily terminal . . . Let us say that empire is a recurrent condition, an extraordinarily adaptive one that grows rapidly in each new manifestation, vicariously consuming the space it occupies . . . yet within imperial space allergy may turn into attraction; traditions may collude and mingle, birthing all manner of strange religio-cultural hybrids.[51]

This "imperial condition" poses a colossal problem for the exiles, not least being the distinctive possibility of such merging, dissolving their identity. Aberbach has observed that "One does not have to be a disciple of Marx to see that, to a large extent, dominant powers and their cultures can crush minority cultures, whether through coercion, social pressure, or the force of their values and aesthetics, or through a mixture of three."[52] This assessment invites the exploration of a parallel view of a radical peace ethic as a basis of survival and life in captivity. Jeremiah's admonition, as if to "rub salt in the wound," is entirely counter-intuitive. Despite the textual acknowledgment that in part this captivity has been brought on by the people themselves, nonetheless, the natural impulse would likely be one of revenge, perhaps a return of the pain and suffering, humiliation and displacement, but Jeremiah, himself being ravished by God, says no. Not that the people had any such power to mete out judgment to their captors. Rather it will be *shalom* for a new worldview. Jeremiah makes it clear that the exiles will not be like their captors. There will be no returning ill for ill. Their identity will not be defined by revenge. Instead, their identity will be redefined, and the source and expression of power will be redefined. Yet, the minority exiled community could not simply routinely impose or

---

50. Ibid., 421.

51. Keller, "Love of Postcolonialism," 221–22.

52. Aberbach, *Revolutionary Hebrew*, 128.

even incorporate the radical *shalom* worldview. While the challenges for the exiles were numerous, there were two in particular.

First, there is no history or indication that admonishing or proclaiming the centrality of *shalom* for all of life would mean that the people necessarily would listen or adhere. Such a dramatic pronouncement with all of the associated pain was not likely to be embraced fully and immediately by everyone. Second, this *shalom* worldview dictated an essential kind of assimilation and an active challenge to the imperial convention of treating the exiled community as a lesser community.[53] The key idea of this new worldview will not only have a life that could be immediately envisioned, but the exiled community must live lives that envision a future beyond themselves. They will have to live lives that are inter-generational, anticipating a future that has a clear and indelible effect on the military imperial complex. It is possible, perhaps even conceivable that members of the dominant community may come to see that there are dramatically different options in which one relates to the other. Neither Jeremiah nor any of the exilic or post-exilic prophets speak to the effect of the new *shalom* ethic on the captors.

In his book *The Rebel*, Albert Camus concluded that years of imprisonment do not in fact produce a very conciliatory form of intelligence. Such an experience has the potential to turn a person into a killer. It is very difficult to argue with Camus' conclusion, and there have certainly been many particular situations or circumstances when the truth of Camus' position has proven indisputable; however, it is precisely the notable exceptions that make his assertion difficult to have universal claims. In a contemporary scenario, one might think of the transformation that Nelson Mandela has lived through and the substantial effects that his transforming philosophy brought into a society that was shaped by a particular brand of power and dominance predicated on divisiveness and hatred, literally captured in the term, *apartheid*. It is precisely such an experience departing from Camus' conclusion that serves as a reminder that there is hope for a redemptive and different way to see the world. When, after twenty-seven years in prison, Nelson Mandela was freed from prison and assumed leadership in South Africa, many imagined, and some even hoped, that he would mete out punishment, perhaps revenge, and rule in the manner of his captors. But Mandela chose otherwise. One unlikely and notable moment vividly illustrates the challenging view that he took. He set out to reshape a society that had only known rule by division and force; violence,

---

53. See Psalm 137.

and oppression. Such was its history. Against the advice of both family and advisors, he pursued a vision of *shalom* in one of the most unlikely places, Springbok rugby. Not surprisingly, the erstwhile ruling group also showed a measurable level of distrust. They could not possibly believe that given this "reversal of fortune" that those once oppressed would not now seek retribution and revenge. But, the vision of the free, once imprisoned, would become the worldview for others. After Mandela shared his impregnable hope for the Springbok rugby team, a sport almost entirely associated with, and dominated by "White South Africa," the captain François Pienaar was inspired and embraced the challenging vision. Against extraordinary odds, the South African Springboks won the World Cup in 1995. In *Playing the Enemy*, John Carlin records the following: "As the captain held the cup, Mandela put his left hand on his right shoulder, fixed him with a fond gaze, shook his right hand and said, 'François, thank you very much for what you have done for our country'. Pienaar meeting Mandela's eyes replied, 'No, Mr. President. Thank you for what you have done for our country.'"[54]

The rarity of such moments has perhaps had the effect of causing interpreters to imagine that the establishment of imperial power, long and deeply entrenched, is intractable. In the ongoing militaristic impulse of the Babylon Empire, there were certainly many opportunities to cast condemnation and criticism and legitimately lay blame, but in Jeremiah's letter, there is no such condemnation. The challenge to live lives of *shalom* was not meant to overlook imperial atrocities, but rather focus on a community predicated on a new *shalom*. While evil is identified for what it is, "name calling" is not a part of *shalom* and cannot be counted as policy. Aberbach argues that "the Jews as a perpetual minority had . . . to base their religious culture not upon military heroism and power but upon a philosophy of life considerably more humane than that of empires. The emphasis [on] . . . demanding truth, faith, love and justice was antithetical to, even subversive of the realities of imperial rule."[55] As counter-intuitive as it might seem to the exiles, this new ethic of *shalom* for all, including in particular the enemy, is essential for their personal well being. And this is possible and does not have to be natural. Aristotle has proposed:

> Virtue, then, being of two kinds, intellectual and moral, intellectual virtue in the main owes both its birth and its growth to teaching (for which reason it requires experience and time), while moral virtue comes about as a result of habit, whence also its name

54. Carlin, *Playing the Enemy*, 245.

55. Aberbach, *Revolutionary Hebrew*, 139.

(ethike) is one that is formed by a slight variation from the word ethos (habit). From this it is also plain that none of the moral virtues arises in us by nature; for nothing that exists by nature can form a habit contrary to its nature. For instance the stone which by nature moves downwards cannot be habituated to move upwards, not even if one tries to train it by throwing it up ten thousand times; nor can fire be habituated to move downwards, nor can anything else that by nature behaves in one way be trained to behave in another. Neither by nature, then, nor contrary to nature do the virtues arise in us; rather we are adapted by nature to receive them, and are made perfect by habit.[56]

Reflecting on the social ethic of Jesus, Stanley Hauerwas suggests it lies in his very story.[57] While one is able to make this claim about Jesus as one whose life generated an ethic, a "social/*shalom* ethic" in Jeremiah's message is neither by nature or within the exiles natural impulse, but must be developed. This letter from Jeremiah invites us to embrace the reality that we live in a pluralistic world where by design or circumstance, we must live with, and relate to those people who we may not like, whom we might deem enemies or who we perceive as different. Bracke suggests that this might be a gift from God, both for our own *shalom* and the *shalom* for all of God's creation. To embrace such exilic experience is to see others as participating in God's ongoing plan for creation.[58] Moreover, there are no exceptions in terms of who must live out the ideals. *Shalom* for all will have to be lived out and embraced by all exiles. Aberbach observes further:

> The need for this egalitarianism appears to have been specially pronounced in crisis when class differences among the Jews could be dangerous. The unity promoted by a common set of beliefs and practices, a collective history, language and literature enhanced the chances of Jewish survival.[59]

Intragroup power within the exiled community will be re-defined. In the context of this radicalizing of a worldview, self identity is essential and the voice and actions of the exiles have to be maintained. "On the social as well as the individual plane, it is the sick organ which creates awareness, and it is in moments of crisis that men are most aware of the enigma of

---

56. Aristotle, *Nicomachean Ethics* II.1.

57. Hauerwas, *A Community of Character*, 40.

58. Bracke, "Justice in the Book of Jeremiah," 203.

59. Aberbach, *Revolutionary Hebrew*, 137.

their presence in the world."[60] The exiled community cannot imagine that they are anyone but who they are. If *shalom* to the other becomes more the cornerstone in trying to ingratiate or collapse their identity, and assimilate, perhaps even for understandable and legitimate reasons, then it would be practically impossible to create an alternative worldview. The living out and pursuit of justice will bear *shalom* (Isa 32:17), and perhaps for a while as the transformation happens, there will be weeping for themselves and the new world in which they find themselves.[61] But in the pursuit of the new *shalom*, weeping will not be the last word (Ps 30:5).

Blame and Self-Critique

The people will have to recognize and acknowledge the magnitude of their loss and collapse of life, temple and land. O'Connor suggests that "By showing them losses, it validates them in their suffering, let them know they are not alone in it, and provides words for them to begin to speak of it. When they accept the magnitude of their disaster, healing can begin."[62] Jeremiah's very specific admonitions ensure that the magnitude and extent of their brokenness is known. The people have desecrated the very name of God through their disingenuity and self-righteousness, and as if the egregious behavior was not enough, it is thinly veiled behind religious language. One thinks of the sharp invectives uttered by Jeremiah's predecessor, the prophet Amos. No amount of ritual propriety (5:21–24) or quantity of offerings and tithes and attendance will suffice in themselves (4:4). The deceptive words, "The Temple of the Lord" howsoever often they are repeated, cannot ever absolve the people of their actions: injustice against widows and orphans; the shedding of innocent blood; idolatry; stealing; murdering; adulterous behavior; perjury while confidently proclaiming, "We are safe." Or, as Sean Freyne has noted regarding Jer 6:14, "They have healed the wound of my people lightly, saying 'peace, peace' when there is no peace."[63] The self-righteous audacity must be faced. O'Connor proposes insightfully an idea that brings with it something of a commensurate pain.

60. Goldman, *Hebrew Prophets*, 49.
61. See Psalm 137.
62. O'Connor, "Surviving Disaster," 371.
63. Freyne, "Bible and Violence," 92.

> Blaming becomes a strategy for survival . . . As a theology of human responsibility for the politics of the world, blaming is a prophetic survival tactic for the nation. As difficult as this blaming might be for some contemporary Christians to understand, Jeremiah's accusations are a balm in Gilead, a healing ointment for the wounds of the people. It is difficult to see Jeremiah's blaming as a healing vision today, except for one important point. Jeremiah's theology of blame insists on the human capacity to shape the course of events. It reminds us of our vocation to live in fidelity, justice and right relationship with others with the cosmos and with God.[64]

Two aspects of O'Connor's proposal are particularly important to emphasize here. First, while the idea of blaming seems inherently inflammatory and incendiary, it must be noted that the blaming is generated by God and the prophet, and not by the enemy or strangers. Whether it is "blaming" or some other euphemism, the responsibility has to be reckoned with as a singular moment to begin a new journey of *shalom*. Second, Jeremiah's admonition and the idea of blaming for our contemporary society and world do have essential importance. Again, while the language of "blame" will likely bring some strong resistance and even an instant defensive mode with *ad hominem* retorts, nonetheless, what has transpired has to be named. Perhaps it will take one with integrity, memory by some, and vision to make the pronouncement of blame.

The first and arguably the most painful and necessary step for personal and collective transformation to occur is to face oneself with honest self critique. This might be forged through personal self-discovery when all of the viable options are exhausted as in the parable of the Prodigal Son (Luke 15), or the prophet Nathan's parable to David (2 Samuel 12) where he creates a path for the king to see and acknowledge the injustice that he initiated and further orchestrated to veil his personal culpability. That acknowledgement, however, is but a step to transformation. As the exiles must face themselves, there are particular and universal questions that must be posed. What does it mean that the enemy's *shalom* is the same as the exiles' *shalom*? How will the people respond in the context of the unimaginable predicament in which they find themselves? O'Connor has noted that "The Babylonian army invaded Jerusalem three times, they destroyed the Temple, the king's palace, the governing system. They undermined ordinary domestic and commercial life and they deported members of the ruling

---

64. O'Connor, "Surviving Disaster," 372.

classes to Babylon."[65] This action by any measure is a disaster; and yet, the reality of this disaster is precisely what sets the stage for survival in a new and dramatic way. O'Connor further iterates, "By disaster I do not mean simply a sorrowful time or a set of tragedies out of which the community or individual expects to emerge. Disaster reflects a colossal collapse of the world, a vast interruption of life as it is known."[66] The extraordinary and daring worldview that emerges from such a disaster will reflect the magnitude of the disaster.

The drama cannot be underestimated. A significant issue in seeking to understand one's response is to have an honest self critique and name the disaster, and begin to ask and pursue the painful questions and events that might have precipitated the calamitous event. Jeremiah is certainly not at a loss to describe the scope of the disaster. The mountains and hills were quaking and swaying; the land was void of people; birds and vegetation have all gone; what was once fruitful is now a desert and in ruins and the anger of the Lord was fierce. There is no mistaking the magnitude of the disaster. Simply repeating the familiar, even when there is some truth and hope in the familiar, is not enough.

Bracke is pointed in what he sees as a narrow preoccupation with self as he reflects on post September 11: "Since September 11, we have devoted our national energies—our wisdom, might and riches—to serve ourselves. To undergird our efforts we regularly invoke a henotheistic deity to bless America."[67] The very survival of a people, of a people deeply broken, wounded, and uprooted must now re-root itself in foreign and unknown territory by uniting with the very nation that created the exile, while maintaining a covenantal relationship with the very God who had uprooted them and now chooses the enemy king as "servant." The exiles' destiny and future are inextricably woven together with the other nations. This experience of "cosmic crumbling" as Louis Stulman calls it, ensures that one cannot continue life without a dramatic transformation. Less, it is unclear, Jeremiah's focus is not only, or for that primarily on the exiles, but the land. His question, wrought with deep emotive content and full of poignancy, "why should this city become a desolation?," does indeed point to the large and pervasive issue of the land.[68] It is the land, the city, the temple, that must be preserved.

65. O'Connor, "Surviving Disaster," 370.

66. Ibid., 369.

67. Bracke, "Justice in the Book of Jeremiah," 395.

68. Stulman, *Order amid Chaos*, 57.

Jeremiah's admonition to submit to the Babylonians is not therefore to acquiesce to a foreign power and their ideology of force and violence but the greater vision of the security and preservation of the land. Yet, as important as it was, returning to the land was not the principal concern of Jeremiah, but rather the ideal of a new worldview in creation. One might say that it was the shaping of life in *a* land that would shape life in *the* land.

Jeremiah's words to the exiles on how to live in harmony with oppressors extend beyond the historical context of 587 BCE, and it may be a good starting place, especially if "memory" itself has nearly been lost. Its open ended language suggests its importance for future generations. That one advocates a "peace ethic" is not an invitation to appease or collapse into a state of pacific inertia; but rather, to embrace a different worldview, with an eye not only for the present and the vital connection to the past, but for a future reality, a future that encompasses both family and the continued regeneration, together with the ongoing care and stewardship of the environment. Brueggemann has observed: "The book of Jeremiah looks beyond Babylonian brutality and acknowledgement that the anguish of Psalm 137 has been embraced, but will be overcome."[69] It is certainly a viable argument that *shalom* could be the essential bonding between disparate and adversarial groups, and stands as a direct challenge to an ideology or perhaps policy of violence, oppression, and militarism. *Shalom* is not seeking the lowest common denominator; but rather with Jeremiah's "welfare ethic," it sets the bar high, and yet, this *shalom* is not utopian. It is an ideal, and as an ideal, must be pursued, perhaps with prudence. An ideal pursued without prudence would be fraught with pitfalls. Speaking in particular to the issue of monarchy, Brueggemann, argues that "the book of Jeremiah may present a theological-political teaching against the royal policies that brought about the destruction of Jerusalem—politically and militarily at the hands of Babylonian, theologically at the hands of YHWH. The work . . . may be durable testimony after the fact to the folly of the monarchy."[70] While the particular monarchy might be the issue here, it is arguable that it is the structure of imperial militarism and the mentality of conquest and domination that is the greater issue. Among the qualities generated by Jeremiah's *shalom* is the landscape that is being reshaped, a landscape where greed and gain at the expense of the other will no longer be the norm. The *shalom* for Jeremiah and the generations following is not mere wishful thinking

---

69. Brueggemann, *Meditation*, 345.

70. Ibid., 344.

with no foundation, but rather an expectation rooted in memory of what was, and, therefore, not what *might* be, but what *will* be. The Hebrew Bible is one of the rare bodies of sacred literature that is so persistently and unequivocally critical of its own people when it is necessary. The demands and expectations are sometimes such that it is difficult and painful to imagine. Thus, it is that, even as Jeremiah and others within the canon are relentless in pointing to, and facing such brutal self-critique, those who embrace and purport to use the Bible as foundation and guide must similarly face themselves before moving forward.[71]

Never has there been an indication that this self critique would be easy. Moreover the very idea of calling a society to face its ills and injustices does not in any way intimate or imply immediate comfort or for that matter protection or the end of exile or wilderness experience. Yet, the word must be spoken and those who speak will do so from a perspective of being a part of the community. Jeremiah uniquely embodied the pain of the people. The particular drama of such an embodiment is intensified in its poignancy given that the prophet was not responsible for the pain and circumstances in which the people found themselves. The proclamation of Jeremiah that it is singularly through *shalom* to create a new ethic is embodied by him. He remains in the land amid the ruins and so speaks very much from within the vortex of pain and loss. He certainly does not make this proclamation lightly for he too will actively live out the *shalom*. There will certainly be ridicule and rebuke, and it will be hurled by his own beloved people. As is clear from the text, Jeremiah would prefer not to speak the difficult word with which he has been entrusted, but knows that he cannot do otherwise. Like Jeremiah, those who embrace an ethic of *shalom*, and speak such a word to those who would prefer not to hear will feel despair, and while the despair will linger, it will not last forever.

71. See Greenspahn, *Syncretism and Idolatry in the Bible.*

7

Challenging the Empire

On April 19th 1985, Elie Wiesel, Shoah Survivor and Nobel Peace Laureate received the Congressional Medal of Achievement at the White House; Ronald Reagan was the President of the United States. In the days surrounding the ceremony President Reagan found himself in a somewhat conflicted situation as to whether he should proceed on a planned trip to Bitburg cemetery, particularly after it was discovered that SS soldiers were buried there. President Reagan decided to proceed with his trip as planned. Wiesel on this public occasion at the White House spoke directly to President Reagan.

> Allow me Mr. President to touch on a matter which is sensitive. I belong to a traumatized generation; to us symbols are important. Following our ancient tradition which commands us to "speak truth to power," may I speak to you of the recent events that have caused so much pain and anguish? We have met four or five times. I know of your commitment to humanity. I am convinced that you were not aware of the presence of SS graves in the Bitburg cemetery. But now we all are aware of that presence. I therefore implore you Mr. President in the spirit of this moment that . . . you will not go there. That place is not your place.[1]

The physical setting with all the grandeur in 1 Kings 22 is described at great length. Like the White House, the King's Court is a place of power and authority. Micaiah is put to the test. Like Wiesel, Micaiah is not with the king for an informal conversation; in fact the agenda is formal and

---

1. Wiesel, *From the Kingdom of Memory*, 176.

155

precise. What is spoken will not be "behind closed doors." This is public. There are moments when one might speak the truth in a neutral or private setting, but not here, for Elie Wiesel chose not to speak privately with the President. When truth that challenges the State and the considerable power of the Office is to be told, it cannot be a private transaction but a public pronouncement. Analogues are hardly perfect and surely the one used here is no exception, but we witness a quality of courage to speak the truth in the face of daunting possibilities. Howsoever one views this, finally there is a palpable element of vulnerability by the one who challenges the source of power. As a world we should not be surprised that the moments of war, some of which have lingered on for a hundred years have punctuated the landscape of world history. It is a tragic commentary that often, though by no means always, have we come to think of war as giving identity and definition to many generations. Presently, numerous countries and various groups in the world are involved in wars and still others employ the rhetoric of war in political discourse and engagement. We have had recent evidence in the United States where even wondering about, let alone questioning war are viewed by some as undermining the direction of the State; some even view these fundamental human principles as subversive. Yet, in such extraordinary circumstances how can there not be questions! Biblical narratives and histories remind us that a nation is propelled into war for a variety of reasons, and in fact a leader of the State might even seek to determine divine assent to justify. In this regard 1 Kings 22, is a narrative that remains remarkably relevant and pointed in its implications.

Notably in 1 Kings 22 King Ahab is the vested subject. An essential component of this is understood principally through the military and the voice of the majority who subscribe to a broad imperial role of government. The challenge by a prophet outside the circle of "assenters" is to redefine "power" and reassert an indispensable role for the "voice of conscience." In matters of truth and the moral conscience of the prophet, there is no retreat. Punishment in the form of imprisonment and the meager rations will be meted out to Micaiah, but the prophet is unflinching in his commitment. In speaking the truth Micaiah will do so at considerable cost, like every other prophet who speaks the truth; again one turns to Jeremiah among others. The prophetic truth must be spoken and once spoken there is no retreat or retraction.

There are different layers of conflict that permeate 1 Kings 22: nation against nation; prophet against prophet; monarchical power against divine power, among others. There is no doubt that there are conflicts of interest. The voices of power that resound out of the halls of power do not necessarily echo the voice of God. Each of these tensions exists independently, and yet each intersects in significant ways. Additionally and worthy of singular note is that of the pervasive tension between truth and lies. There are numerous surprising revelations regarding those who seek the truth and those who tell the truth, and those involved in deceit and lies. Micaiah insists that he must speak the truth (v. 14) and then immediately proceeds to do otherwise (v. 15). Ahab does not want to hear the truth, but rather he wants to hear *his* truth; truth based on what he has already determined. Part of the complexity here is that Ahab, the king, insists on the truth—but in fact he really only wants confirmation for his decision to enter into war. Thus, what he insists on publicly is not what he wants to hear. The king wants the truth, in the public, for this is what the public must hear and believe. But this drama is doubly disingenuous for not only is the king not interested in the truth, but he sees the truth as a mere tool to be navigated around, negotiated away, and finally to become a casualty. The king simply cannot have a prophetic challenge to his authority. Even the "propping up" of Ahab at the end of the narrative is a deception in order to perpetuate the truth of the power of the State. To the degree Ahab is the principal representative of State power, then the power is sustained only by a lie, before the truth is known, for even the State can only feign death for so long. Ahab's war is ill conceived and unwise, and God will use it to destroy the king.

Labyrinth of Truth and Lies

When the king of Israel is asked to inquire of God, the immediate response is to ask those who are employed by Ahab. The guild of prophets is clearly in the king's employment. It is evident that their role is not to speak on behalf of God, but on behalf of the king, though even here, unbeknownst to them and to Ahab, God placed "lying spirits" within them. The manner in which the question is asked makes it clear where the focus is. Not unlike some poll questions, this one too is designed to elicit a particular answer. They assure the king, unanimously, in one voice that this is a good idea, and that indeed God will deliver Ramoth-Gilead into his hands. There are no qualifications; no stipulations. Go to war, and the city will be yours. Such is the immediate and uncritical response. They do not ponder; they do not take it to God and wonder, they simply apply the answer that the king is seeking, and thus it is the case that in this instance, it seems that the collective prophetic voice is collapsed under the force of imperial power. Four hundred advocated in the "war room" in unison, "Go up; go up; go up." Ahab intentionally determines what he will do and places restrictions on a divinely shaped and guided future. Listening to the report of the four hundred voices of Ahab's prophets, Jehoshaphat knows instinctively that all is not well. Certainly this kind of hasty and grand unanimity cannot be the voice of God, and thus he asks for another prophet who might be available. What he seeks is one who does not appear to be a surrogate of the State. There is an ongoing intrigue/tension/conflict between "truth" and "the labyrinth of lies" in this story. This is the point at which Micaiah ben Imlah enters the scenario. The king of Israel knows Micaiah, and it is clear that he intentionally seeks to keep his voice silent. If there is something to be said about the king of Israel, he does not finally seek to hide Micaiah, or his deep disdain for the prophet. Even Jehoshaphat chastises him for ridiculing Micaiah in this manner. He knows that his history is such that Micaiah is fearless in the telling of truth and thus he hides him. The imperial power seeks to hide the prophetic power. What is a king to do, he knows the prophet is telling the truth but whose very words he knew will spell disaster? Ahab does what those in power typically do, namely, either vilify the critic or as was the case with Jeremiah, silence him. This is often done through marginalizing the person or persons or placing them in physical or figurative places where they cannot be heard from. But such a course inevitably fails. We have seen examples throughout history, and if there is in fact a particularly demoralization quality to this kind of action, it is that it continues to this day as if those with power have not learned an iota of the lesson that it is a ultimately a destructive code of operating and sustaining power. Such is the situation with Ahab and Micaiah.

One should certainly not confuse Micaiah the prophet as being the "enemy of the State" as perhaps Ahab would like to identify him. Ahab deems him to be so even before Micaiah makes any pronouncements. This prophecy regarding Ahab's fate does not in any way reflect a condemnation of the people. It is true that as the king, Ahab is a "corporate personality," but in this case the king's punishment is not a reflection of the people, for as Nelson suggests the "fate of the people is separate from that of the monarch, the leader."[2] Indeed from the beginning Ahab pronounces his hatred for Micaiah. Whatever the earlier prophecies might have been, the

2. Nelson, *I & II Kings*, 150.

hatred appears to be personal and thus intentionally distinguishes him from the people. Even though there is no biblical record, it is indisputably clear that Ahab and Micaiah had a prior relationship, a tempestuous one from all account one that existed before the recorded encounter in 1 Kings 22. Given the nature of the reference it seems that there must have been several encounters and the animosity has heightened. Had it not been for Jehoshaphat's inquiry, Ahab would not have mentioned Micaiah. In fact if Jehoshaphat is unaware of Micaiah, one is left to wonder why Ahab would have mentioned him. Again Ahab's interest in "truth" surfaces, and the question as to what this means for him emerges. The issue as to why Ahab would make this known is something of a mystery. He might have felt compelled to speak the truth despite his personal disinclination to do so. The prophet's pronouncements will not be determined on the basis of whether he is liked or disliked by Ahab or whether he believed that he would not prophesy good. Indeed by whose standard is "good" defined? What does it mean for the prophet to prophesy "good?" From Ahab's perspective "good" is equated with agreement with him. "Good" for Ahab is the sustaining and sanctioning of monarchical power. The king's personal inclination, disinclination or his personal animosity cannot be the ultimate guiding principles on which the decisions are made.

Perhaps it is the case that it has been historically true that a leader's deeply entrenched ideological foundation is such that when she/he hears the truth from one who is deemed the enemy, he/she cannot bring himself to accept such a truth. Thus ego overpowers the truth and in so doing the leader places himself and invariably his people in grave danger. In the case of Ahab, the king perishes, but the people are saved; certainly that is more the exception rather than the rule. If we have learned anything in the last several years in the Middle East, it is at the very core the idea that the fate of a people while at important points is inextricably linked to its ruler, ultimately it is not the case that how goes the ruler so goes the fate of the people in every instance. God is a discerning God, who in fact makes decisions not on the basis of perfection or on the basis that since the ruler is something of a corporate personality that the punishment of the ruler parallels that of the people. Among other lessons to be learned from this experience that outlines much about God and therefore how human must act, is the fact that generalizations are not to be made wantonly and without reflection. God is discerning and does the challenging work of ensuring that the innocent are not cast with the guilty. It is a common axiom that says that a person is judged by the company he/she keeps, and while there might be some truth to this, punishment by association no more than virtue by association is essentially true. Such is the egotistical notion that some leaders believe that they are the only ones that have the power to rule and only they have the reservoir of truth. To put it somewhat differently, how could truth be generated from one who is hated or one who might be deemed the enemy? It is important to note that YHWH is not spoken of as the enemy by Ahab and Jezebel; indeed despite her odious actions Jezebel calls upon God. Yet, despite the placing of the blame on Micaiah and his predecessor Elijah, they surely must know that finally it is YHWH who metes out such punishment.

Ahab cannot claim by any measure that he does not know the truth, for in fact he *does* know the truth; he insists on being told the truth, but really has no discernible interest in the truth. It is instructive that Ahab does not insist on the truth by the four hundred prophets, and when Micaiah tells him the truth he nonetheless proceeds as if he had not heard anything new or different from the four hundred prophets. Ahab wants a war and a war he will have, but as in all wars there are vagaries over which a leader might not have any control. It is true that the declaration of war is the prerogative of the leader of a nation; advisory or legislative bodies may suggest or opine; debate or vote, but finally the leader decides. A nation or a people may be given particular or general reasons for a war or talk of war, but in the case of Ahab there is no reason given and it is his decision entirely, and he anticipates the outcome. What he does not know or anticipate is the singular unknown element that YHWH plans to use the war for Ahab's final demise. No war comes without a price, and if the only casualty in the military undertaking would be the life of Ahab, then perhaps one might argue that this is justifiable. However the death of Ahab would not be the only cost, but the often overlooked or neglected cost of the peace that exists between the countries. Certainly given the history between Aram and Israel one might be led to believe that this was a tenuous peace, but a three year old peace it was, nonetheless.

How important is Ramoth-Gilead that peace between the nations must be sacrificed? The narrator of this text deems it significant enough to mention that these nations coexisted peaceably for a duration of three years. This, I would argue is more than passing in importance, and certainly not to be construed as incidental. Assuming that the narrative only has material relevant for the story then it is incumbent upon readers to ponder on the significance of such a reference. This is not a trifling feat as Israel and

Aram (Syria) seemed to be constantly at war. This lengthy narrative follows on the heels of an alliance between Aram and Israel, as together they held off the powerful imperial army of Assyria. Moberly suggests:

> The king is willing to sacrifice peace for the arguable benefit of regaining disputed territory; arguable because no benefit is specified for anyone, except, implicit the king in his reputation and power. Moreover, if one allows the placement of this story next to the preceding story of Naboth's vineyard to bear upon its interpretation, then the reader will be less inclined to see territorial responsibility as the prime royal motive. Thus the king may implicitly be abusing royal prerogative in lightly sacrificing peace and greedily undertaking war.[3]

Moberly is substantially correct in his assessment of how one might intersect these events. The textual placement of these stories alongside each other certainly aid tremendously in the interpretation that Ahab was not only selfish, but utterly destructive in his pursuit of a war and the sacrifice of peace for a stretch of land that at best can be described as disputed. Power is such that he is willing to sacrifice peace and certainly the lives of his people for the sake of his sense of power.

One might legitimately argue that the very act of war between nations, especially when there is peace between the particular nations, creates fear, pain and suffering for the citizens of the respective nations. Whatever has been the history between Aram and Israel what we know is that the people were in a peaceful existence with each other when Ahab made his decision to go to war. There is no textual indication or inference that there is a royal envoy, conversations or negotiations from Ahab to the king of Aram. When nations are adversaries, diplomacy and conversations are important; here peace exists, and this would arguably be the principal reason for diplomacy. But none of these principles appear to matter to Ahab, and the unsuspecting attack seems to be his guiding principle. What precipitated the change from a peaceful relationship to one of war was the decision by King Ahab to recapture the disputed territory of Ramoth-Gilead, the value of which has not been determined in the scheme of national identity. Moberly suggests that the juxtaposition of Ramoth-Gilead and Naboth's Vineyard, both involving Ahab and land acquisition, might indicate an abuse of power.[4] The pursuit and conquest of territory in both instances do not suggest any

---

3. Moberly, *Prophecy and Discernment*, 110.

4. Ibid., 4.

particular benefit, except the building of political power and capital. This disputed territory has precipitated a call to war, and Israelite, Judahite, and Aramean blood will all stain the land before it is all over.

Ahab seeks a partnership with Judah and its king, Jehoshaphat. As new alliances between Judah and Israel are made, old ones disintegrate, and a former peace partner becomes the adversary. Jehoshaphat immediately, without any intervening question establishes that his military force is at the disposal of Ahab. Ahab's coalition with Jehoshaphat certainly brings about the desired alliance though it meets with an unexpected and compelling request by the latter. Jehoshaphat does not engage with the king of Israel as to the reason for the sudden interest in, or arguments for war, but rather the matter hinges on the issue as to whether this might be God's intent. "Inquire first for the word of the Lord" insists Jehoshaphat. The fact that YHWH is the covenanted God of Israel and Judah, is not enough to enter into war against an enemy. Jehoshaphat does not trust the "truth" of Ahab's 400 prophets; God will not simply sanction State power for its own sake. Jehoshaphat knows that in matters of truth neither the voice of the majority nor the voice of power will suffice.

While imperial power has structural support, prophetic power is invariably embodied in a voice beyond the center. Jehoshaphat seeks to do the right thing, and ascertain what God desires, for he knows that in both national and international matters, God is the central player, and it is God's word that constitutes ultimacy. What is the divine purpose at this point, and importantly, who might speak on behalf of God? Can the voice of the imperial power also be the voice of God? Can the political establishment speak on behalf of God? Is the voice of God simply meant to sanction what has already been decided? Then and now, discerning and determining who speaks on behalf of God has been a point of dissention.

A Promethean Struggle

Ahab is not only willing to go to war, but there seems to be an urgency to do so. The pace is only slowed down through the engagement of the prophet and the ensuing conflict. There is a seemingly promethean struggle between the king, the imperial force with the support of the structure of government, and the prophet who functions without structure or institution. The one who initially caused the pace to be slowed down is the one coalition partner, Jehoshaphat, and when he receives the truth that he too seeks and perhaps might even have believed, it still does not matter, and he follows Ahab anyway. As devastating as the call to war is, the narrative renders it as a critical point of departure for something greater and more urgently challenging. Among other trajectories within the text, a tension of great magnitude looms between imperial power and prophetic power.

While the kings sit on their thrones arrayed in their royal robes, with the guild of prophets telling the king what he wishes to hear, a messenger is sent to Micaiah to seek his prophetic word regarding the war that is about to be waged. But the reality is that the messenger has no intention of eliciting a genuinely prophetic word from Micaiah. Zedekiah, clearly a "yes man" for the king, even symbolically displays a horn to gore Aram. The imperial power seeks unanimous approval, but prophetic power cannot be collapsed under such pressure. The imperial prophets have spoken with one accord, and this is the pressure that is levied against Micaiah. The messenger does not even formally ask Micaiah to seek God's word; he is simply told what the imperial majority has pronounced and what he should likewise do. When Zedekiah approaches Micaiah there is clearly an unveiled "arm twisting" and the message is perfectly scripted.

Preparations for war, in both theatre and rhetoric are well underway as the machinery of the State has been effected. It is a shocking realization that the king has no intention of hearing what the word of God is, for he has already determined what he will do. Moberly suggests: "To challenge the complacencies and self deceptions of the human heart and mind with the searching truth of God will regularly provoke a hostility whose consequences may be devastating. To try to avoid this by being more accommodating risks becoming a prophet whose message is ultimately self serving."[5] Micaiah's initial response is exactly as one would expect. "As the Lord lives, whatever the Lord says to me, that I will speak." Yet when Micaiah comes before the king, his word is exactly as the other prophets have spoken. There is the peculiar situation of knowing that Micaiah will speak the truth, and yet, in the face of imperial power, he says what the king wishes to hear. To simply agree as he did initially is immediately seen for its transparency, even by Ahab who seeks such approval.

Contrary to his imperial trappings, the king of Israel knows that Micaiah's initial word is not true, and he seeks *the truth* despite himself. But Micaiah's response is instructive. Perhaps it is the case that Micaiah shrinks in the face of imperial power. One should not imagine that prophetic

5. Ibid., 15.

testimony is oblivious of the power of the State, for Micaiah is aware of the danger, and his initial response demonstrates self-preservation. The narrative leading to this point has made it altogether clear that Ahab and Jezebel are utterly unscrupulous and violent. Micaiah's initial response is understandable. The history of the Crown's actions when it is challenged and confronted, even in the name of God, is to resort to violence. Micaiah has good reason to be reluctant, and yet he must speak the truth. There is nothing that Micaiah is able to say that will align him with the Crown. The voice of the prophet is not the voice of the State, and Ahab feels vindicated that indeed in his estimation Micaiah turns out to be an enemy of the State. Yet, the enemy of the State as Ahab sees him is the one who speaks on behalf of God. So the quest for truth is made public, but when the truth comes, the one who bears it must be silenced. Micaiah is thus placed in detention.[6] Micaiah is imprisoned; he is given "prisoner food" and the idea is that in the imprisonment and demoralizing of Micaiah, the word that he speaks will be discounted, discredited and discarded. The larger issue of course is not simply the feud between the Prophet and the State; the mouthpiece of the king and God's prophet Micaiah, but in reality the silencing of God. The belief is that in silencing the prophet, the prophetic oracle will also recede if not disappear. One thinks of Solzhenitsyn and Havel, both of whom have written so remarkably poignantly about such silencing. Moreover, as we see in contemporary society, when there is disagreement with those who bring a prophetic voice, then the powers that be, vilify and ostracize them and often call them "crazy." Perhaps in doing so, the general public will believe that the prophetic word has been weakened. Here too, one is reminded that Elisha is called "mad" also by the establishment because of his prophetic words.

When he outlines his vision that speaks of a scattering, a people without a king and a society that will collapse into chaos, he is imprisoned and physically weakened. Despite what Micaiah pronounces, Jehoshaphat maintains his alliance with Ahab and follows him into war. But we know that Jehoshaphat does have a vision that contains a striking and dramatic component that God in fact will use the war for the death of Ahab. Not only will the policy of Ahab not succeed, but death will come to Ahab because of an unwise, self-indulgent act. There is thus a clash of two designs of foreign policy, Ahab's and God's. Shalom is beyond Ahab, and ultimately his warring intent will lead to his death, for he has been enticed, seduced

6. 1 Kgs 22:26–28.

and finally blinded by his own military machinations. His justification is not predicated on any kind of genuine discussion or listening, but rather territorial dispute has expanded itself into the realm of certitude regarding ownership and belonging.

Given what Micaiah has spoken regarding Ahab, one is not surprised that Micaiah is imprisoned for his words. The Crown has the power to silence, in the hopes of undermining or even unraveling the truth. In the face of challenges, the State seeks to silence the voice of the critics and those who pose an alternative. Thus even as Micaiah is silenced the vision not only lives on, but it is directed by God. In a striking juxtaposition of two powers, both State and God prepare for war and while Ahab imagines and anticipates, God already knows the outcome. This war will ultimately not be about the disputed land of Ramoth-Gilead, or Israel versus Aram, but about Ahab; he realizes this as he disguises himself as a peasant soldier. But external changes and disguises will not do, for this war is out of his hands and is guided by God. His fate has been sealed. The war which he himself initiated would lead to his death, and there is nothing to stem the tide of his demise.

In some countries, including the United States patriotism is narrowly construed and understood as that which lends support to the State-sanctioned position. Voices that challenge such state sanctioned positions are deemed unpatriotic, often silenced, and frequently demonized. Micaiah's pronouncement establishes with unencumbered clarity that State ideology as powerful as it may be, and as widely as it is embraced by operatives of the State, must not be confused with divine affirmation. We know that with all of the State planning, the military alliances, the political maneuvering, and the rhetoric of peace through war, ultimately this is neither the only word nor the final word. As this narrative comes at an end there is an enduring message. The destiny of a people which is often viewed as tied to its leader is not necessarily so. In the case of Ahab's undertaking the leader dies and the people return home in peace. The alignment of God with the goals of the State cannot be assumed and there are moments when God will protect the people from their leaders. The people will survive in peace despite an ideology of war. In many respects our society and aspects of the Church have formed the notion that YHWH's interests and the wellbeing of the State and its power have the same interests. Perhaps one might argue that in an ideal world, it might be the case that both interests should converge. But in reality, the State's interest is often at odds with that of the Church, but nonetheless claims a close identification. This is, in a way, a usurping of God's role and the taking on of divine purpose and voice. Except, the State cannot be confused with the interest of God. We inhale it every day. It is the assumption that dominant economic power allied with the State power needs always to act to protect its own interests, to sustain its honor and to maintain its credibility.

> All manner of brutality and stupidity can be done in the interest of such "reasons of state." Even in a democracy, moreover, permission and support for such ventures is relatively easy to muster, given propaganda, sloganeering, and manipulation of public opinion. As with the 400 prophets, the religious is widely expected to follow the line of dominant ideology . . . and almost always does. . . . What is unfamiliar to us is the prophetic resistance of Elijah and Micaiah and the ground for such resistance. The resistance itself is the insistence that Yahweh's purposes are not readily collapsible into state policy, thus countering the royal assumption. Yahweh is not simply an echo of dominant opinion and is not primarily a legitimator of entrenched power.[7]

At the end, as Ahab is wounded by accident, and he dies in the process of a "lie" even as he is being propped up in his chariot. The irony is that he is being overlooked as the king, and yet he is killed. The tensions and layers in the narrative are multiple; certainly among them is the ever present question: "who will speak for God"? The four hundred prophets claim to speak for God, but in reality in this instance they represent a thinly veiled collective mouthpiece for the crown even as they are used by God. The voice of the prophet on God's behalf need not be measured quantitatively or by decibels, but by truth, even quiet and devastating truth. This is the measure. God will use whatever measures, whether a truth speaking prophet or lying spirits to bring about the demise of Ahab. God's "lying spirits" work; Ahab's "lying" through his disguise does not. He dies, despite himself. In both "truth" and "lie" Ahab is outdone.

7. Brueggemann, *I & II Kings*, 278.

8

Justice and Redemption

It is the case today that a discernible percentage of the rhetoric about who one might vote for, as President of the United States or a national legislator and who might best represent particular ideological and theological ideals, is being espoused from pulpits and podiums frequently from a variety of settings. In itself, this is probably enough to lead one to conclude that it is, and has always been, the conservative movement that has embraced the notion of the United States as having a "Manifest Destiny," though this is not true historically. In large part Progressives are likely to feel somewhat righteous if not self righteous about the fact they are the ones who are the contrarians and the ones whose principles best reflect the true message of the Hebrew prophets. However, this is not entirely true either. In Josiah Strong's *Our Country*, he espoused precisely this idea, and given that he was widely regarded, his ideas were very influential. He argued that God had commissioned the United States as the nation "to dispossess the many weaker races, assimilate others, and mold the remainder."[1] My point here is that many within the Church and religious institutions were caught up in the fervor of a nation that was set apart as the New Jerusalem so to speak, the light on the hill, a phrase that is being touted today in particular circles.

In broad strokes, Progressives are more likely to be in favor of regulations while Conservatives are typically opposed to regulations, as Conservatives would view this as government yet again interfering in the affairs of the people when there is neither need nor warrant. One thinks of Nehemiah returning to Jerusalem in the midst of a people rebuilding but have

1. As cited in Horsley, *In the Shadow of the Empire*, 5.

for the most part lost the direction of their lives and the connection with Torah. So then what? Nehemiah's actions are, I believe, is instructive for us in that they point to the importance of the fact that there are moments in which leaders must act to ensure that which is necessary for the health and wellbeing of relationships. Nehemiah the governor imposed regulations, some of which have been used over time to fuel a particular ideology and abuse. There was clearly a need for a regulation, for systemic guidance, and it was clear that the people could not simply do as they pleased, as if they had no responsibility and connection with the other. In the Nehemiah regulations, all of which are driven by covenantal expectations, the point is to bring the people back to a place of caring and living in the present in a proper and meaningful relationship, and envisioning a future that will again restore what was intended. However as is sometimes the case, such ancient regulations and modern day iterations have a way of lingering, and being misconstrued, and even abused along the way beyond their original intent.

Ultimately no one owns God, nor should God be viewed as simply one who supports a person, a movement, or a nation's ideology. "The effort to domesticate God, to tie the deity to one's own aims and desires, which is a catastrophic consequence of the total failure of human beings as moral agents, results in a chaotically disordered political and social life . . . The failure of human beings to know themselves and to know God results in idolatry, injustice, and violence."[2] One of the issues that Ezekiel speaks to is that of taking personal responsibility, and it is certainly one of the issues that is very much in the forefront of our consciousness today. To be sure there are problems, challenges and other realities that are painful that we have inherited. But, then, other generations have also inherited challenging issues. But as Ezekiel notes, the people are eager to embrace the now axiomatic statement, "The parents have eaten sour grapes, and the children's teeth are set on edge."[3] We have also inherited this notion, and thus it seems convenient to shift blame to others and not take any responsibility for what transpires.

One of the questions that continues to be in the forefront of our consciousness and one that needs to be reckoned with, is that of redemption, and whether redemption is possible in every instance? To point to the defining moment of our time, the Shoah, is it possible to imagine redemption

2. Lapsley, "Genius of the Mad Prophet," 132–33.

3. Ezek 18:2.

for Hitler and the Nazis? Is the mercy shown to Nineveh an indication that even for the Ninevites, knowing their historical propensity for evil and what in fact they did to Israel later, that there is still hope for transformation? Can such redemption be justified? In a dialogue between Origen and Jerome regarding this very issue, the two early Church Fathers came to radically different conclusions.

"Origen insisted upon the full pardon of the repentant sinner; at the end even the devil will be converted. Jerome reacted to this opinion with indignation, rhetorically asking whether ultimately there will be no difference between the Virgin Mary and a prostitute, between the angel Gabriel and the devil, between the martyrs and their torturers."[4] When one considers the depth and expanse of the punishment that is meted out to the people as they are led into exile, not least the loss of the land, the abandonment and razing of Jerusalem and the Temple, one might be right to wonder why such devastation. This kind of punishment must at the very least raise the specter of the expanse and depravity of the human condition in terms of the lack of a moral compass. It is important for those of us who seek to interpret the prophetic texts for our time, to have a discerning sense of the difference between the manner in which the prophet might have seen the expression of even one act of injustice and how such an act might be regarded today.

> I will restore the fortunes of my people Israel,
>> and they shall rebuild the ruined cities and inhabit them;
> they shall plant vineyards and drink their wine,
>> and they shall make gardens and eat their fruit.
> I will plant them upon their land,
>> and they shall never again be plucked up
>> out of the land which I have given them,
>>> says the LORD your God.[5]

And yet again . . .

> How shall I give you up, O Ephraim!
>> How shall I surrender you, O Israel!
> How can I make you like Admah!
>> How can I treat you like Zeboiim!
> My heart recoils within me,
>> my compassion grows warm and tender.

---

4. LaCocque and LaCocque, *Jonah*, 145.

5. Amos 9:14–15.

> I will not execute my fierce anger,
> > I will not again destroy Ephraim;
> For I am God and no mortal,
> > the Holy One in your midst,
> > and I will not come in wrath.[6]

These words by Amos and Hosea among others have to be read and understood contextually. These are extraordinary reminders that the punishment that has been meted out, devastating as it was in so many instances, is not the last word. This restoration and redemption, notably is at the behest and initiative of God. Moreover, one notes the definitive, "they shall never again be plucked up"; "I will not again destroy Ephraim." And yet, one knows equally well, that the people, both guilty and innocent were plucked up and sent into exile. Perhaps it is the case that one does not wish to consider the complexity of these prophetic promises that are seemingly etched in stone, but also are seemingly cast aside in time. By the time of Jeremiah, not only will the Temple be destroyed and Jerusalem razed to the ground; indeed despite the word of Amos (9:15), the people will be plucked up from the land. One cannot help but then wonder whether in fact the actions of the people across the generations have the capacity to change the manner in which God intended to act and indeed alter the promises that God had made?

> Because you are precious in MY eyes,
> > and honored, and I love you . . .

> For a brief moment I forsook you,
> > but with great compassion I will gather you.
> In overflowing wrath for a moment
> > I hid my face from you,
> But with everlasting love I will have compassion on you,
> > says the Lord, your Redeemer.

> Can a woman forget her suckling child,
> > that she should have no compassion on the son of her womb?
> Even these will forget,
> > but I will not forget you.

> For the mountains may depart,
> > and the hill be removed,
> but my steadfast love shall not depart for you.[7]

---

6. Hos 11:8–9.

7. Isa 43:4; 54:7–8; 49:15; 54:10.

When one sees the devastation that God brought on the people because of the injustice and the corruption in their lives, it is sometimes difficult to imagine that God's anger will ever relent, and whether God will stop being indignant. But indeed despite all of this, not least the exile, this is not YHWH's fundamental inclination.

> In a very little while my indignation will come to an end . . .

> Come, My people, enter your chambers,
>   and shut your doors behind you;
> hide yourselves for a little while
>   until the indignation is passed.[8]

> Therefore the LORD waits to be gracious to you;
>   therefore he exalts himself to show you mercy.
> For the LORD is a God of justice
>   blessed are all those who wait for him.[9]

As is so often the case, there is a "yet" from YHWH, a "yet" of grace that is as surprising as it is demanding. Just when it appears that the door is closed to any further relationship between Judah and YHWH, hope comes in the form of a dramatic requirement for reorientation that must be rooted in worship, and inextricably expressed in justice. The relationship between the two cannot be negotiated or overlooked. Anyone who is to take this biblical text seriously must do so on the principle that it is only on the basis of a just society, where the afflicted, the marginalized, and the impoverished are attended to and brought into proper relationship; it is only on these terms that cultic activities will have any meaning. To divorce cultic activities from social justice, is to continue in the same vein as the ancient societies of Sodom and Gomorrah. For the Hebrew prophets doom is not the last word. Perhaps it is the case that it is the last thing that one hears, but is not the last word.

> Why have you forgotten us completely?
>   Why have you forsaken us these many days?
> Restore us yourself, O Lord, that we may be restored;
>   renew our days as of old—
> unless you have utterly rejected us,
>   and are angry with us beyond measure.[10]

8. Isa 10:25; 26:20.

9. Isa 30:18.

10. Lam 5:20–22.

There is a word of hope, but it never comes automatically because of "time served." It comes on the basis of change, or turning around and recasting oneself into living out the qualities inherent in the relationship we have with each other. To remain at "doom" is to miss the final word. In what might appear to be a counterintuitive decision to many, Jeremiah in the midst of making devastating pronouncements to the people, and with exile on the very near horizon, surprisingly buys a plot of land. One wonders who buys a plot of land under these circumstances? Does Jeremiah know something that the people do not, or perhaps we do not? There is a sense that not only does he seem to know something, but this very act of buying a plot of land is foundational in the construction of a fabric of hope. Could there be a better or more appropriate time for hope than in a time of sheer despair, pain and exile? Jeremiah's action, is a profound expression of hope in a time when hope would be the very last thing on the horizon. But there is a divine reminder immediately as the transaction ends, almost as if to anticipate the questions that would be generated. "For thus says the Lord of Hosts, the God of Israel: Houses and fields and vineyards shall again be bought in this land."[11] Yes, indeed there must be an element of madness to the quality of hope. "In the midst of the national catastrophe, one must continue to teach and study, bake and sell bread, plant trees and count on the future. One must not wait for the tragedy to end before building or rebuilding life; one must do it in the very face of tragedy."[12]

Moreover, there are any number of prophetic texts that speak to the various elements of restoration after God's punishment has been meted out. As we have noted above, even as the created order is involved in the punishment, so also the land will be involved in restoration.[13] One of the many effects of the 9/11 terror attack on the World Trade Center and the Pentagon is that it created within the United States a sense of vulnerability, a sense that the veil with which the nation protected itself and which seemed for a while to be impossible to breach, was in fact breached. An inevitable reminder of such horror is the very idea of what it means to be vulnerable, not only on a global scale, but within one's community. This might have been a platform for a prophetic word to ensure that the vulnerable do not become invisible, and thus casualties. Vulnerability has the potential and possibility to guide us in at least two different directions. It

11. Jer 32:15.
12. Wiesel, *Five Biblical Portraits*, 121.
13. E.g., see Isa 29:17–21; 30:18.

certainly gives cause and opportunity for introspection, to wonder what might have been instrumental in creating such a moment. Alternatively, it might propel a kind of external "lashing out," casting blame on others with the possibility for violence and hatred of the *other*. When one is weak, and vulnerability is something of a constant companion, there is ample time for hope and introspection, for the quest for community and compassion. However, when vulnerability is experienced by the powerful and those who occupy the center by circumstances of force, the response invariably is that of a show of force and the exercise of power. For those who are entrenched in power, vulnerability is viewed as a sign of weakness, and it is one of the most fearful realities. The role of truth telling and vulnerability is best captured through the expression of divine truth telling, which also has a quality of divine vulnerability. God tells the truth about a period of abandonment, as painful as it is to do so. Indeed where does one go to hear the truth, the truth that is not distilled and framed to fit an ideology that is not painful or offensive? Truth must be a message that is not based on the interpreter's inclination or preference or posturing.

> For a brief moment I abandoned you,
> but with great compassion I will gather you.
> In overflowing wrath for a moment
> I hid my face from you
> But with everlasting love I will have compassion on you,
> says the LORD, your Redeemer.[14]

The good news here and for those who would dare and have the courage to proclaim the prophetic word is that this is neither the only word, nor the last word. Hope is born out of despair and depression, vulnerability and abandonment. But the word is not simply to become empty optimism, platitudes, or clichés. Instead, the hope that is born out of such calamities must be predicated on YHWH's promises, whose very words serve as a moment of fulfillment. Thus, when the word from the prophet is "do not fear" a pronouncement predicated on the promises of YHWH, it is not simply a human wish for newness, as heartfelt as such a wish might be, but rather a hope in the face of despair and hope in the midst of a wilderness experience.

> Do not fear, for I am with you,
> do not be afraid for I am your God, . . .

14. Isa 54:7–8.

> it is I who say to you, "do not fear,
>> I will help you."[15]

> Do not fear, for I have redeemed you,
>> I have called you by name, you are mine . . .[16]

> Do not fear, for I am with you;
>> I will bring your offspring from the east,
>> And from the West I will gather you.[17]

In these texts from Isaiah, the divine assurance of "do not fear" is accompanied with six respective promises, each with a restorative quality and presence of God; relationship with God, divine help; redemption; naming and belonging; promise of generation; gathering to come home. The only way "do not fear" finds meaning is in the context of circumstances or situations that indeed are fearful. Out of these circumstances, the quality of restoration takes on a particularly significant meaning.

> Let those who boast, boast in this, that they understand and know me, that I am the LORD; I act with steadfast love, justice and righteousness in the earth, for in these things I delight, says the LORD.[18]

> The LORD enters into judgment
>> with the elders and princes of his people:
> It is you who have devoured the vineyard;
>> the spoil of the poor is in your houses.[19]

> Therefore the days are surely coming . . .
> The corpses of this people will be food
>> for the birds of the air,
> and for the animals of the earth;
>> and no one will frighten them away.
> And I will bring to an end the sound of mirth and gladness,
>> the voice of the bride and bridegroom
> in the cities of Judah
>> and in the streets of Jerusalem;
> for the land shall become a waste.[20]

15. Isa 41:10a, 13b.

16. Isa 43:1b.

17. Isa 43:5.

18. Jer 9:24.

19. Isa 3:14.

20. Jer 7:32a, 33–34.

9

Postscript

"Truth stumbles in the Public Square." (Isa 59:14b)

For interpreters of the Hebrew prophets in today's post Shoah world, silence with regard to the role of God and our understanding of God as one who punishes in such a devastating manner, but is also silent in the face of violence and genocide, must be seriously reckoned with. There must be questions about God, about loss of faith, about trauma, about genocide, about displacement, about the use of evil power for divine purposes. At the very least, we are forced to redefine the meaning of ubiquitous phrases such as "God of justice," "God of love," "merciful God." To do so would be a healthy reckoning of our understanding of and our relationship with God.

It might be easy for some to see the Hebrew prophets as angry and raging wild persons who did not invest themselves with the people. That would be misplaced and biblically untenable. As counter intuitive as it might appear, the prophets were principally persons of hope—who in delivering this message of punishment or doom or exile also held out a word of hope and redemption. Occasionally this word of hope is lost along the way, when only the harsh rhetoric is heard and remembered. As we listen to the words of the prophet, and in the midst of the intense invectives, the people are not abandoned in the darkness of a tunnel without an occasion to see the light again. For there will be tearing down and building up, but the latter cannot happen without the former. For Christians it is simply not possible to journey to the glory of Easter without facing the reality of Good Friday, and the long, sometimes tortuous journey through the liminal

Saturday. The light will come, but not before the darkness is lived through. The message of the Hebrew prophets has had an enduring and lasting quality over the centuries in a variety of circumstances, settings, and situations. Today, the message of the Hebrew prophets continues to have remarkable relevance, again in a variety of settings, and is cited and used in multiple ways. In particular, themes such as justice, mercy, love, peace, and equality all have a striking resonance within the global community.

One of the arguments that one often hears when the prophets' words are being applied to issues in contemporary society is the fact that it is a different time and place. Some say that the prophets' pronouncements regarding social transformation, oppression, injustices, feeding the hungry, clothing the naked, including the foreigners, is unrealistic and unattainable. It is an ideal, or even more so, utopian. Perhaps it is ideal in the sense that the ideal is exactly what we must pursue because it always seems elusive, but of course it is not out of reach. But the prophets' message is certainly not utopian.

What should be a basic and non-negotiable standard for the care of the other? Perhaps sharing a meal as an act of simplicity and shared intimacy. To share a meal then is seen as collapsing a social class, economic barrier that for many is the final line of defense. The idea of a shared meal is not one that is central to the prophets' message and yet there are both allusions and indeed references to this moment of significant connection.

Bibliography

Aberbach, David. "Revolutionary Hebrew, Empire and Crisis: Towards a Sociological Gestalt." *British Journal of Sociology* 48 (1997) 128–48.

Ajzenstat, O. E. "Beyond Totality: The Shoah and the Biblical Ethics of Emanuel Levinas." In *Strange Fire: Reading the Bible after the Holocaust*, edited by Tod Linafelt, 106–20. New York: New York University Press, 2000.

Allen, Leslie. *Jeremiah: A Commentary*. Old Testament Library. Louisville: Westminster John Knox, 2008.

Anderson, Bradford A. "Poetic Justice in Obadiah." *Journal for the Study of the Old Testament* 32 (2010) 247–55.

Aristotle. *Nicomachean Ethics*. Newburyport, MA: Focus, 2008.

Bard, Mitchell G., ed. "The Nazi Olympics." Jewish Virtual Library. www.jewish virtuallibrary.org/jsource/Shoah/olympics.html.

Bartusch, Mark W. "From Honor Challenge to False Prophecy: Rereading Jeremiah 28's Story of Prophetic Conflict in Light of Social-Science Models." *Currents in Theology and Mission* 36 (2009) 455–63.

Ben Zvi, Ehud. "Wrongdoers, Wrongdoings and Righting Wrongs in Micah 2." *Biblical Interpretation* 7 (1999) 87–10.

Berges, Ulrich. "How Babylon Became Merciless: A Subversive Re-Reading of Isaiah 47:6." In *The Centre and the Periphery: A European Tribute to Walter Brueggemann*, edited by Jill Middlemas et al., 145–58. Sheffield: Sheffield Phoenix, 2010.

Berlin, Adele. "A Rejoinder to John A. Miles, Jr., With Some Observations on the Nature of Prophecy." *Jewish Quarterly Review* 66 (1976) 227–37.

Birch, Bruce C. *Let Justice Roll Down: The Old Testament, Ethics, and Christian Life*. Louisville: Westminster John Knox, 1991.

Blumenthal, David. *Facing the Abusing God: A Theology of Protest*. Louisville: Westminster John Knox, 1993.

Bodner, Keith. "The Locutions of I Kings 22:28: A New Proposal." *Journal of Biblical Literature* 122 (2003) 533–46.

Borg, Marcus J. *Reading the Bible Again for the First Time*. New York: HarperCollins, 2001.

Bracke, John M. *Jeremiah 1–29*. Westminster Bible Companion. Louisville: Westminster John Knox, 2000.

———. "Justice in the Book of Jeremiah." *Word and World* 22 (2002) 387–95.

Brueggemann, Walter. *A Commentary on Jeremiah: Exile and Homecoming*. Grand Rapids: Eerdmans, 1998.

————. "The Costly Loss of Lament." In *The Psalms and the Life of Faith*, edited by Patrick D. Miller, 98–111. Minneapolis: Fortress, 1995.

————. *Deep Memory, Exuberant Hope: Contested Truth in a Post-Christian World*. Minneapolis: Fortress, 2000.

————. *Divine Presence amid Violence: Contextualizing the Book of Joshua*. Eugene, OR: Cascade, 2009.

————. *I & II Kings*. Smyth & Helwys Bible Commentaries. Macon, GA: Smyth & Helwys, 2000.

————. "A Fissure Always Uncontained." In *Strange Fire: Reading the Bible after the Holocaust*, edited by Tod Linafelt, 62–75. New York: New York University Press, 2000.

————. *Isaiah 1–39*. Westminster Bible Companion. Louisville: Westminster John Knox, 1998.

————. *Isaiah 40–66*. Westminster Bible Companion. Louisville: Westminster John Knox, 1998.

————. "Meditation upon the Abyss: The Book of Jeremiah." *Word and World* 22 (2002) 340–50.

————. "Prophetic Leadership: Engagement in Counter-Imagination." *Journal of Religious Leadership* 10 (2011) 1–23.

————. "Recovering from the Long Nightmare of Amnesia." In *The Bible and the American Future*, edited by Robert L. Jewett et al., 1–21. Eugene, OR: Cascade Books, 2009.

————. *Testimony to Otherwise: The Witness of Elijah and Elisha*. St. Louis: Chalice, 2001.

————. *Theology of the Old Testament: Testimony, Dispute, Advocacy*. Minneapolis: Fortress, 1997.

————. "Together in the Spirit—Beyond Seductive Quarrels." In *Deep Memory, Exuberant Hope: Contested Truth in a Post-Christian World*, edited by Patrick D. Miller, 29–41. Minneapolis: Fortress, 2000.

————. *The Word Militant: Preaching a Decentering Word*. Minneapolis: Fortress, 2007.

Buber, Martin. *The Eclipse of God: Studies in the Relation between Religion and Philosophy* New York: Harper & Row, 1952.

Callaway, Mary Chilton. "Exegesis as Banquet: Reading Jeremiah with the Rabbis." In *A Gift of God in Due Season: Essays on Scripture and Community in Honor of James A. Sanders*, edited by Richard D. Weis and David M. Carr, 219–30. Sheffield: Sheffield Academic, 1996.

Camus, Albert. *The Rebel*. New York: Vintage, 1992.

Carlin, John. *Playing the Enemy: Nelson Mandela and the Game that Made a Nation*. New York: Penguin, 2008.

Carroll, Robert P. *Chaos to Covenant: Uses of Prophecy in the Book of Jeremiah*. London: SCM, 1981.

————. *Jeremiah*. Old Testament Library. Philadelphia: Westminster, 1986.

Carroll, R. M. Daniel. "A Passion for Justice and the Conflicted Self: Lessons from the Book of Micah." *Journal of Psychology and Christianity* 26 (2006) 169–76.

Caruth, Cathy, ed. *Trauma: Explorations in Memory*. Baltimore: Johns Hopkins University Press, 1995.

Chaney, Marvin L. "Bitter Bounty: The Dynamics of Political Economy Critiqued by the Eighth-Century Prophets." In *Reformed Faith and Economics*, edited by Robert L. Stivers, 15–30. Lanham, MD: University Press of America, 1989.

————. "Whose Sour Grapes: The Addresses of Isaiah 5.1–7 in the Light of Political Economy." *Semeia* 87 (1999) 105–23.

Clabeaux, John. "The Demands of Justice and the Practice of the Presence of God: A Biblical Theology of Sinai and Zion." *Josephinum Journal of Theology* 17 (2010) 41–56.

Clements, Ronald E. "Prophecy, Ethics and Divine Anger." In *Ethical and Unethical in the Old Testament: God and Humans in Dialogue,* edited by Katherine J. Dell, 88–102. Library of Hebrew Bible/Old Testament Studies 528. New York: T. & T. Clark, 2010.

Cochran, Clark E. "Political Science Confronts the Book: Recent Work on Scripture and Politics." *Journal of Politics* 50 (1988) 219–34.

Coles, Robert. *Handing One Another Along: Literature and Social Reflection.* New York: Random House, 2010.

Coomber, Matthew J. M. "Caught in the Crossfire? Economic Injustice and Prophetic Motivation in Eighth-Century Judah." *Biblical Interpretation* 19 (2011) 396–432.

Coote, Robert B. *Amos among the Prophets: Composition and Theology.* Philadelphia: Fortress, 1981.

Crenshaw, James L. *Prophetic Conflict: Its Effect on Israelite Religion.* Beihefte zur Zeitschrift für die alttestamentliche Wissenschaft 24. Berlin: de Gruyter, 1971.

Crossan, John Dominic. *God and Empire: Jesus against Rome, Then and Now.* New York: HarperCollins, 2007.

———. *Jesus: A Revolutionary Biography.* New York: HarperCollins, 1994.

Dearman, John Andrew. *Property Rights in the Eighth-Century Prophets.* SBL Dissertation Series 106. Atlanta: Scholars, 1988.

Dell, Katherine, ed. *Ethical and Unethical in the Old Testament: God and Humans in Dialogue.* Library of Hebrew Bible/Old Testament Studies 528. New York: T. & T. Clark, 2010.

Dempsey, Carol J. *Hope amid the Ruins: The Ethics of Israel's Prophets.* St. Louis: Chalice, 2000.

De Vries, Simon J. *Prophet against Prophet: The Role of the Micaiah Narrative (I Kings 22) in the Development of Early Prophetic Tradition.* Grand Rapids: Eerdmans, 1978.

Dobbs-Allsopp, F. W. *Lamentations.* Interpretation. Louisville: Westminster John Knox, 2002.

Elgin, Duane. *Promise Ahead: A Vision of Hope and Action for Humanity's Future.* New York: HarperCollins, 2000.

Eliot, T. S. *Christianity and Culture.* London: Harcourt, 1948.

Erikson, Kai. "Notes on Trauma and Community." In *Trauma:Explorations in Memory,* edited by Cathy Caruth, 183–99. Baltimore: Johns Hopkins University Press, 1995.

Fowl, Stephen. "Texts Don't Have Ideologies." *Biblical Interpretation* 3 (1995) 15–34.

Fretheim, Terence E. "Caught in the Middle: Jeremiah's Vocational Crisis." *Word and World* 22 (2002) 351–60.

———. *Creation Untamed: The Bible, God and Natural Disasters.* Grand Rapids: Baker Academic, 2010.

———. "'I Was Only a Little Angry': Divine Violence in the Prophets," *Interpretation* 58 (2004) 365–75.

———. "Interpreting the Prophets and Issues of Social Justice." In *The Bible and the American Future,* edited by Robert L. Jewett et al., 92–107. Eugene, OR: Cascade, 2009.

———. *Jeremiah.* Smyth & Helwys Bible Commentary. Macon, GA: Smyth & Helwys, 2002.

———. "The Prophets and Social Justice: A Conservative Agenda." *Word and World* 28 (2008) 159–68.

Bibliography

Freyne, Sean. "The Bible and Violence." *Furrow* 26 (1975) 88–94.

Goldmann, Lucien. *The Hebrew Prophets of Muslim Spain*. Hammondsworth, UK: Penguin, 1964.

Gossai, Hemchand. "Challenging the Empire: The Conscience of the Prophet and Prophetic Dissent." In *Postcolonial Interventions: Festschrift for R. S. Sugirtharajah*, edited by Tat-Siong Benny Liew, 98–108. Bible in the Modern World 23. Sheffield: Sheffield Phoenix, 2009.

———. "Jeremiah's Welfare Ethic and the Challenge to Imperial Protocol." In *A Postcolonial Commentary on the Old Testament*, edited by Leo G. Perdue and Archie Lee. Bible & Postcolonialism. Edinburgh: T. & T. Clark, forthcoming.

———. *Social Critique by Israel's Eighth-Century Prophets: Justice and Righteousness in Context*. 2nd ed. Eugene, OR: Wipf and Stock Publishers, 2006.

Gowan, Donald E. *Theology of the Prophetic Books: The Death and Resurrection of Israel*. Louisville: Westminster John Knox, 1998.

Gray, Mark. "Justice with Reconciliation: A Text for Our Times. The Rhetoric of Isaiah 58:6–10." In *The Centre and Periphery: A European Tribute to Walter Brueggemann*, edited by Jill Middlemas et al., 159–78. Sheffield Phoenix, 2010.

Greenspahn, Frederick E. "Syncretism and Idolatry in the Bible." *Vetus Testamentum* 54 (2004) 480–94.

Hall, Douglas John. *God and Human Suffering: An Exercise in the Theology of the Cross*. Minneapolis: Augsburg, 1986.

Hamilton, Jefferies M. "Caught in the Nets of Prophecy? The Death of King Ahab and the Character of God." *Catholic Biblical Quarterly* 56 (1994) 1–9.

Hanson, Paul D. *Isaiah 40–66*. Interpretation. Louisville: Westminster John Knox, 1995.

———. *Political Engagement as Biblical Mandate*. Eugene, OR: Cascade Books, 2010.

Hauerwas, Stanley. *A Community of Character*. Notre Dame: University of Notre Dame Press, 1981.

Herder, J. G. "Ueber Begeisterung, Offenbarung." *Werke XI*, Stuttgart, 1852.

Heschel, Abraham J. *The Prophets: An Introduction*. New York: Harper & Row, 1969.

Hillers, Delbert R. *Micah: A Commentary on the Book of the Prophet Micah*. Hermeneia. Minneapolis: Fortress, 1984.

Hirsch, Eric D. *Validity in Interpretation*. New Haven: Yale University Press, 1967.

Holladay, William L. "God Writes a Rude Letter (Jeremiah 29:1–23)." *Biblical Archaeologist* 46 (1983) 145–46.

———. *Long Ago God Spoke: How Christians May Hear the Old Testament Today*. Minneapolis: Fortress, 1995.

Horsley, Richard A. "Ethics and Exegesis: 'Love your Enemies' and the Doctrine of Non-Violence." *Journal of the American Academy of Religion* 54 (1986) 3–31.

———, ed. *In the Shadow of the Empire: Reclaiming the Bible as a History of Faithful Resistance*. Louisville: Westminster John Knox Press, 2008.

———. "Jesus and the Renewal of Covenantal Economics." In *The Bible and the American Future*, edited by Robert L. Jewett et al., 181–208. Eugene, OR: Cascade, 2009.

Houston, Walter J. *Contending for Justice: Ideologies and Theologies of Social Justice in the Old Testament*. New York: T. & T. Clark, 2006.

Jewett, Robert L., ed. *The Bible and the American Future*. Eugene, OR: Cascade Books, 2009.

Kast, Verena. *Joy, Inspiration and Hope*. Translated by Douglas Whitcher. New York: Fromm, 1994.

Keller, Catherine. "The Love of Postcolonialism: Theology in the Interstices of Empire." In *Postcolonial Theologies: Divinity and Empire*, edited by Michael Nausner and Mayra Rivera, 221–42. St. Louis: Chalice, 2004.

Knierim, Rolf P. "Justice in Old Testament Theology." In *The Task of Old Testament Theology: Method and Cases*, 86–122. Grand Rapids: Eerdmans, 1995.

LaCocque, André, and Pierre-Emmanuel LaCocque. *Jonah: A Psycho-Religious Approach to the Prophet*. Studies on Personalities of the Old Testament. Columbia: University of South Carolina Press, 1990.

Langer, Lawrence L. *Shoah Testimonies: The Ruins of Memory*. New Haven: Yale University Press, 2001.

Lapsley, Jacqueline. "The Genius of the Mad Prophet: Ezekiel and the New Moral Self." In *The Bible and the American Future*, edited by Robert L. Jewett et al., 130–45. Eugene, OR: Cascade, 2009.

Lash, Nicholas. "The Church in the State We're In." In *Spirituality and Social Embodiment*, edited by L. Gregory Jones and James J. Buckley, 121–37. Oxford: Blackwell, 1997.

Levenson, Jon D. "Is Brueggemann Really a Pluralist?" *Harvard Theological Review* 93 (2000) 265–94.

Lindberg, Tod. *The Political Teachings of Jesus*. New York: HarperCollins, 2007.

Maguire, Daniel C. "The Lies of War: Building an Ethics of Peace." *Furrow* 56 (2005) 550–59.

Mandolfo, Carleen. "Talking Back: The Perseverance of Justice in Lamentation." In *Lamentations in Ancient and Contemporary Cultural Contexts*, edited by Nancy C. Lee and Carleen Mandolfo, 47–56. Atlanta: SBL, 2008.

Marlow, Hilary. *Biblical Prophets and Contemporary Environmental Ethics: Re-Reading Amos, Hosea, and First Isaiah*. Oxford: Oxford University Press, 2009.

———. "Justice for Whom? Social and Environmental Ethics and the Hebrew Prophets." In *Ethical and Unethical in the Old Testament: God and Humans in Dialogue*, edited by Katherine J. Dell, 103–21. New York: T. & T. Clark, 2010.

Mays, James Luther. "Justice: Perspectives from the Prophetic Tradition." In *Prophecy in Ancient Israel*, edited by David L. Petersen, 147–58. Philadelphia: Fortress, 1987.

———. *Psalms*. Interpretation. Louisville: Westminster John Knox, 1994.

McCann, J. Clinton, Jr. "'The Way of the Righteous' in the Psalms: Character Formation and Cultural Crisis." In *Character and Scripture: Moral Formation, Community and Biblical Interpretation*, edited by William P. Brown, 135–49. Grand Rapids: Eerdmans, 2002.

McKenzie, Steven L. *How to Read the Bible*. Oxford: Oxford University Press, 2005.

Moberly, R. W. L. "Does God Lie to His Prophets? The Story of Micaiah ben Imlah as a Test Case." *Harvard Theological Review* 96 (2003) 1–23.

———. *Prophecy and Discernment*. Cambridge: Cambridge University Press, 2006.

Muilenburg, James. *The Way of Israel: Biblical Faith and Ethics*. New York: Harper & Row, 1961.

Nelson, Richard. *First and Second Kings*. Interpretation. Louisville: Westminster John Knox, 1987.

Nicholson, E. W. *Preaching to the Exiles: A Study of the Prose Tradition in the Book of Jeremiah*. Oxford: Blackwell, 1970.

Niedner, Frederick A., Jr. "Rachel's Lament." *Word and World* 22 (2002) 406–14.

Nussbaum, Martha. *Love's Knowledge: Essays on Philosophy and Literature*. New York: Oxford University Press, 1990.

Bibliography

Nwaoru, Emmanuel O. "A Fresh Look at Amos 4:1–3 and Its Imagery." *Vetus Testamentum* 59 (2009) 460–74.

O'Brien, Julia M. *Challenging Prophetic Metaphor: Theology and Ideology in the Prophets.* Louisville: Westminster John Knox, 2008.

O'Connor, Kathleen M. "Surviving Disaster in the Book of Jeremiah." *Word and World* 22 (2002) 369–77.

———. "Teaching Jeremiah." *Perspectives in Religious Studies* 36 (2009) 273–87.

Ogletree, Thomas W. *The Use of the Bible in Christian Ethics.* Philadelphia: Fortress, 1983.

Olyan, Saul. *Biblical Mourning: Ritual and Social Dimensions.* Oxford: Oxford University Press, 2004.

Pipher, Mary. *The Shelter of Each Other: Rebuilding Our Families.* New York: Putnam, 1996.

Podhoretz, Norman. *The Prophets.* New York: Free Press, 2002.

Polkinghorne, John. *Quarks, Chaos, and Christianity: Questions to Science and Religion.* New York: Crossroad, 1994.

Premnath, D. N. "Latifundialization in Isaiah 5.8–10." In *Social-Scientific Old Testament Criticism*, edited by David J. Chalcraft, 301–13. Biblical Seminar 47. Sheffield: Sheffield Academic, 1997.

Quarantelli, E. E., ed. *What Is Disaster? Perspectives on the Question.* London: Routledge, 1998.

Rieger, Joerg. "Liberating God-Talk: Postcolonialism and the Challenge of the Margins." In *Postcolonial Theologies: Divinity and Empire*, edited by Michael Nausner and Mayra Rivera, 204–20. St. Louis: Chalice, 2004.

Roberts, J. J. M. "Does God Lie? Divine Deceit as a Theological Problem in Israelite Prophetic Literature." In *Congress Volume: Jerusalem, 1986*, edited by J. A. Emerton, 211–20. Vetus Testamentum Supplements 40. Leiden: Brill, 1988.

———. "Security and Justice in Isaiah." *Stone-Campbell Journal* 13 (2010) 71–79.

Robertson, David. "Micaiah ben Imlah: A Literary View." In *The Biblical Mosaic: Changing Perspectives*, edited by R. Polzin and E. Rothman, 139–46. Philadelphia: Fortress, 1982.

Rubenstein, Richard L. *After Auschwitz: Radical Theology and Contemporary Judaism.* Indianapolis: Bobbs-Merill, 1966.

Scalise, Pamela J. "The Way of Weeping: Reading the Path of Grief in Jeremiah." *Word and World* 22 (2002) 415–22.

Schmidt, N., ed. *Die Schriften des Alten Testaments in Auswahl.* Göttingen, 1910.

Schneidau, Herbert N. *Sacred Discontent: The Bible and Western Tradition.* Berkeley: University of California Press, 1976.

Schüssler Fiorenza, Elisabeth. *Bread Not Stone: The Challenge of Feminist Biblical Interpretation.* Boston: Beacon, 1984.

Searcy, Edwin "'A People, a Name, a Praise, and a Glory': False and True Faith in Jeremiah." *Word and World* 22 (2002) 333–39.

Seitz, Christopher R. "The Crisis of Interpretation and the Meaning and Purpose of the Exile: A Redactional Study of Jeremiah XXI–XLIII." *Vetus Testamentum* 35 (1985) 78–97.

Sells, Michael. "Kosovo Mythology and the Bosnian Genocide." In *In God's Name: Genocide and Religion in the Twentieth Century*, edited by O. Bartov and P. Mack, 180–207. New York: Berghahn, 2001.

Sharp, Carolyn J. "The Call of Jeremiah and Diaspora Politics." *Journal of Biblical Literature* 19 (2000) 421–38.

———. *Old Testament Prophets for Today*. Louisville: Westminster John Knox, 2009.

Sisson, Jonathan Paige. "Jeremiah and the Jerusalem Conception of Peace." *Journal of Biblical Literature* 105 (1986) 429–42.

Slessarev-Jamir, Helene. "Prophetic Activism in an Age of Empire." *Political Theology* 11 (2010) 674–90.

Smith, Daniel L. "Jeremiah as Prophet of Nonviolent Resistance." *Journal for the Study of the Old Testament* 13 (1989) 95–107.

Smith-Christopher, Daniel L. *A Biblical Theology of Exile*. Overtures to Biblical Theology. Minneapolis: Fortress, 2002.

Stulman, Louis. *Order amid Chaos: Jeremiah as Symbolic Tapestry*. Biblical Seminar 57. Sheffield: Sheffield Academic, 1998.

Sugirtharajah, R. S. "Complacencies and Cul-de-sacs: Christian Theologies and Colonialism." In *Postcolonial Theologies: Divinity and Empire*, edited by Michael Nausner and Mayra Rivera, 22–38. St. Louis: Chalice, 2004.

———. *The Postcolonial Biblical Reader*. Oxford: Blackwell, 2006.

Sweeney, Marvin. *I & II Kings: A Commentary*. Old Testament Library. Louisville: Westminster John Knox, 2007.

———. *Reading the Hebrew Bible After the Shoah: Engaging Holocaust Theology*. Minneapolis: Fortress, 2008.

Tollington, Janet. "The Ethics of Warfare and the Holy War Tradition in the Book of Judges." In *Ethical and Unethical in the Old Testament: God and Humans in Dialogue*, edited by Katherine J. Dell, 71–87. New York: T. & T. Clark, 2010.

Tracy, David. "The Hidden God: The Divine Other of Liberation." *Cross Currents* 46 (1996) 5–16.

Walsh, Jerome T. *I Kings*. Berit Olam. Collegeville, MN: Liturgical, 1996.

Weber, Max. *The Sociology of Religion*. Boston: Beacon, 1993.

Weil, Simone. *Gravity and Grace*. London: Routledge, 2002.

Wessels, Wilhelm J. "Prophet versus Prophet in the Book of Jeremiah: In Search of the True Prophets." *Old Testament Essays* 22 (2009) 733–51.

Williams, James G. *The Bible, Violence and the Sacred: Liberation from the Myth of Sanctioned Violence*. San Francisco: HarperSanFrancisco, 1995.

Williams, Rowan. *Dostoevsky: Language, Faith and Fiction*. Waco, TX: Baylor University Press, 2008.

———. *Writing in the Dust: After September 11*. Grand Rapid: Eerdmans 2002.

Wiesel, Elie. *The Accident*. New York: Hill & Wang, 1962.

———. *Five Biblical Portraits*. Notre Dame: University of Notre Dame Press, 1981.

———. *From the Kingdom of Memory*. New York: Summit, 1990.

Wiesel, Elie, and Timothy K. Beal. "Matters of Survival: A Conversation." In *Strange Fire: Reading the Bible after the Holcaust*, edited by Tod Linafelt, 22–35. New York: New York University Press, 2000.

Author and Subject Index

Scripture Index

~

NEW TESTAMENT